MW01077316

STAR TREK
THE NEXT GENERATION®

OMNIBUS

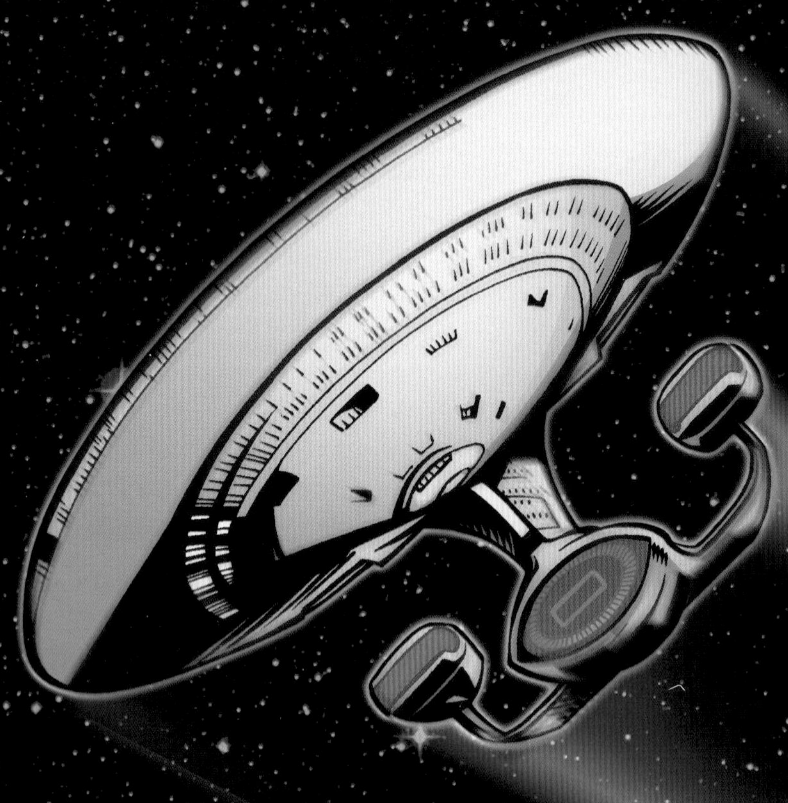

Collection Edits by Justin Eisinger and Alonzo Simon
Collection Production by Chris Mowry

Star Trek created by Gene Roddenberry.
Special thanks to Risa Kessler and John Van Citters of CBS Consumer Products for their invaluable assistance.

IDW founded by Ted Adams, Alex Garner, Kris Oprisko, and Robbie Robbins

ISBN: 978-1-61377-537-0

15 14 13 12 1 2 3 4

IDW®

Ted Adams, CEO & Publisher
Greg Goldstein, President & COO
Robbie Robbins, EVP/Sr. Graphic Artist
Chris Ryall, Chief Creative Officer/Editor-in-Chief
Matthew Ruzicka, CPA, Chief Financial Officer
Alan Payne, VP of Sales
Dirk Wood, VP of Marketing
Lorelei Bunjes, VP of Digital Services

Become our fan on Facebook **facebook.com/idwpublishing**
Follow us on Twitter **@idwpublishing**
Check us out on YouTube **youtube.com/idwpublishing**
www.IDWPUBLISHING.com

STAR TREK: THE NEXT GENERATION OMNIBUS. DECEMBER 2012. FIRST PRINTING. ® & © 2012 CBS Studios Inc. STAR TREK and related marks are trademarks of CBS Studios Inc. All Rights Reserved. IDW Publishing, a division of Idea and Design Works, LLC. Editorial offices: 5080 Santa Fe St., San Diego, CA 92109. The IDW logo is registered in the U.S. Patent and Trademark Office. Any similarities to persons living or dead are purely coincidental. With the exception of artwork used for review purposes, none of the contents of this publication may be reprinted without the permission of Idea and Design Works, LLC. Printed in Korea. IDW Publishing does not read or accept unsolicited submissions of ideas, stories, or artwork.

Originally published as STAR TREK: THE NEXT GENERATION: THE SPACE BETWEEN Issues #1–6, STAR TREK: THE NEXT GENERATION: INTELLIGENCE GATHERING Issues #1–5, STAR TREK: THE NEXT GENERATION: THE LAST GENERATION Issues #1–5, and STAR TREK: THE NEXT GENERATION: GHOSTS Issues #1–5.

STAR TREK
THE NEXT GENERATION®
THE SPACE BETWEEN

Art by Dennis Calero

1
CAPTAIN'S LOG:
STARDATE 41590.8.
THE *ENTERPRISE* IS IN ORBIT OVER TIGAN, A TECHNOLOGICALLY ADVANCED BUT TRADITIONALLY ISOLATIONIST WORLD...

...WHICH HAS ONLY RECENTLY OPENED COMMUNICATIONS WITH THE FEDERATION.
WE HAVE MUCH TO OFFER, CAPTAIN PICARD.
INDEED, CHANCELLOR LOMAC, THE FEDERATION IS HONORED TO BE CONSIDERED.
IF YOU'LL SEND US THE COORDINATES...

...MY FIRST OFFICER IS READY TO BEAM DOWN.

TASHA, DATA—YOU'RE WITH ME.

CAPTAIN— I'M PICKING UP AN ENERGY READING ON THE SURFACE.
A WEAPON, MR. LA FORGE?
MORE LIKE A PULSE OF SOME KIND.
IT'S GONE.
TRANSPORTER ROOM—
WHAT IS THE STATUS OF COMMANDER RIKER AND THE AWAY TEAM?
"THEY'RE ON THE SURFACE, SIR."
NHHHNNNHHNNNNNNNNHHH

SKRREEHHK
ENTERPRISE TO RIKER— REPORT!

SKRREEHHK
WE'RE AT THE COORDINATES, CAPTAIN. WAITING FOR OUR ESCORT—

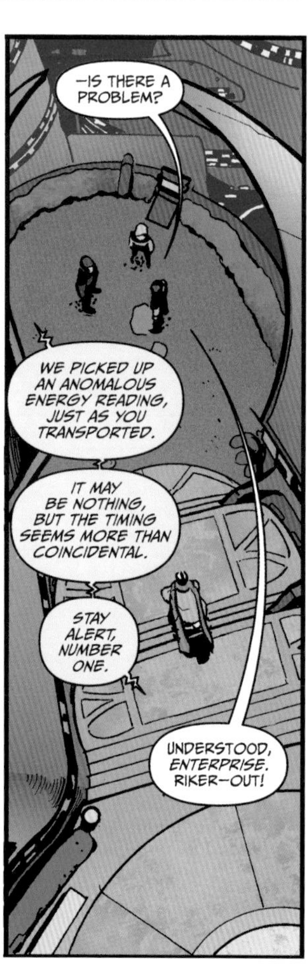
—IS THERE A PROBLEM?
WE PICKED UP AN ANOMALOUS ENERGY READING, JUST AS YOU TRANSPORTED.
IT MAY BE NOTHING, BUT THE TIMING SEEMS MORE THAN COINCIDENTAL.
STAY ALERT, NUMBER ONE.
UNDERSTOOD, ENTERPRISE. RIKER—OUT!

WELCOME, TO TIGAN.
I AM EDIC.
COMMANDER WILLIAM T. RIKER, OF THE FEDERATION STARSHIP ENTERPRISE—
—THIS IS MY SECOND OFFICER, LIEUTENANT COMMANDER DATA...
AND MY SECURITY CHIEF, LIEUTENANT TASHA YAR.

I WOULD BE PLEASED IF YOU WOULD FOLLOW ME.
AFTER YOU.
KEEP YOUR EYES OPEN, SIR.
I ALWAYS DO, LIEUTENANT—
—I WOULD NOT BE ABLE TO SEE, IF I DID NOT.

WE'VE HEARD A LOT ABOUT TIGAN'S ENERGY FACILITY.
THE GRAVIMATRIX.
I AM INTRIGUED BY ITS USE OF A MICROSCOPIC BLACK HOLE AS A POWER SOURCE—

—STARFLEET HAS BEEN UNABLE TO CREATE A STABLE CONTAINMENT FIELD TO MAKE ITS APPLICATION SAFE.
TIGAN'S GEOTHERMIC ENERGY POWERS THE CONTAINMENT FIELD—

—AS LONG AS THE PLANET STANDS, THE STAR CAN BE HARNESSED.
DATA—?
YOU'RE STARING.

I AM SORRY, EDIC—MY INTENTION WAS NOT TO BE RUDE.
AHHHH—

—YOU NOTICED MY INTERFACE.

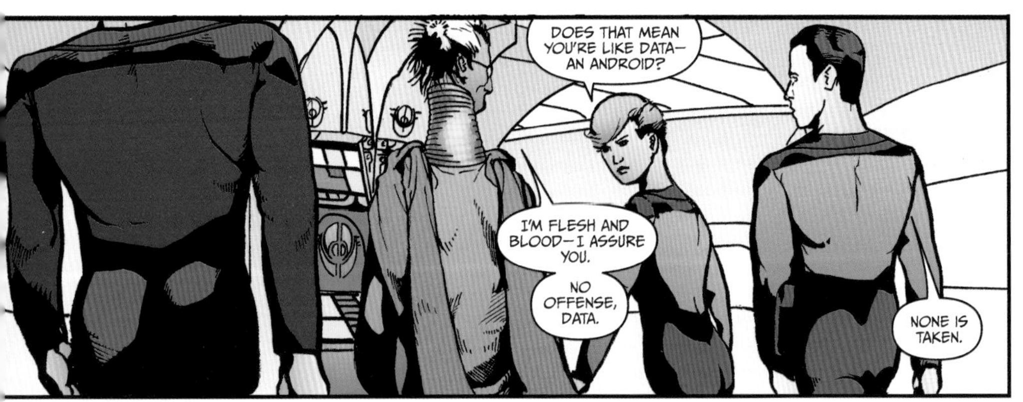
DOES THAT MEAN YOU'RE LIKE DATA— AN ANDROID?
I'M FLESH AND BLOOD—I ASSURE YOU.
NO OFFENSE, DATA.
NONE IS TAKEN.

IT'S A SURGICAL IMPLANT. EVERYONE ON TIGAN HAS ONE...
INFORMATION, ENTERTAINMENT, COMMUNICATION, EVEN FINANCIAL TRANSACTIONS—
ALL RECEIVED FROM THE CENTRAL COMPUTER IN MINUTE TACHYON BURSTS AND DOWNLOADED DIRECTLY INTO THE CEREBRAL CORTEX.

AN IMPRESSIVE FEAT, EDIC—BUT VULNERABLE TO CORRUPTED INFORMATION...
...A CLOSED SYSTEM, LIKE MY POSITRONIC BRAIN, IS BETTER PROTECTED.

THE CHANCELLOR WILL SEE YOU NOW.

THERE MUST BE SOME MISTAKE....

...*WHERE* IS CHANCELLOR LOMAC?
I AM CHANCELLOR KADEC, OF TIGAN.
WE ARE LOOKING FOR CHANCELLOR LOMAC, THE ELECTED LEADER OF TIGAN.
I LEAD THE PEOPLE HERE.

A COUP?
MAYBE. OR SOME KIND OF MIND CONTROL.
LOMAC CONTACTED THE FEDERATION—
LOMAC AND LOMAC—

—THERE IS NO LOMAC!
I ASSURE YOU, COMMANDER RIKER—CHANCELLOR KADEC IS THE LEADER OF THIS PLANET.
DATA—CHECK THE CONSOLE, SEE WHAT YOU CAN FIND OUT.

THERE IS NO RECORD OF CHANCELLOR LOMAC, OR HIS ADMINISTRATION—
NOR IS THERE ANY RECORD OF HIS COMMUNICATIONS WITH THE FEDERATION.
THE ORDER OF THE TIGAN FLAG HAS ALSO CHANGED SINCE WE LEFT THE ENTERPRISE.
THAT DOESN'T MAKE ANY SENSE.

I BELIEVE IT MEANS THAT WE ARE ALL TELLING THE TRUTH.

THERE'S A SECOND ENERGY READING, CAPTAIN.

ANOTHER PULSE?

WEAPONS HAVE BEEN FIRED!

WE ARE UNDER ATTACK!

SHIELDS UP—!

—RED ALERT!

SKRREEAAK
ENTERPRISE, THIS IS RIKER—
—COME IN, ENTERPRISE.

SKRREEAAK
NOTHING.
THE ENTERPRISE WOULD RESPOND IF IT COULD.
AND THE TIGANS AREN'T GOING TO LET US POKE AROUND IN THEIR CENTRAL COMPUTER ALL DAY...

...I NEED ANSWERS NOW, DATA.
THESE READINGS PROVE THE COMPUTER WAS EXPOSED TO A LOW-GRADE GRAVIMETRIC PULSE AT APPROXIMATELY THE SAME TIME WE BEAMED DOWN.

THE ENERGY READING THE ENTERPRISE PICKED UP.
I BELIEVE SO.
IT IS POSSIBLE A PULSE LIKE THAT COULD BE USED TO WIPE THE COMPUTER CORE CLEAN...
...SO THAT SOMEONE COULD REWRITE THE CORE WITH NEW INFORMATION.

THE HUMANS ARE ASKING QUESTIONS....
THE ENTIRE CORE? IT'S ENORMOUS.
THE MEMORY CORE BECAME 1.3 TRILLION MEGA-BITS SMALLER AFTER THE PULSE.
THE TIGANS HAVEN'T USED A WRITTEN HISTORY IN CENTURIES—
IT'S ALL STORED ON THESE COMPTERS.

IF WHAT YOU'RE SAYING IS TRUE, DATA...
...SOMEONE MAY BE REWRITING WHOLE PIECES OF TIGAN HISTORY.

ACCORDING TO THE SECURITY LOGS, THE SYSTEM'S BEEN AFFECTED BY A PULSE LIKE THIS BEFORE.
TEN TIMES IN THE LAST TWO HUNDRED YEARS, SIX IN THE LAST DECADE.

IDEAS?
IT WOULD TAKE A LARGE BURST TO REWRITE THE ENTIRE COMPUTER CORE.
MY TRICORDER SHOULD BE ABLE TO TRACK THE SOURCE OF THE ENERGY.

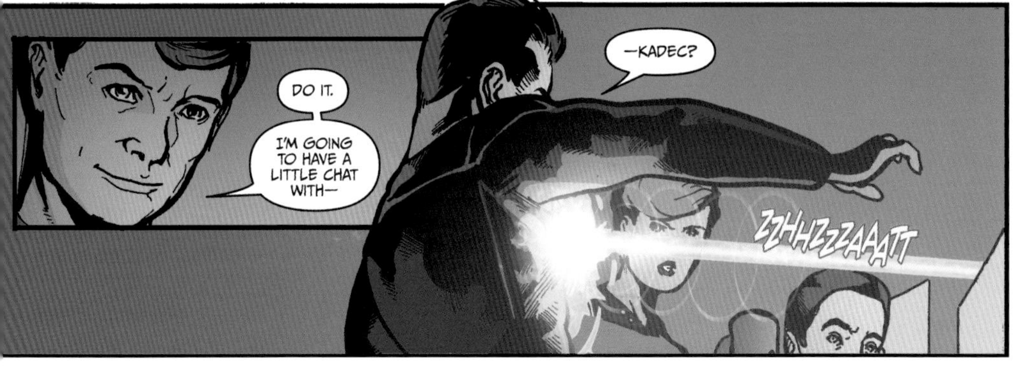
DO IT.
I'M GOING TO HAVE A LITTLE CHAT WITH—
—KADEC?
ZZHHZZZAAATT

UGHHHH!
ZZHHZZAAATT
ZZHHZZAAATT

USE THE GRAVITON GUN.

FWWWOOOHHM

I AM LOMAC, CHANCELLOR.
LOMAC? YES, I THINK I'VE HEARD OF YOU. GOOD WORK—
THANK YOU, CHANCELLOR.

—NOW HELP GET THESE PRISONERS TO A CELL.

CAPTAIN'S LOG: SUPPLEMENTAL—
THE *ENTERPRISE* HAS BEEN HIT BY A MASSIVE GRAVIMETRIC PULSE, WHICH IS PUSHING US ACROSS THE GALAXY AT NEAR-LIGHT SPEEDS.

THE CHIEF SAYS IT'S NO USE, CAPTAIN.
EVEN AT FULL WARP POWER, WE CAN'T BEAT THE FORCE OF THE PULSE. ALL WE'RE DOING IS BURNING OUT THE WARP DRIVE.
IF WE DO NOT ACT SOON, WE WILL END UP IN THE GAMMA QUADRANT...
AND I, FOR ONE, DO NOT WISH TO GO THERE.

ENGINEERING— THIS IS THE CAPTAIN...
IF WE INCREASE OUR SPEED TO FULL WARP POWER, AND ADD IT TO THE MOMENTUM OF THE GRAVIMETRIC WAVE, CAN YOU CALCULATE THE ADDITIONAL VELOCITY?
THAT'D PUSH US CLOSE TO WARP 10, SIR... BUT I DON'T RECOMMEND—
STAND BY.

CAN THE SHIP TAKE THAT KIND OF STRESS?
MY PEOPLE ARE ON THAT PLANET, COUNSELOR.
I'D RATHER BLOW THE *ENTERPRISE* TO KINGDOM COME THAN LEAVE THEM BEHIND.

IF WE CAN GET TO THAT SPEED, THEN BREAK AWAY...
WE COULD SLINGSHOT BACK AROUND...
QUITE RIGHT, GEORDI.
SNAP

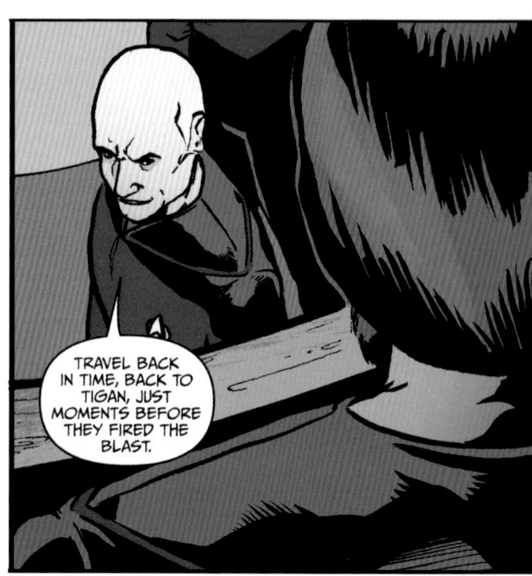
TRAVEL BACK IN TIME, BACK TO TIGAN, JUST MOMENTS BEFORE THEY FIRED THE BLAST.

THE EXACT TIME DILATION WILL REQUIRE A ONE-IN-A-MILLION CALCULATION, CAPTAIN.
EVEN IF WE SUCCEED, WE WILL HAVE ONLY ONE CHANCE TO DISABLE THEIR SHIELDS.

THEN I SUGGEST YOU START BRUSHING UP ON YOUR MATH, MR. WORF.
YES, SIR.

"MAKE IT SO."

WE WERE TOLD THE TIGANS NO LONGER USED BOOKS.
THE PEOPLE ARE TOLD WHAT THEY NEED TO KNOW.
IT WAS AN ACCIDENT—THE FIRST TIME...

...WE WERE TESTING THE GRAVIMATRIX, AND THERE WAS A PULSE. WE LOST EVERYTHING.
AS WE INPUT THE INFORMATION BY HAND, THERE WERE SOME—THE ONES IN GOVERNMENT—WHO THOUGHT WE COULD MAKE THINGS BETTER.

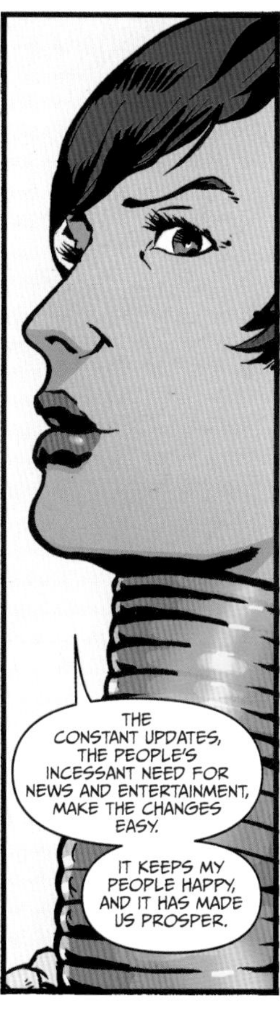
THE CONSTANT UPDATES, THE PEOPLE'S INCESSANT NEED FOR NEWS AND ENTERTAINMENT, MAKE THE CHANGES EASY.
IT KEEPS MY PEOPLE HAPPY, AND IT HAS MADE US PROSPER.

IS THAT WHAT HAPPENED TO CHANCELLOR LOMAC?
MY FAMILY HAS BEEN ENTRUSTED WITH THE REVISIONS FOR CENTURIES—

—MANY DO NOT EVER NEED TO DO WHAT MUST BE DONE. I HAVE BEEN CALLED TO SERVE MANY TIMES.
ALL OF THOSE BATTLES AND HEROES LOST IN TIME—MAY I ASK YOU, CHANCELLOR KADEC...
...WHAT HAPPENS WHEN SOMEONE REWRITES YOU?

ENOUGH.
YOU'VE DELAYED THIS TOO LONG, ALREADY.
YOUR PLAN WILL NOT SUCCEED.

YOU SHOULD HOPE IT DOES.
ONCE YOUR BRAIN ACQUIRES THE NEW UPDATE, WE WILL SEND YOU BACK TO THE *ENTERPRISE*, SO YOU CAN TELL THEM OF YOUR PLEASANT VISIT ON TIGAN.

IF NOT, WE WILL KILL YOU, ALONG WITH THE OTHERS, AND TELL YOUR CAPTAIN OF THE TRAGIC ACCIDENT AT THE GRAVIMATRIX.

YOU SHOULD BE FLATTERED— NOT MANY WATCH HISTORY BEING MADE.
IT IS MY EXPERIENCE THAT KNOWLEDGE MAY BE SUPPRESSED, BUT THAT IT ALWAYS ENDURES.

DO IT, EDIC. NOW!

I TRUST OUR NEXT CONVERSATION WILL BE MORE PLEASANT.

ANOTHER PULSE?
NO WAY OF KNOWING WHAT THAT'LL BRING—

—WE NEED TO GET OUT OF HERE, NOW.

I'VE ALTERED MY COMBADGE.
YOU'LL HAVE A HEADACHE FOR A WEEK, BUT IT'LL DO THE TRICK.
GOOD WORK, LIEUTENANT.
WHEN THE GUARD COMES WITH THE NEXT MEAL, I NEED YOU TO DISTRACT HIM—

WITH ALL DUE RESPECT, SIR...
...I THINK YOU MAY BE BETTER EQUIPPED TO DISTRACT THIS PARTICULAR GUARD.
REALLY?

"REALLY."

I'D LIKE TO TALK ABOUT SOME DIETARY CHANGES FOR THE FOOD—
IF YOU HAVE A MINUTE.
I'M SURE THE CHEF CAN ACCOMMODATE—

TAK
ARRGGHHH!
NOW!

WE HAVE ABOUT AN HOUR BEFORE THE GUARDS WAKE UP.
TCK

PLENTY OF TIME TO FIND DATA AND GET THE HELL OUT OF HERE.
YES, SIR.

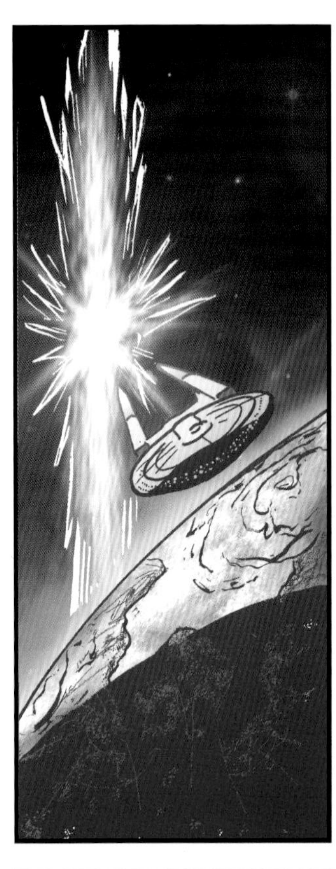

SIR! I DON'T KNOW HOW...
...BUT THE ENTERPRISE JUST APPEARED IN ORBIT!

FIRE AT WILL, MR. WORF.
AYE, SIR!

HHWAAUUGHHHHH

HHWAAAUUGHHHHHH

BOOOM

TZHHZZAAT
BOOOMMM

YOU'RE TOO LATE, COMMANDER RIKER.

WHAT DID YOU DO TO DATA?

IF HE'S HURT, KADEC—
YOU WILL DO NOTHING.
HE *CAN'T*—

—BUT I *WILL*.

EDIC—
WHAT DO YOU
THINK YOU'RE
DOING?
I'M TAKING
CONTROL,
KADEC.
SOMETHING
MY FAMILY
SHOULD HAVE
DONE A LONG
TIME AGO.

WE ARE
ARRESTING FORMER
CHANCELLOR KADEC
FOR CRIMES AGAINST
THE STATE.
...DID ANYONE
GET THE NAME OF
THAT SEHLAT?

DATA—!
I AM HAVING
TROUBLE ADJUSTING MY
AUDITORY INPUT SETTINGS...

THAT LAST
PULSE—?
I MADE A FEW
ADJUSTMENTS.
BUT JUST
A FEW.

AND,
DATA?
HE'LL BE
FINE—

—HIS
POSITRONIC BRAIN
IS A BETTER
SYSTEM THAN OUR
INTERFACE.

ONCE AGAIN, COMMANDER RIKER, YOU HAVE TIGAN'S MOST SINCERE APOLOGY—
AND MY GOVERNMENT LOOKS FORWARD TO WORKING WITH THE FEDERATION.
STARFLEET STILL HAS SOME CONCERNS, BUT IT SHOULD ALL WORK ITSELF OUT.

GOOD LUCK, EDIC.

SKRREEHHK
RIKER TO *ENTERPRISE*—
THREE TO BEAM UP!

NHHHNNNHHNNNNNNNNHHH

WELCOME BACK, NUMBER ONE!
AND WELL DONE.
THANK YOU, SIR.
IT'S GOOD TO BE REMEMBERED.

DATA—?

—WHAT ARE YOU DOING IN THE DARK?

SANTAYANA SAID "THOSE WHO DO NOT LEARN FROM HISTORY ARE DOOMED TO REPEAT IT."

MY POSITRONIC BRAIN REMEMBERS EVERYTHING, SO PERHAPS I CAN LEARN HOW TO BE HUMAN...

...ALTHOUGH I MUST ADMIT, SOMETIMES IT DOES NOT SEEM WORTH THE TROUBLE.

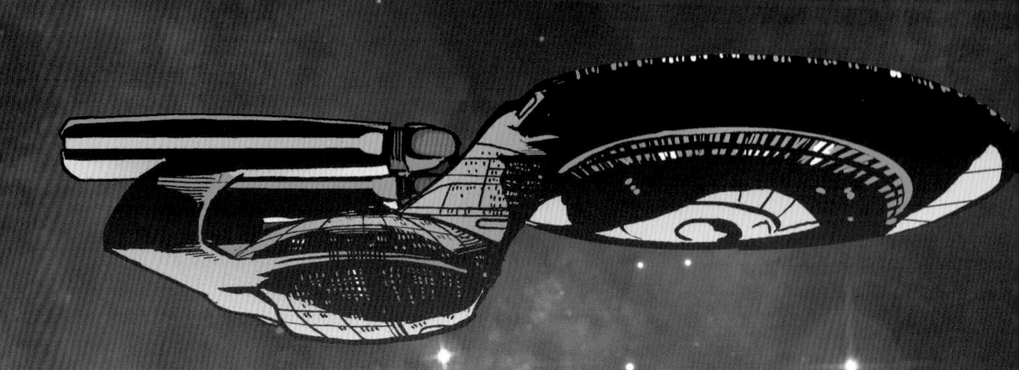

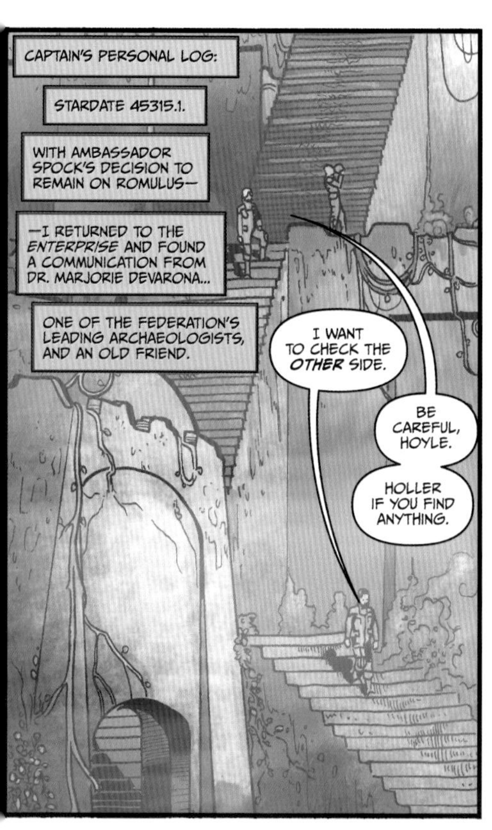
CAPTAIN'S PERSONAL LOG:
STARDATE 45315.1.
WITH AMBASSADOR SPOCK'S DECISION TO REMAIN ON ROMULUS—
—I RETURNED TO THE *ENTERPRISE* AND FOUND A COMMUNICATION FROM DR. MARJORIE DEVARONA...
ONE OF THE FEDERATION'S LEADING ARCHAEOLOGISTS, AND AN OLD FRIEND.
I WANT TO CHECK THE ***OTHER*** SIDE.
BE CAREFUL, HOYLE.
HOLLER IF YOU FIND ANYTHING.

HOW YOU DOING UP THERE, KOB?
SHE HAD DISCOVERED THE RUINS OF AN ANCIENT CITY ON RAJATHA PRIME—

2
THE PROPHETS SHINE ON ME TODAY, DR. DEVARONA.
—BECAUSE OF THE PLANET'S UNIQUE IONOSPHERE, ACCURATE SCANS COULD NOT BE TAKEN FROM ORBIT—

—AND THE CHANCE TO EXPLORE A PRISTINE SITE IS AS RARE AS THE ARTIFACTS OUR TEAM HAS UNCOVERED.
I HAVE LEFT COMMANDER RIKER IN COMMAND OF THE *ENTERPRISE*, WITH ORDERS TO RETURN HERE IN A WEEK—
I FOUND SOMETHING!
HURRY!
—UNTIL THEN, I INTEND TO ENJOY MYSELF.

I SAW THE HOLE—THOUGHT IT MIGHT'VE BEEN A METEOR.
A STARFLEET SHUTTLECRAFT.
NX-02
SHUTTLE POD, ACTUALLY. AN ANTIQUE—
—WHICH MEANS THESE SKELETONS HAVE BEEN HERE FOR MORE THAN TWO CENTURIES.
WE SHOULD CHECK THE—
DO YOU HEAR SOMETHING?
HARMONIC DIAMONDS. FROM THE SOUND, THEY'RE FLAWLESS.
A KING'S RANSOM, IN A DIFFERENT ERA.
MEN HAVE KILLED FOR LESS.
WE SHOULD FIND OUT WHO THESE MEN WERE. IT APPEARS THEY SURVIVED THE CRASH—

THE GEMS ARE *PROBABLY* STOLEN.
I WONDER WHO THEY BELONG TO.
THERE'RE *FIVE*—

—ONE FOR EACH OF US.
WHAT ABOUT *SCHWIN?*

THOSE GEMS WILL BE *RETURNED* TO THEIR RIGHTFUL OWNER.
I BELIEVE THE EARTH PHRASE IS "FINDERS-KEEPERS."

WE CAN *DISCUSS* THIS LATER.
LET'S GET BACK TO *CAMP*—

—WE'RE LOSING THE LIGHT.

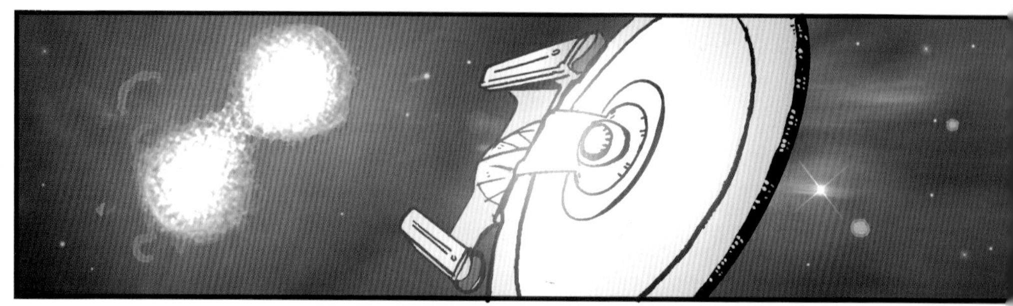

COMPUTER—
OPEN DOOR
TO PROGRAM,
CRUSHER 54.

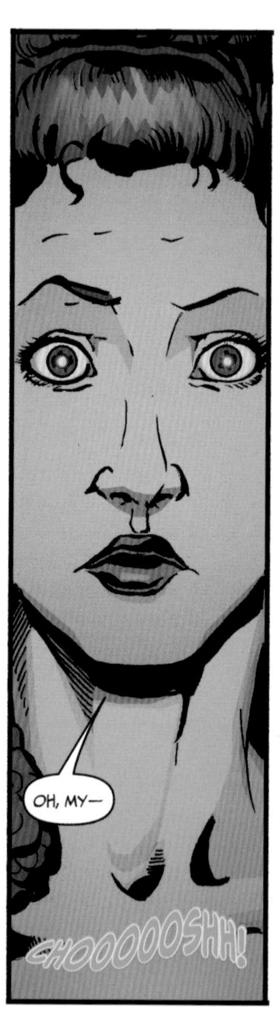
OH, MY—
CHOOOOOOSHH!

IT'S ANOTHER DISCO SATURDAY NIGHT, HERE AT THE BRIDGE CLUB...
SO LET'S GIVE IT UP FOR BROOKLYN'S BEST—
COMPUTER... WHAT YEAR IS THIS?

THE YEAR IS 1975.
—MIKEY AND BEVERLY!

YOU BAJORANS THINK SMALL, KOB.

SOME OF THE GREATEST SCIENTIFIC MINDS IN THE GALAXY—AT A DISCOVERY OF TREMENDOUS IMPORTANCE...

...WASTING THEIR TIME OVER DIAMONDS NO ONE CAN KEEP.

PERHAPS ONE OF THEM WILL FIND A WAY, PICARD.

THAT'S THE KIND OF THINKING THAT KEEPS YOU WORKING AS A COOK, SCHWIN—

AND WANTED BY THE KLINGONS.

WHAT WOULD YOU DO WITH THE MONEY, DR. DEVARONA?

I'D SET UP A FOUNDATION, TO FINANCE HUNDREDS OF DIGS, ALL ACROSS THE QUADRANT. THE INSTITUTE ONLY FUNDS A FEW EACH YEAR.
OR I MIGHT BUY A *MOON*.

YOU, *TOO*, MARJORIE?
THERE'S A LITTLE *FERENGI* IN ALL OF US, JEAN-LUC.

AFTER OUR CHECK-IN *TOMORROW*, THE POINT IS MOOT.
THE *REAL* OWNERS ARE LONG DEAD—YOU SAID SO *YOURSELF*.
TAKE IT UP WITH THE FEDERATION.

BUT FOR *TONIGHT*—HOW DO WE DIVIDE THEM?
I'LL KEEP THEM *SAFE*.
I FOUND THEM.

WHY DON'T YOU *EACH* TAKE ONE? THEN YOU DON'T HAVE TO TRUST *ANYONE*.
ANYONE BUT *YOU*.
YOU CAN GIVE MINE TO SCHWIN.

A WISE *MOVE*, PICARD.
GOOD NIGHT.

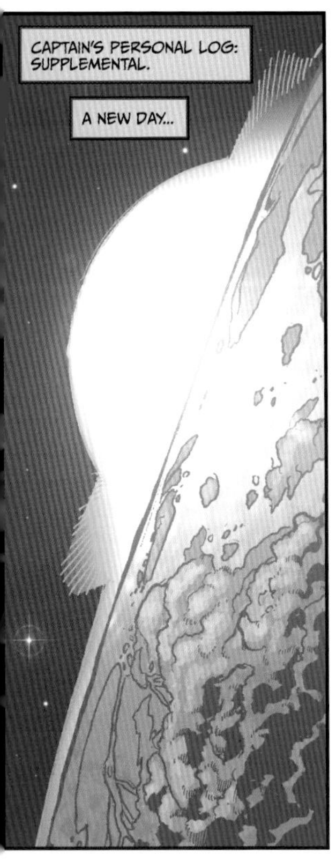
CAPTAIN'S PERSONAL LOG: SUPPLEMENTAL.
A NEW DAY...

...I ONLY HOPE THE MORNING RAIN WASHES AWAY LAST NIGHT'S RANCOR, SO WE CAN ALL GET BACK TO WORK.

I WENT TO CHECK-IN THIS MORNING—BUT THE COMM SYSTEM WON'T WORK.
ONE OF THE CHIPS IS MISSING.
WHO HAS ACCESS TO THE RADIO?
WE ALL DO.

HAS ANYONE SEEN DR. DEVARONA—?
WE WERE SUPPOSED TO MEET AN HOUR AGO.
FIND GEST AND SCHWIN...
...I WANT TO SEE EVERYONE BACK HERE IN FIVE MINUTES—WITH THOSE DIAMONDS!

MARJORIE WAS AN EXCELLENT CLIMBER...

THIS DID NOT HAPPEN BY ACCIDENT. SHE WAS *PUSHED*. OR THROWN.

YOU THINK ONE OF *US* DID THIS?

WITHOUT A PROPER AUTOPSY, IT'S HARD TO SAY *WHAT* HAPPENED.

HER DIAMOND'S *GONE*. OF COURSE IT WAS ONE OF US.

THERE IS ONE *OTHER* EXPLANATION—

—WE'RE NOT THE ONLY PEOPLE ON THIS PLANET.

SOMEONE GOT THE PHASERS, TOO.
I CHECKED THOSE CONTAINERS *YESTERDAY*.

I'M GOING *BACK* TO THE ZIGGURAT.
THAT SHUTTLE POD IS OLD, BUT WE MAY BE ABLE TO USE SOME OF ITS *PARTS* FOR THE COMM...

I MAY BE ABLE TO GET THAT PHASE PISTOL WORKING, TOO.
IF IT'S *STILL* THERE.

DOES ANYONE WANT TO COME WITH ME?
I THINK WE SHOULD STAY *TOGETHER*.

LET HIM GO.

–I WILL SURVIVE!
IT'S CALLED DISCO—A LATE 20TH CENTURY DANCE STYLE.
SOMETIMES TAP AND JAZZ CAN FEEL RESTRICTIVE—
IT'S CERTAINLY COLORFUL.
TUESDA NIGH IS LAD S NI T!

—DISCO IS MORE "FREESTYLE." AND I'VE LOST FIVE POUNDS.
YOU SHOULD TRY IT.
MAYBE I WILL.

HEY, BEV—YOU WANNA DANCE?
MIKEY, THIS IS MY FRIEND, DEANNA—
NICE TO MEET YOU.

JUST STAY AWAY FROM ANYONE NAMED "CARLOS"...
HE HAS TWO LEFT FEET—AND HE'S A GRABBER.
I'LL BE FINE, BEVERLY.

WHO'S THE NEW GIRL WITH BEV—?
YOU SHOULD ASK HER TO DANCE, CARLOS.

AS SOON AS STARBASE 14 FAILED TO GET OUR SCHEDULED TRANSMISSION, I KNEW THE *ENTERPRISE* WOULD BE ON ITS WAY.

SNAP

ZZZZZAAATTTTT!
I JUST HAD TO SURVIVE UNTIL THEN.

ZZZZZAAAATTTT!

ZZZZZZAAATTTTT!
KRASHHH

ZZZZZZAAATTTTT!

THE RAJATHAN CITY WENT UNDISCOVERED FOR TWO THOUSAND YEARS...

...I COULD WAIT ONE DAY TO FIND OUT WHO WANTED ME DEAD.

WHAM
UGGHHHH!

NOOOOO!

ALL RIGHT, DR. HOYLE—
—LET'S TAKE A WALK, SHALL WE?

IT *WASN'T* ME.
LOOK AT MY PHASER— IT HASN'T BEEN FIRED.

AND THE PHASE PISTOL IS *GONE*—
—AS YOU PREDICTED.
IT WAS A GUESS!

SCHWIN'S DEAD...

...AND THE COMM SYSTEM'S BEEN DESTROYED.
I MAY BE ABLE TO ACCESS THE POD'S DATA RECORDER...

ZZHHZZZAAATT!
-AAAAAHHHHH!
HOYLE—?!

LET ME—!
NO!

HHNNNNMMHHHH—!

ZZZZZAAATTTTT!

THAT'S *ENOUGH*, GEST!

HOYLE ATTACKED ME.
HE KILLED KOB.

LET ME PROVE IT TO YOU—
EASY...

—HERE. THIS IS THE PHASER HE USED TO SHOOT AT YOU.
BUT THE DIAMONDS ARE GONE—
—HE HID THEM, AND NOW WE'LL NEVER FIND THEM.
GEST—FOR HEAVEN'S SAKE, OF ALL THE CHILDISH—

I SAW HIM KILL SCHWIN IN THE SHUTTLE POD—AND HE KILLED KOB.
AND, DR. DEVARONA?
HOYLE DID ALL OF IT—YES.
YOU'VE CONVINCED ME, GEST—

—BUT I THINK I'VE MADE A BIGGER DISCOVERY...
...AND I NEED YOUR HELP.

DANCE CONTEST TONIGHT!

RIKER TO DR. CRUSHER—

CRUSHER, HERE.

—I NEED YOU IN TRANSPORTER ROOM THREE IN TEN MINUTES, DOCTOR.

ACKNOWLEDGED.

COMPUTER—

—SAVE PROGRAM, CRUSHER 54.

READY?
WE GO ON *THREE.*

ONE...
...TWO—

—*PUSH!*
WAS THAT "THREE?"

HNNNNNN!

RHHHNNNMMMMBBBLL

WHAAAA-BOOMMHH!

THE RAJATHANS WERE PATHOLOGICALLY NON-JUDGEMENTAL—
—IT MAKES SENSE THAT THEY'D LEAVE THEIR DEAD ENTRANCES TO HEAVEN **AND** THE UNDERWORLD.
IT GOES TO THE **SAME** ROOM AS THE TEMPLE ENTRANCE, UP TOP?
THEY HAVE THE **SAME** MARKINGS—

—LET'S SEE IF WE CAN OPEN IT.

CLK

IT WORKED!
I FOUND AN ENTRY ABOUT THIS ENTRANCE IN THE SHUTTLE POD'S DATA RECORDER...

...THE PILOTS ***KILLED*** EACH OTHER BEFORE THEY COULD DECIPHER THE DESIGNS.
COMPLETELY ***UNDISTURBED.***
WE ARE THE FIRST PEOPLE TO WALK ***THESE*** HALLS IN OVER TWO MILLENNIA.

IT'S AN AMAZING FIND, AND ***IRONIC***...
...THIS ROOM IS MORE VALUABLE THAN A ***STARSHIP*** FULL OF HARMONIC DIAMONDS.
SPEAKING OF THAT—
—I WANT YOU TO HAVE ***THIS.***

WHY?
HOYLE HAD THE OTHER GEMS.
YES, YOU MENTIONED THAT—

STANDING HERE, I REMEMBER WHY I BECAME AN ARCHAEOLOGIST.
TAKE IT.
I'VE ACTED TERRIBLY. THIS IS WHAT'S IMPORTANT TO ME.

WELL DONE, GEST.
WHAT ARE YOU TALKING ABOUT?
CLAP CLAP CLAP CLAP

YOU WANT ME TO BELIEVE HOYLE HID ALL THE GEMS—
—THAT THEY ARE ALL LOST...
...SO YOU GIVE ME ONE STONE, AND YOU WALK OFF THIS PLANET WITH THE OTHER FOUR.

I DON'T KNOW WHAT YOU'RE TALKING ABOUT.
MY GUESS IS THE DIAMONDS ARE SAFE, AT THE BOTTOM OF YOUR CANTEEN—
—WHICH YOU DRANK FROM EACH DAY BEFORE WE FOUND THE GEMS, BUT NOT SINCE.

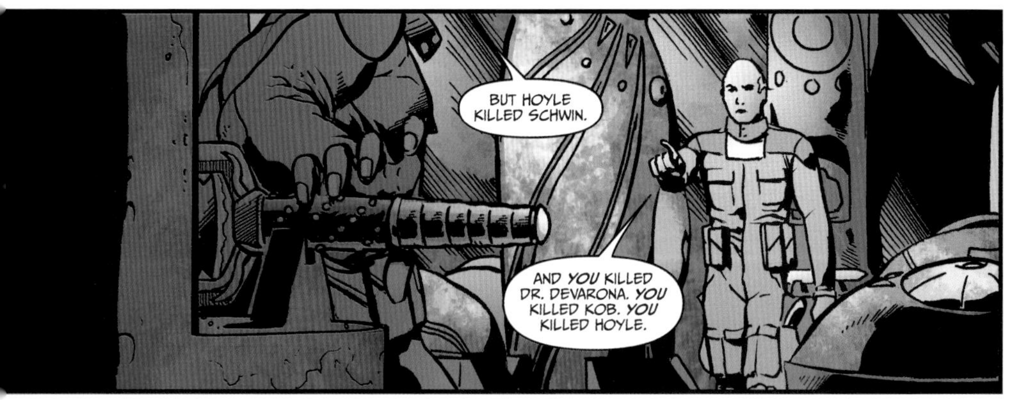
BUT HOYLE KILLED SCHWIN.
AND *YOU* KILLED DR. DEVARONA. *YOU* KILLED KOB. *YOU* KILLED HOYLE.

WOULD YOU LIKE THE PHASER?
DON'T *MOVE*.
WHERE WILL YOU GO?

I CONTACTED MY SHIP BEFORE I DISABLED THE COMM SYSTEM—
—THEY'LL BE HERE BEFORE THE *ENTERPRISE*...

...WHO WILL NEVER FIND YOU TRAPPED IN THIS TOMB.
ENJOY THE RELICS, PICARD.

CAN WE *HELP* YOU WITH SOMETHING, DR. GEST?
CAPTAIN'S LOG:

...STARDATE 45317.8.
THE SHUTTLE WAS REPORTED STOLEN FROM THE *NX-2 COLUMBIA* IN 2296—
—BUT THE DIAMONDS WERE ***UNREGISTERED***.

DR. CRUSHER FOUND THE JEWELS EMIT A LOW-LEVEL ENERGY WAVE...
THE WEALTH WOULD HAVE BEEN THEIRS.
HAVE YOU GIVEN ANY THOUGHT TO WHAT YOU'LL DO WITH THE TREASURE?

...STIMULATING AREAS OF THE BRAIN ASSOCIATED WITH PRIMITIVE EMOTIONS, INCLUDING ANGER, ENVY, AND GREED.
PER DR. DEVARONA'S LAST REQUEST, THE DAYSTROM INSTITUTE IS FINANCING ADDITIONAL ARCHAEOLOGICAL DIGS ACROSS THE QUADRANT...

...AND I MAY BUY A MOON.
A MOON, SIR?
THERE'S A LITTLE FERENGI IN ALL OF US, NUMBER ONE.

I HAVE WONDERED WHY THE GEMS DIDN'T AFFECT ME. PERHAPS IT WAS BECAUSE I NEVER PHYSICALLY HELD THEM, AS THE OTHERS DID.
OR PERHAPS A STARSHIP CAPTAIN CRAVES SOMETHING MORE.
HELM, AHEAD WARP FACTOR THREE—!

LIEUTENANT.
ENSIGN.

BOOOOMM

WUUHRRAHHHRRRR WUUHRRAHHHRRRR

WUUHRRRHHHRRRRR WUUHRRRHHHRRRRR

SKRREEKKK
LIEUTENANT WORF—REPORT TO THE BRIDGE!

DEANNA!

SKRREEKKK
WORF TO SICKBAY—
—MEDICAL EMERGENCY IN COUNSELOR TROI'S QUARTERS!
WUUHRRRHHHRRRRR WUUHRRRHHHRRRRR

SKKRRAATTKKKT
THE WARP ENGINES ARE OFF-LINE, CAPTAIN—
BOOMM
—ALL AVAILABLE POWER'S BEEN REROUTED TO THE SHIELDS.
HOW LONG BEFORE THE ENGINES ARE REPAIRED, MR. LA FORGE?
SIX HOURS— MINIMUM.
SENSORS ARE BACK ON-LINE, CAPTAIN.
VISUAL, MR. DATA—QUICKLY.
BE READY TO FIRE ON MY MARK, ENSIGN—
AYE, SIR.
—FIRE!
WHAT THE HELL IS *THAT?*

CAPTAIN'S LOG:
STARDATE 47630.1.
ZZZZZZHHHHHHHHHTTTTT
THE *ENTERPRISE* IS ON A MISSION TO MAP THE BANDOR SYSTEM, A REMOTE AREA OF SPACE WHICH RECENTLY CAME UNDER FEDERATION JURISDICTION.
THOOOM
THOOOM
NCC-1701-D
WE HAVE BEEN ATTACKED BY AN UNKNOWN ASSAILANT.
THE *ENTERPRISE* HAS BEEN DAMAGED AND CREWMEN ARE INJURED.

BRING US AROUND, MR. KARP.

YOU'RE *LATE, MR.* WORF—
—TAKE YOUR STATION.

GGRRRRR—!

TTTHHNUGHT
TTTHHNUGHT
NCC-1701-D

FIRE!

NCC-1701-D
ZZZZZZOAAAAAAHHHHHHTTT

TTTHHHOOUUG
TTTHHHOOUUG

"HOLD YOUR FIRE–!"

OPEN A HAILING FREQUENCY.
CAPTAIN, THE ALIEN VESSEL IS POWERING ENGINES...

ZZZZZHHHHHMMMMM

THAT LAST ATTACK TOOK OUT THE SUB-LIGHT ENGINES.
SHIELDS ARE HOLDING AT TWENTY-FOUR PERCENT, BUT IF WE PUSH IT ANY MORE THAN THAT, WE'LL START LOSING OTHER SYSTEMS.

THERE IS NO SIGN OF THE ALIEN VESSEL'S RETURN, AND LONG-RANGE SENSORS HAVE BEEN RECONFIGURED TO DETECT ITS WARP SIGNATURE.

WE HAVE WEAPONS, BUT COMMUNICATIONS ARE INOPERATIVE.

THE *ENTERPRISE* IS CUT OFF FROM STARFLEET—
—A SITTING DUCK!
WHAMMP

THAT SHIP HAS THE DISRUPTOR NACELLES AND THE WARP CORE OF A ROMULAN WARBIRD, A STARFLEET-STYLE SAUCER SECTION—ALL OF IT PROTECTED BY THE SHIELD STRUCTURE OF A BORG CUBE.

THE ROMULAN PART OF THE SHIP—
—DO WE KNOW IF THEY HAVE A CLOAKING DEVICE?

WE DON'T THINK SO...
...BUT THEIR SHIELD FREQUENCIES MODULATE SO OFTEN, IT'S HARD FOR OUR SENSORS TO GET AN ACCURATE LOCK.

WHOEVER THEY ARE, THEY HAVE *NO* HONOR.
WE MUST ALERT STARFLEET—

—WE COULD BE LOOKING AT SOME KIND OF ROMULAN-BORG ALLIANCE.

A CLASS-9 PROBE COULD CARRY THE INFORMATION.
FROM THIS POSITION, IT SHOULD REACH STARBASE 122 IN ABOUT TWO DAYS.
ONE DAY, NINETEEN HOURS, AND FORTY-SEVEN MINUTES, TO BE EXACT.
MAKE IT SO, MR. LA FORGE.
NUMBER ONE, WORK WITH MR. DATA AND MR. WORF. GO THROUGH THE SENSOR LOGS.
WE'LL FIND *SOMETHING* WE CAN USE.
EVERY SHIP HAS A WEAK SPOT. SOMEWHERE.
YOU HAVE YOUR ASSIGNMENTS.
A MOMENT, MR. WORF...?

CAPTAIN... ABOUT MY ARRIVAL ON THE BRIDGE—
WE ALL CERTAINLY *APPRECIATE* THE HELP YOU GAVE COUNSELOR TROI.
INDEED, YOUR ACTIONS MAY HAVE *SAVED* HER LIFE...
TINK

...BUT WHEN MY FIRST OFFICER GIVES YOU AN ORDER, YOU RESPOND—
—*IMMEDIATELY*, AND WITHOUT HESITATION...

...REGARDLESS OF PERSONAL RELATIONSHIPS.
YES, SIR. UNDERSTOOD.
IT WILL *NOT* HAPPEN AGAIN.

SEE THAT IT DOESN'T.

DISMISSED.

SHOULDN'T YOU BE ON THE BRIDGE?

I'M SORRY, WILL...
...I HAVE 110 PEOPLE ALL SCREAMING FOR A DOCTOR— AND NO TIME FOR A BEDSIDE MANNER.
HOW IS SHE?

WE ALMOST LOST HER. TWICE. CRANIAL TRAUMA, MASSIVE INTERNAL HEMORRHAGING—
SKRREEEKKK
SICKBAY, THIS IS ENGINEERING—
—I'VE GOT AN ENSIGN WITH PLASMA BURNS DOWN HERE, DOCTOR!

SKRREEKKK
ON MY WAY!
GO.
UGGHHHHHH...

...WORF...

SENSORS . DETECT SEVERAL SUBSPACE COMMUNICATIONS RECEIVED BY THE VESSEL—

—BUT I AM UNABLE TO DETERMINE A POINT OF ORIGIN.
WHAT PUZZLES ME IS WHY THE ENTERPRISE WAS ATTACKED.

THE BANDOR SYSTEM IS UNINHABITED, AND OF LITTLE STRATEGIC VALUE.
PERHAPS IT IS AN OLD ENEMY OF CAPTAIN PICARD'S...
THEN WHY BREAK OFF THE ATTACK WHEN THE ENTERPRISE WAS AT A DISADVANTAGE?
A TEST?

THE FIRST BLAST WAS DIRECTED SEVERAL DECKS AWAY FROM THE CAPTAIN'S QUARTERS—
—AND YET OUR ATTACKER KNEW EXACTLY WHERE TO TARGET WEAPONS TO DISABLE THE WARP DRIVE AND COMMUNICATIONS.

ARE YOU SAYING THEY PURPOSELY TARGETED COUNSELOR TROI?
OR SOMEONE THEY KNOW TO BE CLOSE TO HER.
TSSSCHHHH

STATUS REPORT, MR. WORF?

THE SENSOR LOGS HAVE GIVEN US NO ANSWERS...
...BUT COMMANDER DATA HAS A THEORY.
THE ATTACK MAY HAVE BEEN DIRECTED AT COUNSELOR TROI.

BASED ON WHAT *EVIDENCE*?
THE *LACK* OF EVIDENCE, ACTUALLY.
"WHEN ALL OPTIONS FAIL, THE TRUE COURSE IS THE ONLY ONE THAT REMAINS."

SHERLOCK HOLMES?
ELEMENTARY, MY DEAR COMMANDER.

WHAMMPH
SKRREEKKK
CAPTAIN TO THE BRIDGE!
WUUHRRHHHRRRR WUUHRRHHHRRRR

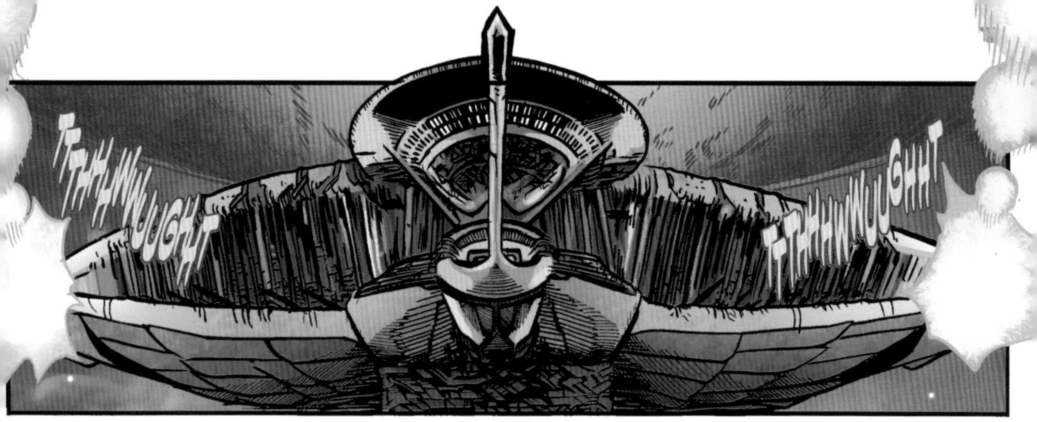
TTHHWWUUGHHT
TTHHWWUUGHHT

BOOOOM

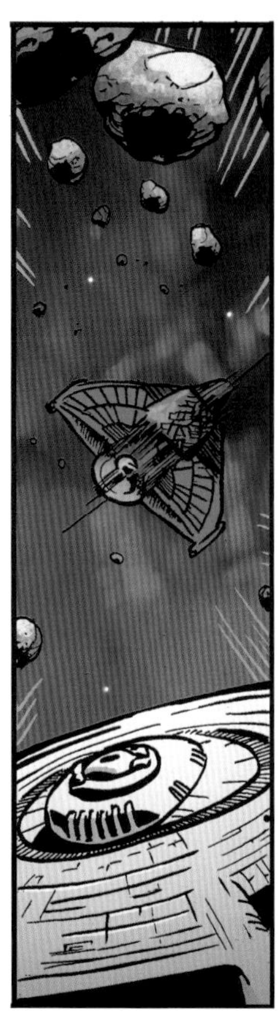

SHIELDS HAVE FALLEN TO SIXTEEN PERCENT.
HELM, EXECUTE MANEUVER EPSILON THETA 3.
MR. WORF— READY PHASERS.
AYE, SIR.

ZZZZAAAAAHHHHHHHHTTTT

PHASER FIRE HAD NO AFFECT.
THE ALIEN VESSEL IS MOVING TO RESPOND.

...HAVE TO TELL YOU...

...THAT SHIP—
DEANNA—!

WORF TO DOCTOR CRUSHER—
—A MEDICAL TEAM IS NEEDED ON THE BRIDGE.
BELAY THAT ORDER, MR. WORF—!
COUNSELOR TROI MAY BE IN FURTHER DANGER, AND I NEED A SECURITY OFFICER TO GET HER TO SICKBAY.
CAN YOU HANDLE THAT?
I'LL TAKE TACTICAL.
QUICKLY, NUMBER ONE!

TTHHWUUGHT
TTHHWUUGHT
NHHHNNNHHNNNNNHHH
ZZZAAKKTT
THANK YOU, WORF.
IN ALL THE CRAZINESS, SHE JUST WALKED OUT THE DOOR!
WWWRRRPP
...NO ONE ON THAT SHIP... NO PEOPLE... TRIED TO TELL...
SKRRREEAAK
WORF TO BRIDGE—
—COUNSELOR TROI BELIEVES THAT SHIP IS RECEIVING ORDERS VIA SOME TYPE OF REMOTE COMMAND—

—THERE IS NO ONE ABOARD.
IF THAT'S TRUE, ALL WE NEED TO DO IS DISRUPT THE SIGNAL.
THE LIEUTENANT SAID THE SHIP RECEIVED SEVERAL COMMUNICATIONS DURING OUR FIRST ENCOUNTER.
MR. DATA, WHAT IS THE MOST EFFECTIVE METHOD OF SEVERING SUB-SPACE COMMUNICATIONS?

SEVERAL TYPES OF RADIATION—
THE MOST EFFECTIVE, DATA.
—AN INTER-RECEPTIVE NETWORK OF SUB-SPACE BEACONS STRATEGICALLY PLACED AT POINTS AROUND THE SHIP'S EXTERIOR WOULD BE BEST...

...INFORMATION WILL JUMP FROM BEACON TO BEACON, CREATING A NEAR-INSTANTANEOUS LOOP—
A WALL OF SOUND.
—A SIMPLISITIC VERSION OF MY OWN POSITRONIC BRAIN...

...POWERFUL ENOUGH TO STOP ANY EXTERIOR COMMUNICATIONS FROM REACHING THE SHIP—
—BUT THE BEACONS NEED TO BE PRECISELY POSITIONED. TO ACCOMPLISH THAT, WE SHOULD GET AS CLOSE TO THE SHIP AS POSSIBLE.

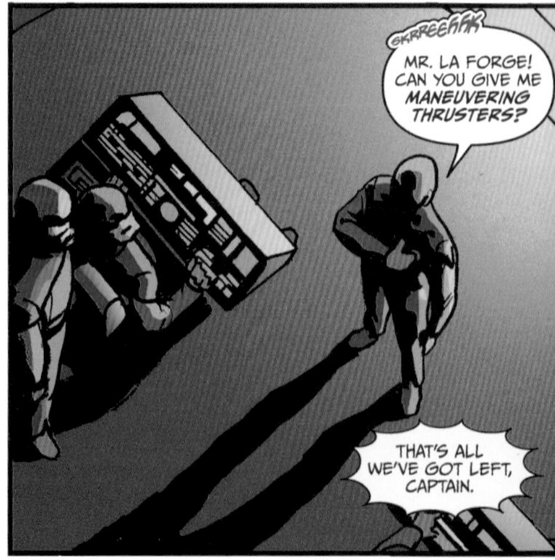
SKRREEEAAK
MR. LA FORGE! CAN YOU GIVE ME MANEUVERING THRUSTERS?
THAT'S ALL WE'VE GOT LEFT, CAPTAIN.

THAT LAST SHOT TOOK OUT THE LEFT NACELLE—
—AND WE'RE WALKING UP AND KNOCKING ON THE FRONT DOOR.

NOW, MR. DATA—!

THUUUHH
THUUUHH
THUUUHH

ZZZAAKKT

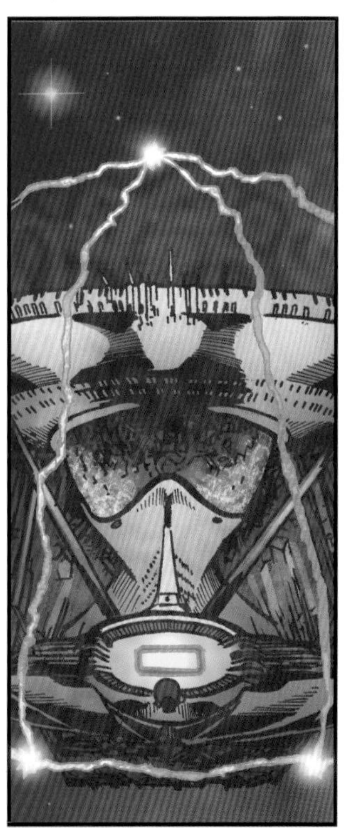

THE SHIP IS POWERING WEAPONS, CAPTAIN.
OUR SHIELDS ARE DOWN TO THREE PERCENT—

"—THE *ENTERPRISE* CANNOT SURVIVE ANOTHER DIRECT HIT."

BHHCCHKKK
BOOOOOOOM

AAAAAHHHHH—!
—STOP!

WHAAMHP
THWAAAPP
WHAAMHP
THWAAAPP
I AM SORRY. I HEARD—
—I DID NOT MEAN TO INTRUDE.

DEANNA AND I WERE TALKING ABOUT OLD TIMES—
OF COURSE. OLD TIMES.
—WE GOT A LITTLE CARRIED AWAY.
CARRIED AWAY. *I SEE.*
THAT'S FOR THE FLOWERS—*AND* THE KTARIAN CHOCOLATE PUFF.
THE *WHAT*—?
THE KTARIAN CHOCOLATE PUFF *YOU* ASKED ME TO BRING DEANNA. YOU SAID IT WAS HER *FAVORITE DESSERT*.
IT WAS DELICIOUS.
REALLY, WORF. YOU'RE SO THOUGHTFUL.

I WAS SO BUSY WORRYING ABOUT A *CLOAKING DEVICE*—I FORGOT THE ROMULANS ALSO HAVE A HISTORY WITH REMOTE-CONTROLLED VESSELS.
WE CAN ONLY SURMISE THE VESSEL HAD A SELF-DESTRUCT PROTOCOL, IN THE EVENT CONTACT WITH ITS CREATOR WAS EVER BROKEN.

AND STARFLEET HAS NO KNOWLEDGE OF ANY VESSEL OF THIS TYPE?
NONE THAT I HAVE BEEN ABLE TO REVEAL.

THAT SHIP WAS DESIGNED TO DESTROY THE *ENTERPRISE*—
—WE GOT ***LUCKY***, DATA.

BUT WE STILL DON'T KNOW WHO OUR ENEMY IS...

"...AND ***THAT*** WILL KEEP ME LOOKING OVER MY SHOULDER FOR QUITE A LONG TIME."

"IT WILL BE *GOOD* TO RETURN TO THE *ENTERPRISE.*"

GODDARD

NCC-1701-D

I'M SURE ***CAPTAIN PICARD*** WILL BE EAGER TO HEAR YOUR REPORT ON OUR STARFLEET BRIEFINGS.

OF COURSE. AS SECURITY CHIEF, IT IS MY ***DUTY***—

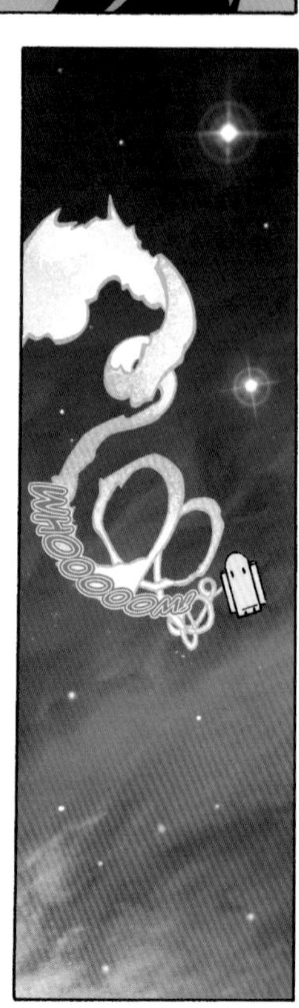

WE'RE NOT GOING *ANYWHERE*.
THE NAVIGATION SYSTEM WAS DAMAGED IN THE CRASH, GEORDI—
—EVEN IF YOU *COULD* FIX THE SHUTTLE, I DON'T KNOW WHERE WE ARE.
WE ARE ALIVE, ENSIGN. AND WE HAVE FOUND SHELTER—
—THAT IS ALL THAT MATTERS.

WE ARE ALMOST THERE.
YOU SAID THAT TWENTY MINUTES AGO.

WHAAK!
WHAAK!
WHAAK!
AAAHHHHH—!
GEORDI!

THE SOLAR ACTIVITY'S INTERFERING WITH MY VISOR.
I'M ADJUSTING THE INPUT, WHICH SHOULD COMPENSATE FOR THE ELECTROMAGNETIC FEEDBACK.

ARE YOU WELL ENOUGH TO CONTINUE?
I'M FINE, WORF. THANKS.

WORF'S RIGHT. SOMETHING MAY HAVE HAPPENED TO THEM.

WE WILL BEGIN A SEARCH OF THE MONASTERY, IMMEDIATELY.

I'VE GOT A *BAD* FEELING ABOUT THIS.

RO, ***STOP WORRYING.***

EVER SINCE WE GOT HERE, I CAN'T EXPLAIN IT...

TCHK-TCHK!

"...IT'S LIKE SOMEONE'S ***WATCHING*** US."

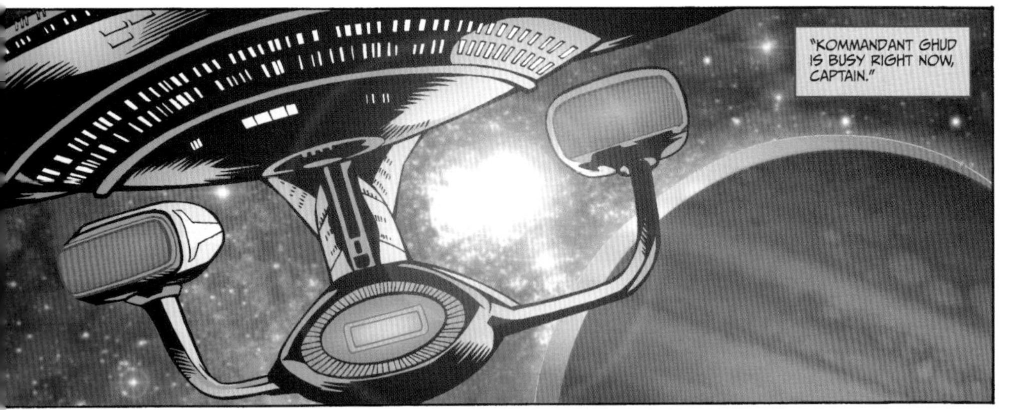
"KOMMANDANT GHUD IS BUSY RIGHT NOW, CAPTAIN."

HIS NAME IS PRONOUNCED "HUD," ENSIGN. ON WYATH, THE "G" IS SILENT...
YES, SIR!
AND, FRANKLY, I DOUBT ANYONE WOULD ACCUSE HIM OF BEING "GOOD."
...MAY THE LIGHT SHINE ON US ALL.

YOU KNOW ME?
KOMMANDANT GHUD, THE SCIENTIST WHO TOOK CONTROL OF THE PLANET WYATH—
—AND DESTROYED THE ECOLOGY OF A DEVELOPING WORLD FOR HIS OWN PROFIT...

...WHEN THE PEOPLE ROSE UP, YOU FLED THE SYSTEM, FUELING A CIVIL WAR.
AND FOR MY RETURN, MY PEOPLE REQUESTED THESE ACCOMMODATIONS?
INDEED, KOMMANDANT. THEY INSISTED.

I AM NOT THE SELFISH DESPOT MY PEOPLE THINK I AM.
I HAVE FOUND THE LIGHT.
AND YET YOU HAVE ALREADY MADE UP YOUR MIND.
I AM NOT HERE TO JUDGE.
SKREEEEET—!
RIKER TO CAPTAIN PICARD—

—WE'RE AT THE RENDEZVOUS POINT, BUT THERE'S NO SIGN OF THE GODDARD.
LONG-RANGE SENSORS ARE PICKING UP SOLAR ACTIVITY AND TRACES OF WARP PLASMA.
ARE THERE ANY OTHER SHIPS IN THE AREA?

THE EXCELSIOR IS TWO DAYS FROM WORF'S LAST REPORTED POSITION.
UNDERSTOOD, NUMBER ONE. MAINTAIN PRESENT COURSE AND SPEED—
—PICARD OUT.

WE CANNOT BE LATE FOR MY HEARING.
I ASSURE YOU, KOMMANDANT— WE WILL REACH WYATH ON TIME.

RIGHT NOW, I AM NEEDED ON THE BRIDGE.
MY APOLOGIES FOR INTERRUPTING YOUR PERSONAL TIME.
IT WASN'T PERSONAL, CAPTAIN. I WAS PRAYING, WHICH IS OPEN TO EVERYONE—

—YOU JUST CAUGHT ME DOING IT WITH MY LEGS CROSSED.
MAY THE LIGHT SHINE ON US ALL.

THIS IS THE THIRD LEVEL DOWN, AND WE HAVEN'T SEEN ANYONE.
WAIT...
WHAT IS IT?

SNNNFF!
SNNNFF!
...I SMELL BLOOD.
A BODY--!

PART OF ONE, AT LEAST.
TORN APART AND EATEN. WHAT KIND OF ANIMAL WOULD DO THIS?
A HUMAN ANIMAL.

TCHK-TCHK!
DON'T WANDER OFF.
I WANT TO SEE WHAT THAT WAS.

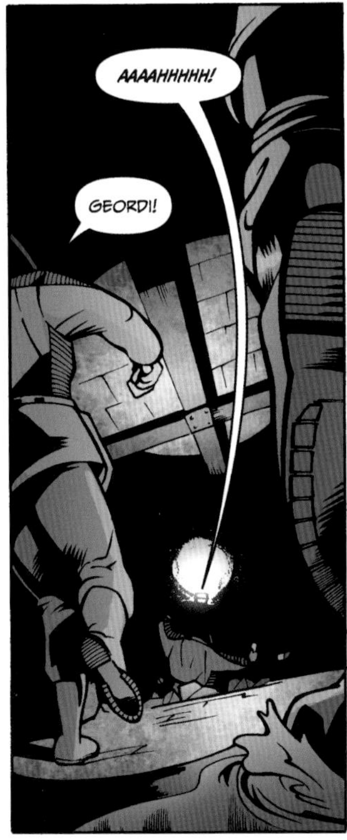
AAAAHHHHH!
GEORDI!

GEORDI—?!
YOU'RE TOO FAR DOWN! WE CAN'T GET YOU OUT!
I'M HERE!

MY VISOR'S PICKING UP SOMETHING IN THE WATER—!
—SOME KIND OF SINGLE-CELLED ALGAE. IT'S GLOWING!

THAT KIND OF PLANT LIFE HASN'T SEEN DAYLIGHT IN THOUSANDS OF YEARS—
—JUST IMAGINE WHAT THE RADIATION FROM A SOLAR FLARE WOULD DO.
AND IF SOMEONE DRANK THAT WATER?

WE'RE GOING TO WORK OUR WAY TOWARD YOU. TRY TO FIND A WAY UP—
—WE'LL MEET YOU IN THE MIDDLE.

WE SHOULD GO RIGHT.
IN SOME CULTURES, EATING THE ENEMY IS CONSIDERED THE ULTIMATE VICTORY.
WE WILL GO LEFT.
THESE PEOPLE AREN'T SOLDIERS, WORF—

—THEY SPEND THEIR DAYS IN QUIET CONTEMPLATION, SEEKING A HIGHER UNDERSTANDING.
WE NEED TO GO RIGHT.
THEY ARE INFECTED NOW. WHAT THEY SEEK MAKES THEM NO LESS DEADLY.

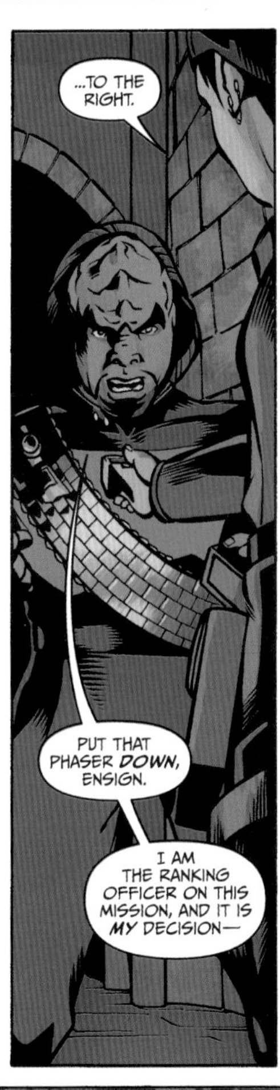
...TO THE RIGHT.
PUT THAT PHASER DOWN, ENSIGN.
I AM THE RANKING OFFICER ON THIS MISSION, AND IT IS MY DECISION—

TCHK-TCHK!

MOVE!

MY PHASER'S SET ON FULL STUN—WITH NO EFFECT!
THEY'RE COMING FROM BOTH TUNNELS!
TCHK-TCHK! TCHK-TCHK! TCHK-TCHK! TCHK-TCHK!
TCHK-TCHK! TCHK-TCHK! TCHK-TCHK! TCHK-TCHK!

KRAK!
WWHHHHOOMMMF!
WHAM
TCHK-TCHK! TCHK-TCHK! TCHK-TCHK! TCHK-TCHK! TCHK-TCHK! TCHK-TCHK! TCHK-TCHK! TCHK-TCHK!

SOLAR ACTIVITY IN THE AREA IS AFFECTING OUR SENSORS. ANY FURTHER SCANS HAVE PROVED INCONCLUSIVE, CAPTAIN.
AND WE NEED TO BE ON WYATH *TOMORROW*.
WYATH LAW IS VERY SPECIFIC IN REGARD TO TIME—

—ARRIVING EVEN A MINUTE LATE COULD RESULT IN THE CHARGES AGAINST GHUD BEING DROPPED.
GHUD BELIEVES HE IS INNOCENT.
BECAUSE OF "THE LIGHT?"
HE WAS INTRODUCED TO ITS PHILOSOPHY WHILE LIVING IN EXILE.

AND THIS BELIEF WIPES AWAY HIS CRIMES?
NO, BUT HE CONSIDERS THEM "IRRELEVANT."
BECAUSE HE COMMITTED THE ACTS *BEFORE* HIS CONVERSION.

WHEN WE SPOKE, GHUD EXHIBITED *JOY* WHEN HE TALKED ABOUT HIS CRIMES. HE BELIEVES WITHOUT THEM, HE WOULD NOT HAVE FOUND THE LIGHT.
IT DOES SEEM TO BE A RATHER CONVENIENT TRANSFORMATION.
SKREEEEET—!
BRIDGE, THIS IS THE BRIG—

GO AHEAD, NEWMAN.
—IT'S KOMMANDANT GHUD, SIR. HE SAYS HE WANTS TO *HELP* US FIND THE *MISSING* SHUTTLECRAFT.

A HIGHER PHASER SETTING WILL *KILL* THEM.

I AM *OPEN* TO SUGGESTIONS.

THE FLOOR—!

GEORDI FELL THROUGH THE FLOOR.

QUICKLY— USE YOUR PHASER!

ZZZZZAAHHHHTTT!

KER- AAHHHHKK!

RUN!

KRRRR-

-AAAHHHHHHK!

WE ARE SAFE, BUT GEORDI REMAINS IN DANGER.
AND POSSIBLY INFECTED.
ONE THING AT A TIME, WORF.
BAJORANS DO *NOT* GLORIFY WAR AS KLINGONS DO.
BUT YOU FIGHT WITH HONOR.

UNDERSTAND, GHUD, I WILL NOT DIVERT OUR COURSE, EVEN IF YOU LOCATE THE MISSING CREWMEN.
THAT WILL BE YOUR CHOICE, PICARD.
THE LIGHT TELLS ME MINE IS TO *HELP* YOU FIND THEM.

BEFORE I BECAME WYATH'S LEADER, I WAS AN ENGINEER.
I *RECONFIGURED* OUR SENSOR ARRAY AND MADE MY PLANET A HUB FOR INTERSTELLAR TRANSPORT.
YOU *USED* THAT ARRAY TO TRACK DOWN YOUR POLITICAL ENEMIES AND *EXECUTE* THEM.

MY CRIMES ARE YESTERDAY'S PROBLEM.

TODAY, I NEED ACCESS TO THE LONG-RANGE SENSORS AND THE DEFLECTOR GRID...
...NOTHING THAT WILL ALLOW ME TO TAKE CONTROL OF YOUR SHIP, PICARD, I ASSURE YOU.
ALL ESSENTIAL SYSTEMS HAVE BEEN LOCKED OUT FROM THIS LOCATION, CAPTAIN.
MAKE IT SO.

IF WE NEED ASSISTANCE, CAPTAIN, I WILL ASK THE SECURITY TEAM YOU'VE PLACED AT THE DOOR.
KEEP ME APPRISED, MR. DATA.
UNDERSTOOD, CAPTAIN.

WHERE IS THE NEAREST STARBASE?
STARBASE 172 IS TWELVE-POINT-SEVEN LIGHT YEARS FROM OUR CURRENT POSITION—

IS THERE MORE?
I BELIEVE IT IS WHAT HUMANS WOULD CALL A *HABIT*...
...I AM ACCUSTOMED TO BEING CUT OFF WHEN I GIVE WHAT OTHERS PERCEIVE AS NON-ESSENTIAL INFORMATION.

WE WILL *SYNC* THE *ENTEPRISE'S* SENSOR INPUT WITH STARBASE 172—
—THEN TRIANGULATE THEM WITH THE ARRAY ON WYATH, AND BOOST THE SIGNAL THROUGH THE DEFLECTOR GRID.

WYATH IS NOT A MEMBER OF THE FEDERATION—
MY POLICIES CAUSED THE DEATH OF FORTY-SEVEN MILLION PEOPLE. YOU ARE BRINGING ME HOME TO STAND TRIAL...
...WYATH WILL GIVE US WHATEVER WE NEED.

YOU SAID ONE OF YOUR FRIENDS WEARS A *VISOR* OF SOME KIND?
GEORDI, YES. IT ENABLES HIM TO SEE.
ONCE WE ESTABLISH THE SENSOR PARAMETER, WE SHOULD BE ABLE TO TRACE THE ENERGY PATTERNS IN HIS DEVICE.

LIEUTENANT COMMANDER WORF WEARS A KLINGON SASH, AND ENSIGN RO IS BAJORAN.
THE METALS IN THE SASH AND IN THE EARRING ARE BOTH UNIQUE TO THOSE HOME WORLDS.
THE *COMBINATION* OF THOSE METALS AND THE VISOR WILL *SHINE* LIKE THE LIGHT.

IT WILL TAKE TIME FOR THE COMPUTER TO SORT THROUGH THE SENSOR INFORMATION.
I STILL DO NOT UNDERSTAND YOUR WILLINGNESS TO HELP US.
BY LOCATING MY FRIENDS, DEAD OR ALIVE, YOU HAVE ASSURED THE *ENTERPRISE* WILL ARRIVE AT WYATH ON TIME...

...YOU WILL BE TRIED FOR YOUR CRIMES.
SSSHHHHUUUUSH!
I SEE THE LIGHT, DATA—

—IT IS ***UNFORTUNATE*** YOUR CAPTAIN IS UNWILLING TO ACCEPT MY EPIPHANY.
I BELIEVE CAPTAIN PICARD REMAINS SKEPTICAL.
AND ***YOU?***

I AM AN ANDROID, SO MY PROGRAMMING CAN BE ALTERED—
—BUT FROM MY EXPERIENCE WITH HUMANS, I KNOW CHANGE IS HARD.
THE LIGHT COMES TO THOSE WHO LOOK FOR IT.

PERHAPS I WILL LOOK HARDER.

"THIS MUST BE WHERE THE MONKS COME TO MEDITATE..."

SKREEEEET—!
LAFORGE TO WORF—!
—RO, DO YOU READ ME?

AHHHH—!

...THE SOLAR ACTIVITY'S GIVING ME A *MAJOR* HEADACHE!
CAN'T SEE A THING—

—WHOOOOAHH!

TCHK-TCHK!

KRAK!

IS ANYONE DOWN THERE?
WHAMMP!
WORF–?

PHASERS DO NOT STOP THEM, BUT ENSIGN RO AND I WERE ABLE TO *PHYSICALLY* SUBDUE ONE OF THE MONKS.
WE WERE WORRIED YOU'D BEEN INFECTED.
MY EXPOSURE PROBABLY WASN'T HIGH ENOUGH TO TRIGGER THE MUTATION.

I AM GLAD YOU ARE SAFE.
FOR THE MOMENT. THERE ARE MORE MONKS IN THESE TUNNELS, AND WE *STILL* NEED TO FIND A WAY OUT.
IF THIS MUTATION IS FUELED BY THE *EXCESS* SOLAR ACTIVITY, ITS EFFECTS MAY ONLY BECOME ACTIVE AT *NIGHT*.

SO WE JUST HAVE TO STAY ALIVE UNTIL MORNING, IS THAT WHAT YOU'RE SAYING?

TCHK-TCHK-I
IT'S JUST A THEORY—

—BUT RIGHT NOW, THAT'S ALL WE'VE GOT.
THE MONKS HAVE RETURNED.
AND WE'RE OUT OF BELTS.

SKREEEEET—!
RIKER TO AWAY TEAM—

WORF HERE, COMMANDER. IT IS GOOD TO HEAR YOUR VOICE.
I'M APPROACHING RIAT NOW. IS EVERYONE ALL RIGHT?

THREE TO BEAM OUT, SIR. AS SOON AS POSSIBLE.
ON MY WAY!

THANK YOU FOR YOUR HELP, GHUD. AND GOOD LUCK AT THE TRIAL.
THERE IS NO LUCK, PICARD. THERE IS ONLY THE LIGHT.
ENERGIZE.

NHHHNNNHHNNNNNHHH

IS SOMETHING TROUBLING YOU, MR. DATA?
DOCTOR SOONG CREATED ME TO BE AN INDIVIDUAL, TO HAVE WHAT MANY CALL "FREE WILL"...
...BUT THAT DOES NOT OVERRIDE THE CONCEPTS OF RIGHT AND WRONG.

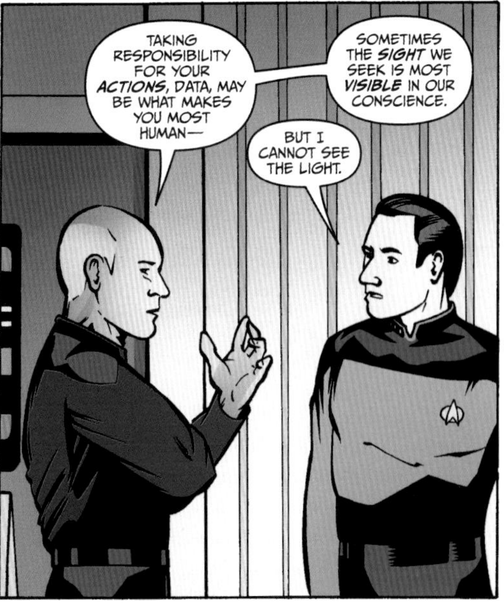
BUT I CANNOT SEE THE LIGHT.
TAKING RESPONSIBILITY FOR YOUR ACTIONS, DATA, MAY BE WHAT MAKES YOU MOST HUMAN—
SOMETIMES THE SIGHT WE SEEK IS MOST VISIBLE IN OUR CONSCIENCE.

THANK YOU, SIR.

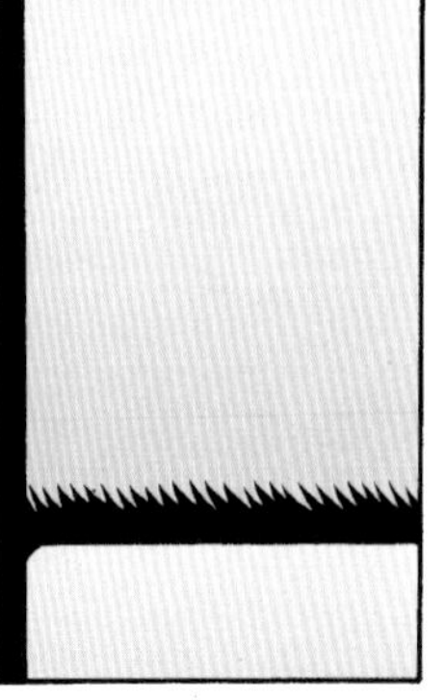

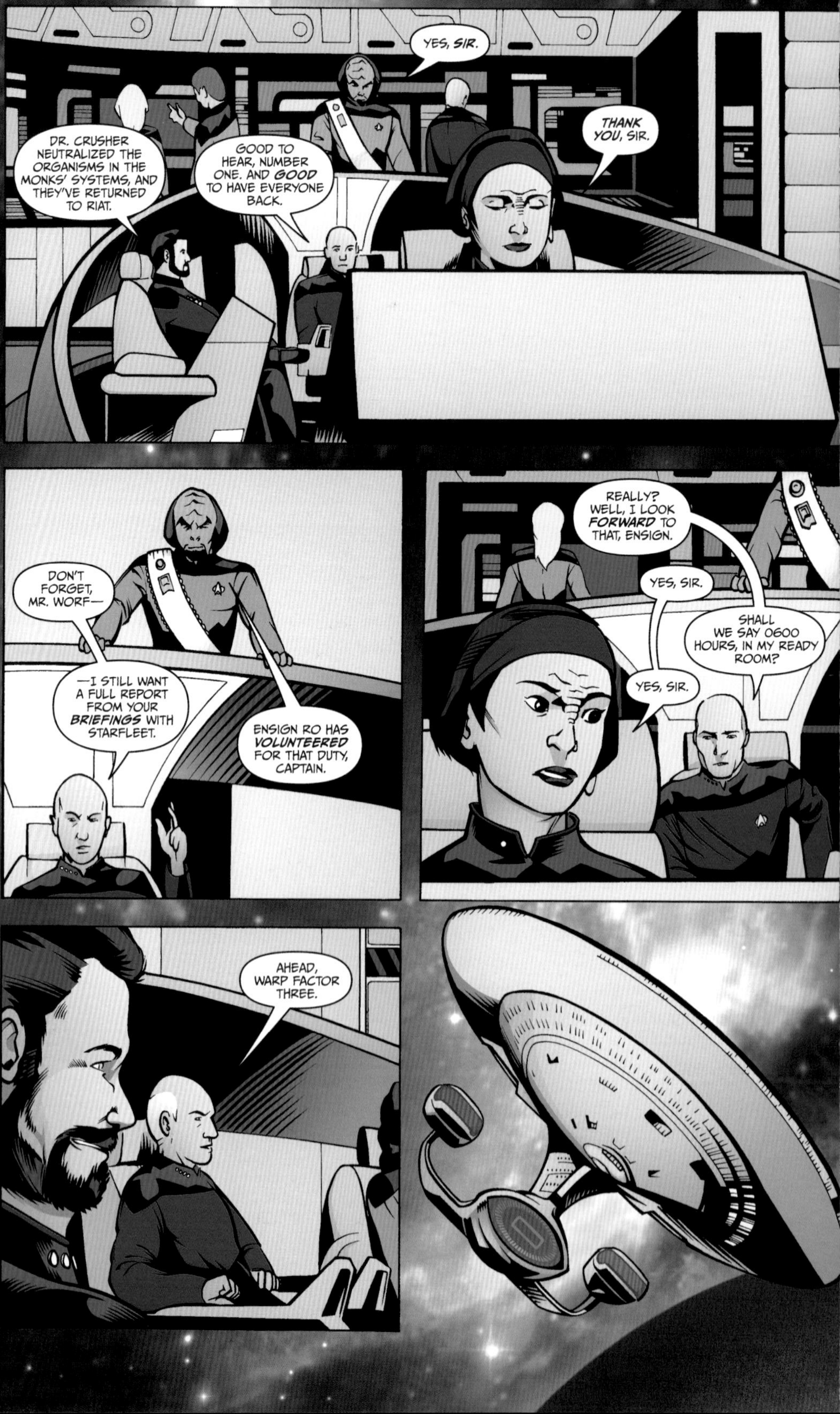

DR. CRUSHER NEUTRALIZED THE ORGANISMS IN THE MONKS' SYSTEMS, AND THEY'VE RETURNED TO RIAT.
GOOD TO HEAR, NUMBER ONE. AND *GOOD* TO HAVE EVERYONE BACK.
YES, *SIR.*
THANK YOU, SIR.

DON'T FORGET, MR. WORF—
—I STILL WANT A FULL REPORT FROM YOUR *BRIEFINGS* WITH STARFLEET.
ENSIGN RO HAS *VOLUNTEERED* FOR THAT DUTY, CAPTAIN.

REALLY? WELL, I LOOK *FORWARD* TO THAT, ENSIGN.
YES, SIR.
SHALL WE SAY 0600 HOURS, IN MY READY ROOM?
YES, SIR.

AHEAD, WARP FACTOR THREE.

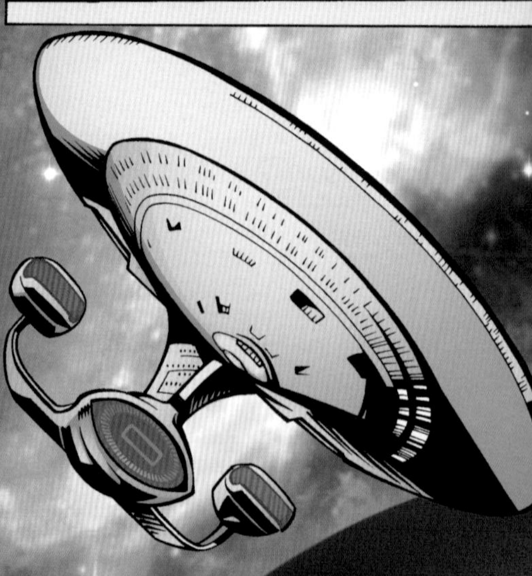

—AND I'LL *RAISE* YOU ANOTHER FIFTY.
TINK TINK TINK

TOO RICH FOR MY BLOOD—
—I'M *OUT*.
ME, TOO.

IT IS YOUR CALL, WESLEY.
WHAT'S IT GONNA BE, WES—?

—YOU READY TO PLAY WITH THE BIG BOYS?

CALL.
TINK TINK TINK

TWO PAIR, QUEENS HIGH.

COME ON, WES....
YOU TAKING SIDES, GEORDI?

NO, SIR!
PLEASE SHOW US YOUR CARDS, WESLEY.

FULL HOUSE.

NOT ONLY DID HE HAVE A GREAT HAND, HE WAS COMPLETELY UNREADABLE!
YES, SIR!
INTRIGUING.

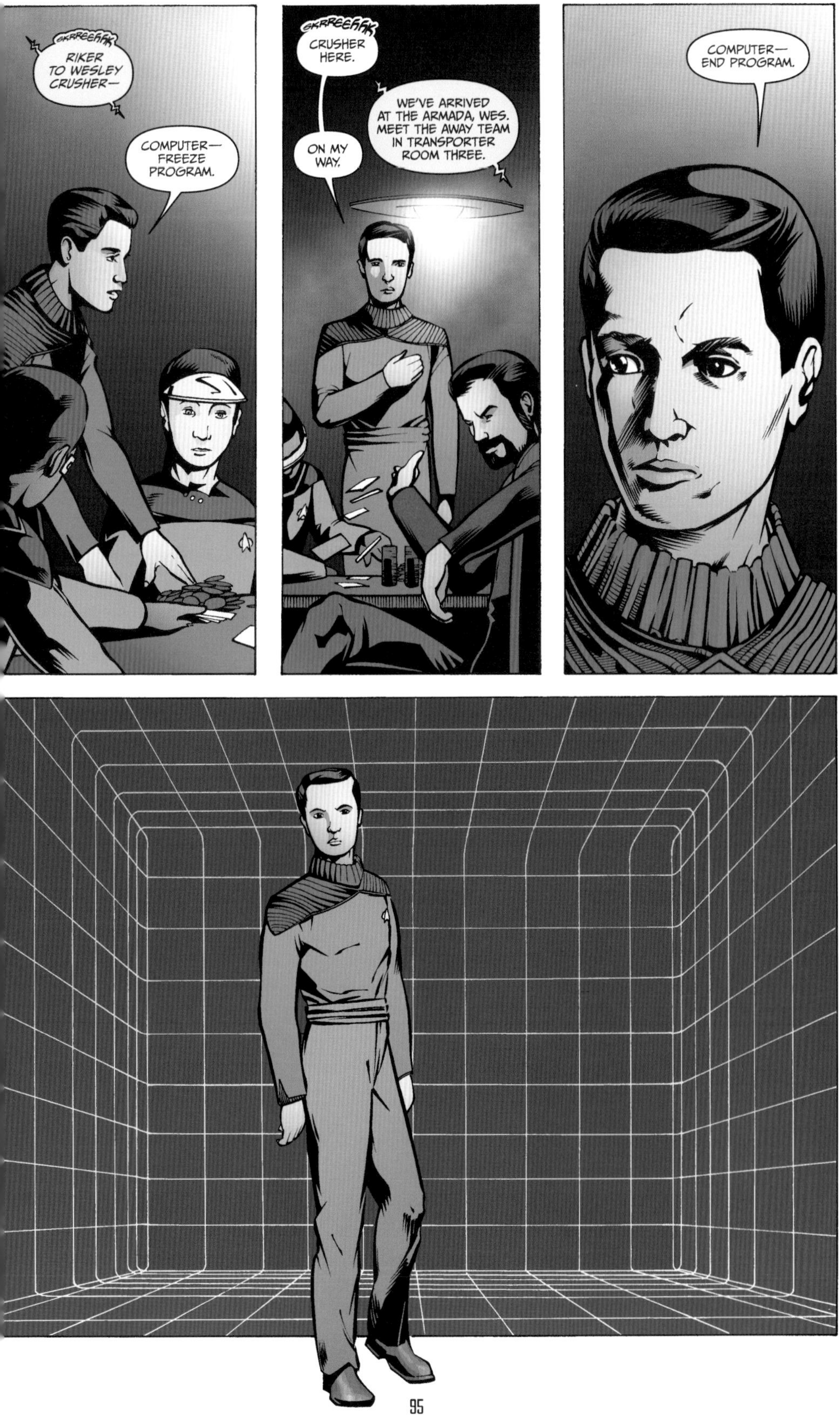

SKRREEEKK
RIKER TO WESLEY CRUSHER—
COMPUTER— FREEZE PROGRAM.

SKRREEEKK
CRUSHER HERE.
WE'VE ARRIVED AT THE ARMADA, WES. MEET THE AWAY TEAM IN TRANSPORTER ROOM THREE.
ON MY WAY.

COMPUTER— END PROGRAM.

CAPTAIN'S LOG: STARDATE 42317.1.
THE ENTERPRISE HAS BEEN CALLED TO THE ARMADA, A COLONY OF AGRICULTURAL DOMES BUILT ON THE MALTESE ASTEROID BELT.
THE FRUITS AND VEGETABLES GROWN ON THESE FARMS FEED MILLIONS OF PEOPLE IN THIS SECTOR...
...BUT UNEXPLAINED CROP FAILURES NOW THREATEN THAT FOOD SUPPLY, AND STARFLEET HAS ASKED THE ENTERPRISE TO INVESTIGATE.

ON A MORE PERSONAL NOTE, COMMANDER RIKER INFORMS ME **WESLEY CRUSHER** IS HAVING DIFFICULTY ADJUSTING TO HIS MOTHER'S ABSENCE.
WESLEY IS AN EXCEPTIONAL YOUNG MAN, AND HE HAS BECOME A VALUED MEMBER OF MY CREW.
I HOPE OUR TIME AT THE ARMADA IS A BREATH OF FRESH AIR, FOR ALL OF US.

EIGHT HUNDRED ACRES OF QUADROTRITICALE, PLOMEEK, AND UTTABERRIES—
—ALL OF IT BRITTLE AS GLASS.
AND JUST AS INEDIBLE. COULD IT BE A MUTATION FROM PESTICIDES OR FERTILIZER?
THESE DOMES ARE FEDERATION-APPROVED *ORGANIC*, COMMANDER RIKER. INSECTS AND BIRDS HAVE BEEN INTRODUCED INTO THE ECOSYSTEM TO PREVENT INFESTATION—
—AND YOU CAN SMELL THE FERTILIZER.
LOUD AND CLEAR.
WE'LL DO WHAT WE CAN, HOMMUN.
YOU'D BEST, PICARD.
ANOTHER CROP LIKE *THIS*, AND A LOT OF PEOPLE START GOING HUNGRY.
RAARGGHH

WHHYPP
CHARMING FELLOW.

HIS FAMILY'S WORKED THIS LAND FOR EIGHT GENERATIONS, NUMBER ONE.
FARMING IS ALL HE'S EVER KNOWN.

CAPTAIN, MY SCANS CONFIRM A CELLULAR BREAKDOWN OF THE MINERALS IN THE SOIL.
BUT I WILL NEED TO RETURN TO THE *ENTERPRISE* FOR FURTHER ANALYSIS.
THANK YOU, MR. DATA. MAKE IT SO.

I'LL SEE YOU BACK ON THE *ENTERPRISE*.
I PROMISED DEANNA I'D PICK UP A JAR OF UTTABERRY PRESERVES.

COMMANDER RIKER—
SIR?
—MAKE SURE YOU WIPE YOUR FEET BEFORE YOU BEAM UP.

RRRHHHHHHHHRRRR
RRRHHHHHHHHRRRR

PCHAHHHRRH

WHAT'S THE POINT?

THE *POINT* IS THAT IT EXPLODES.
WHAT ELSE IS THERE TO DO ON THIS *ROCK?*

YOU'RE PRETTY YOUNG TO BE AN ENSIGN.
CAPTAIN PICARD MADE ME AN *ACTING* ENSIGN.

CUMIN WAS ACCEPTED TO STARFLEET ACADEMY—
SHUT UP, ASTRA.

—BUT HIS FATHER WOULDN'T LET HIM GO.
I SAID, SHUT *UP*, ASTRA.

HEY— LEAVE HER ALONE.
HEY—YOU GOING TO DO SOMETHING ABOUT IT?
HAY IS FOR HORSES.

BACK OFF, ACTING ENSIGN.
CUMIN—GIVE THE MAN A DRINK.

KORI RIGGED UP A *STILL*, WITH THE CONDENSER FROM AN OLD ROMULAN MISSILE WE FOUND.
SMART ENOUGH TO BUILD IT, TOO YOUNG TO DRINK IT.
GRAIN ALCOHOL, FROM THE QUADROTRITICALE--?
NO THANKS.

I PREFER UTTABERRY WINE, MYSELF...
...BUT SINCE THE BERRIES WENT BAD, WE DON'T HAVE ENOUGH TO SPARE.
CAPTAIN PICARD WILL FIGURE OUT THE CROP PROBLEM.

I HOPE HE DOESN'T.
THEN WE CAN *ALL* LEAVE.
WOULDN'T EVEN WAIT TO PACK.

I DON'T KNOW--LIFE HERE LOOKS PRETTY GREAT TO ME.
WELL, IT ISN'T--

--ME AND KORI WORK THE FIELDS TEN HOURS A DAY, THEN SCHOOL FOR ANOTHER FOUR.
NO TIME FOR FRIENDS, OR *FUN*--
YOU *SAID* I WAS FUN...

MY LIFE ISN'T PERFECT.
THERE'S A WHOLE GALAXY OUT THERE, AND I'M STUCK UNDER GLASS...
...YOUR LIFE SURE *LOOKS* PERFECT TO ME.

TRAVELING AT WARP SPEED MAKES THE TRIP GO *FASTER*—
—BUT WHEN YOU GET THERE, IT HAS TO *MEAN* SOMETHING.
WITHOUT YOUR *FAMILY*, THERE'S NO POINT.

I BET YOUR DAD DOESN'T MAKE YOU SLEEP WITH THE *LIZARDS* WHEN THEY'RE PREGNANT.
MY DAD'S DEAD.

STUPID!
I'M SORRY. I DIDN'T *KNOW*.
...THANKS FOR THE DRINK.

SKRREEKKK
ENTERPRISE, THIS IS CRUSHER— ONE TO BEAM UP.

BUT HE DIDN'T *HAVE* A DRINK...
NHHHNNNNHHNNNNNHHH

PULASKI TO BRIDGE—

—LIEUTENANT COMMANDER DATA JUST BARGED INTO SICKBAY AND PUT MY RESEARCH ON HOLD SO HE COULD ANALYZE SOIL SAMPLES.
DATA WAS ACTING UNDER *MY* ORDERS, DOCTOR.

I HAVEN'T REVIEWED THE SPECS FOR A GALAXY CLASS STARSHIP, COMMANDER, BUT THE *ENTERPRISE* MUST HAVE MORE THAN ONE SCIENCE LAB.

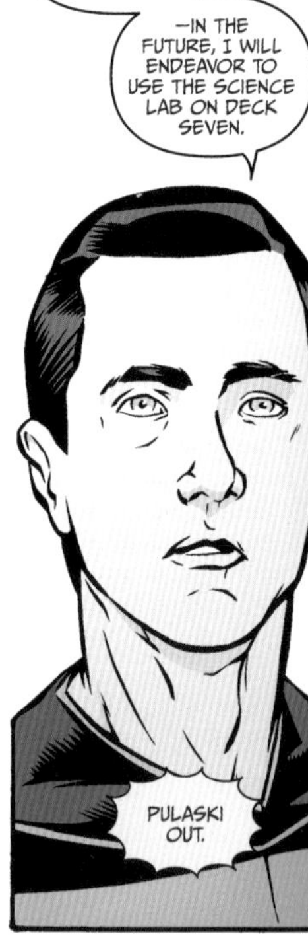
DOCTOR PULASKI, THIS IS DATA—
—IN THE FUTURE, I WILL ENDEAVOR TO USE THE SCIENCE LAB ON DECK SEVEN.
PULASKI OUT.

COMMANDER, DR. PULANSKI SHOULD NOT SPEAK OF LIEUTENANT COMMANDER DATA IN THAT WAY.
THANK YOU, LIEUTENANT, BUT AS DR. PULASKI IS SO QUICK TO REMIND ME, I AM A MACHINE—
AND AS THE OLD EARTH SAYING GOES, "STICKS AND STONES MAY BREAK MY POLYALLOY INFRASTRUCTURE...
"...BUT WORDS WILL NEVER HURT ME."

WHAT ABOUT THE SOIL SAMPLES?
A CELLULAR ANALYSIS DISCOVERED MINUTE LEVELS OF CHRONITON PARTICLES.

CHRONITON PARTICLES? BUT HUMMON SAID THE FARMS ARE *ORGANIC*.
I FOUND TRACES OF THE SAME RADIATION IN ALL THE DOMES.
I BELIEVE THE FARMERS ARE USING THE TIME PARTICLES TO GROW THEIR PRODUCE AT ACCELERATED RATES.

AND WHAT HAPPENS WHEN CHRONITON PARTICLES ARE INGESTED?
RESEARCH IS INCONCLUSIVE.

SKRREEEAAK
RIKER TO COUNSELOR TROI—REPORT TO SICKBAY, *IMMEDIATELY*...

"...THE UTTERBERRY JAM MAY HAVE BEEN CONTAMINATED."

IT FEELS GOOD TO USE MY HANDS.
THANK YOU, PICARD, FOR THE ASSISTANCE. MY CHILDREN NEVER SEEM TO HAVE THE TIME.

I NEVER WANTED TO HELP MY FATHER, WHEN I WAS GROWING UP.
NOW THAT I'M OLDER, I MISS THAT.
WE SHOULD FINISH.

NHHHNNNHHNNNNNHHH

WHAT IS IT, NUMBER ONE?
DATA FOUND CHRONITON PARTICLES IN THE SOIL. HOMMUN AND THE OTHER FARMERS HAVE BEEN LYING TO US.

IS THAT *TRUE*, HOMMUN?
THE GALAXY IS MORE COMPLICATED THAN WHEN WE WERE GROWING UP, PICARD.
WE ALL DID WHAT WE THOUGHT WE HAD TO DO, FOR OUR FAMILIES.

COME ON, KORI—WE GOTTA GO!
YOU TOOK TIME TO PACK.

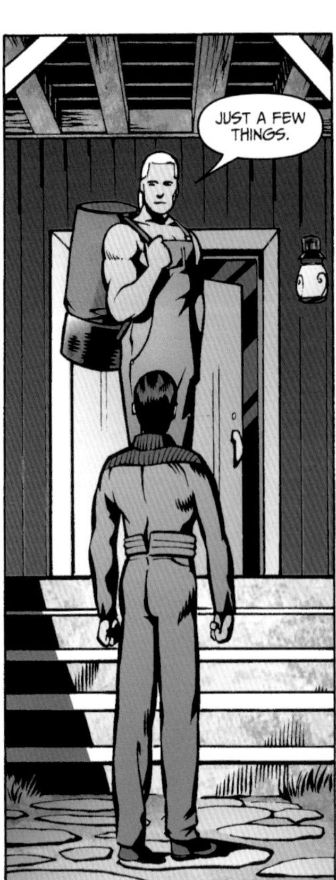
JUST A FEW THINGS.

WHAT'S *HE* DOING HERE?

DON'T YOU CARE WHAT'S GOING TO HAPPEN TO YOUR FATHER?
HE AND THE REST OF THE FARMERS'LL BE OKAY.
IT'S NOT LIKE THEY DID ANYTHING REALLY WRONG.
NO, *THEY* DIDN'T...

YOU FOUND THE CHRONITON PARTICLES IN THAT ROMULAN TORPEDO.
WHATEVER.

IF YOUR FATHER AND THE OTHER FARMERS COULD SPEED UP THE GROWING TIME, YOU'D HAVE MORE FREE TIME—YOU MIGHT EVEN WANT TO STAY.
THEY MADE THAT DECISION, NOT US.

BUT KORI TINKERED WITH THE FORMULA, DIDN'T HE? SO THE FOOD WOULD ROT—SO YOU'D *HAVE* TO LEAVE.
SO HIS BIG BROTHER COULD GO TO STARFLEET.
ARE YOU GONNA TELL ON US, ACTING ENSIGN?

NOT *ME*—
—BUT YOU'RE GOING TO SQUEAL LIKE A ROMULAN *PIG*.
I DON'T THINK SO.

I'M NOT ASKING.
YOU'RE BLUFFING.

TRY ME.

SWOOSH

KRAK

UUNNGHH!

WHAK

—TROI IS FINE, CAPTAIN. THE UTTABERRIES WERE FROM LAST YEAR'S CROP, BEFORE THE CONTAMINATION.
THANK YOU, DOCTOR. PLEASE MAKE SURE TO BRIEF MR. DATA WITH ANY ADDITIONAL INFORMATION.
PULASKI OUT.

WE MUST CONTACT STARFLEET, AND CHECK FOR ANY CONTAMINATED FOOD.
WE ALERTED *STARBASE 112* BEFORE WE BEAMED DOWN.

CAPTAIN PICARD—?
—MY FATHER AND THE OTHER FARMERS... THEY DIDN'T DO THIS.

THEY DID IT, BUT WE—MY BROTHER AND I—WE MADE IT WORSE.

I SEE.
I APPRECIATE YOUR COMING FORWARD LIKE THIS. AND I THINK YOUR FATHER WILL, AS WELL—

—RIGHT NOW, I NEED YOU TO FIND LIEUTENANT WORF, AND TELL HIM EVERYTHING YOU JUST TOLD ME.
YES, SIR.
THANK YOU, CAPTAIN.

CAPTAIN. COMMANDER RIKER.
WES.
IT WAS VERY BRAVE FOR KORI TO COME FORWARD LIKE THAT—

—YOU SPENT SOME TIME WITH THE BOYS, WESLEY, DID YOU GET ANY SENSE OF THEIR INVOLVEMENT?
NO, SIR.
THAT'S SOME SHINER ON CUMIN.

I DIDN'T NOTICE, SIR.
IF YOU NEED ME FOR ANYTHING ELSE, I'LL BE ON THE ENTERPRISE.
OF COURSE, WESLEY. AND THANK YOU.

THAT'S ODD.
THAT A TEENAGER TELLS THE TRUTH WITHOUT BEING FORCED?
NO— THAT WESLEY IGNORED CUMIN'S VERY OBVIOUS BLACK EYE.

IS IT POSSIBLE ENSIGN CRUSHER JUST LIED TO US, NUMBER ONE?
I CAN'T BE SURE, CAPTAIN, BUT I WILL SAY THIS—

"—HE'S GOT ONE HELL OF A POKER FACE."

FIVE YEARS LATER.

...CROSS-REFERENCE THE *ENTERPRISE'S* MISSION LOGS OVER THE LAST SEVEN YEARS WITH THE REST OF THE LOGS IN THE FLEET.

AND INCLUDE REPORTS FROM KLINGON AND VULCAN SHIPS, TOO.

THIS MAY TAKE SOME TIME, CAPTAIN.

IT'S IMPORTANT, DATA. TAKE AS MUCH—

THERE ARE TWO OTHER INSTANCES FROM THE *ENTERPRISE'S* LOGS THAT HAVE CORRESPONDING EVENTS IN THE ALPHA AND BETA QUADRANTS...

THE TECHNOLOGY USED ON TIGAN-7 WAS REPLICATED ON LANGER 14, WHERE ELECTION RESULTS WERE REPLACED—
—AND A MAQUIS SHIP DESTROYED ITSELF DAYS AFTER DISCOVERING A CACHE OF *HARMONIC DIAMONDS*.
FROM RAJATHA PRIME!

IF THIS IS TRUE, CAPTAIN, SOMEONE IS USING THE INFORMATION FROM STARFLEET LOGS TO CREATE OFFENSIVE WEAPONS.
OUR MISSION—OUR PURPOSE—IS EXPLORATION.
THAT ANYONE WOULD PERVERT THAT INFORMATION FOR POLITICAL OR MILITARY PURPOSES COULD DESTROY EVERYTHING THE FEDERATION'S BUILT.

ONLY STARFLEET PERSONNEL WOULD HAVE ACCESS TO THOSE RECORDS, CAPTAIN.

THAT'S WHAT WORRIES ME *MOST*, DATA. UNTIL WE'RE CERTAIN, WE MUST ACT WITH SUPREME CAUTION.

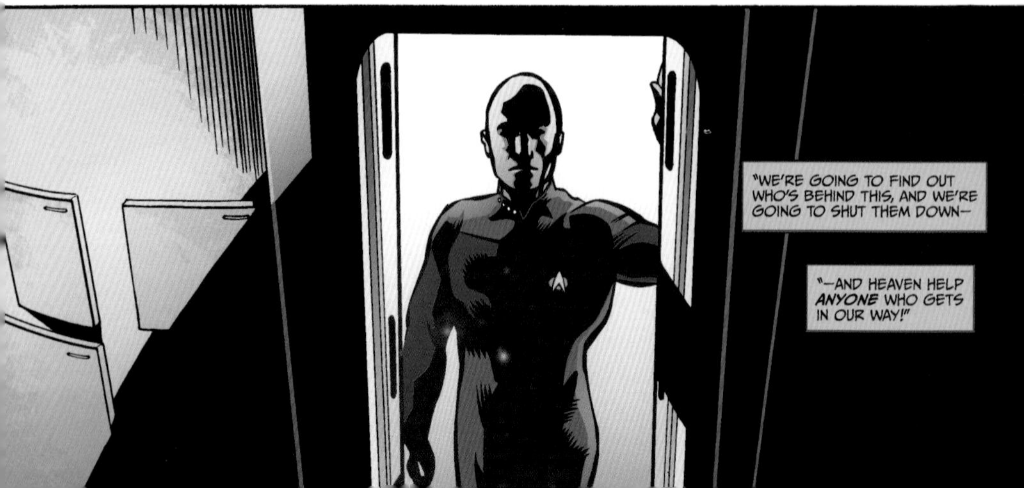
"WE'RE GOING TO FIND OUT WHO'S BEHIND THIS, AND WE'RE GOING TO SHUT THEM DOWN—
"—AND HEAVEN HELP *ANYONE* WHO GETS IN OUR WAY!"

SENSORS ARE *DOWN!*
I'M READING A BURST OF ***THORON RADIATION*** ON THE PERIMETER.
GO TO RED ALERT!

NHHHNNNHHNNNNHHH
IT'S PROBABLY JUST A GLITCH IN THE RELAY—

HOLD IT RIGHT THERE—!

KRAK!—

COMMANDER LA FORGE WAS ***SUCCESSFUL*** IN BLINDING THEIR SENSORS.
WE HAVE ***NOT*** BEEN DETECTED.
LET'S GET TO WORK.

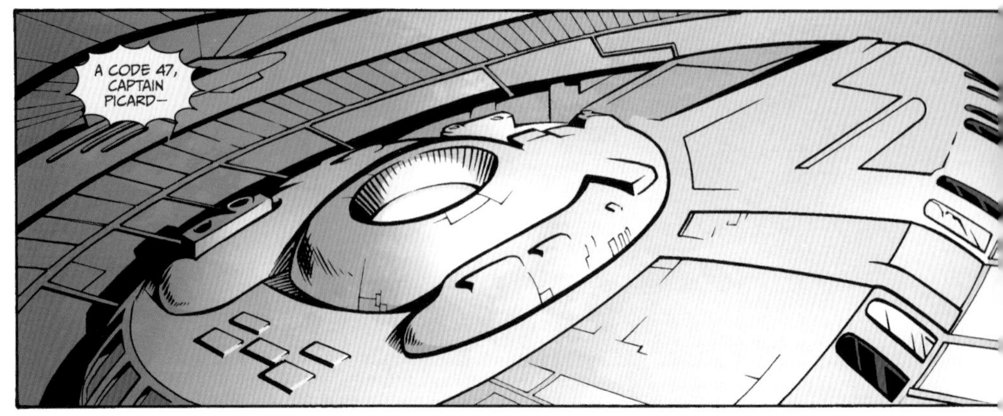
A CODE 47, CAPTAIN PICARD—

—THIS MUST BE IMPORTANT.
INDEED, ADMIRAL.

I RECENTLY DISCOVERED INFORMATION FROM THE *ENTERPRISE'S* MISSION LOGS IS BEING USED FOR ***OFFENSIVE*** PURPOSES—
—TO FORWARD A POLITICAL ***AGENDA*** ON SEVERAL PLANETS IN THE ALPHA QUADRANT... AND PERHAPS ***BEYOND.***

DID YOU ***HEAR*** WHAT I—
YES.

WHAT DO YOU PLAN TO ***DO*** WITH THIS INFORMATION?
THAT DEPENDS A GREAT DEAL ON WHAT ***YOU*** INTEND ON DOING WITH THIS INFORMATION, ADMIRAL NECHAYEV.

HE KNOWS.

IT WAS ONLY A MATTER OF TIME, REALLY.

DON'T WORRY—

—I'LL HANDLE JEAN-LUC PICARD *AND* THE *ENTERPRISE*.

CAPTAIN'S PERSONAL LOG:
STARDATE: 47993.3.
SIX YEARS AGO, THE *ENTERPRISE* FOUGHT AN ALIEN CONSPIRACY THAT THREATENED STARFLEET AND THE FEDERATION.

TODAY WE FIGHT AGAIN, BUT THIS TIME I FEAR IT IS AGAINST OUR OWN—
—MEN AND WOMEN WHO DISREGARD THE PRIME DIRECTIVE AND SEEK TO MAINTAIN *THEIR* VERSION OF A GALACTIC STATUS QUO.
I NO LONGER KNOW WHO IS FRIEND OR FOE, BUT IT ENDS *HERE*.

TSSSSCHHH

LOOKS LIKE THE MODIFIED THORON BURST WORKED.
IT SCRAMBLED THEIR SENSORS AND ALLOWED US TO BEAM IN, UNDETECTED.

GEORDI...
...I'M *SENSING* SOMEONE NEARBY.

TSSSSCHHHH

WHAMMPH!
OUR COMM BADGES ARE BEING MASKED FROM THE INTERNAL SENSORS. I DO NOT THINK ANYONE ELSE WILL BOTHER US.

IT'S GOOD TO SEE YOU, DATA.
THANK YOU, COUNSELOR.
I WAS ABLE TO GET PAST ALL THE SECURITY MEASURES—

—BUT IT'S AS IF THERE'S NOTHING THERE.
THE COMPUTERS ARE *EMPTY*.

COMPUTER—ACCESS PERSONNEL LOGS FOR THIS FACILITY.
PERSONNEL LOGS DO NOT EXIST.
ACCESS SCHEMATICS FOR THIS FACILITY.
SCHEMATICS DO NOT EXIST.

COMPUTER—ACCESS LAST ENTRY.
ENTRIES DO NOT EXIST.

WHAT DOES IT MEAN?
THE ONLY CONCLUSION IS THAT WE HAVE BEEN MISLED.
IT'S A *TRAP*.

YOU SHOULD'VE SEEN NECHAYEV WHEN SHE ENTERED THE ACADEMY—A CHIP ON HER SHOULDER THE SIZE OF JUPITER...
...SO READY TO PROVE A BEAUTIFUL WOMAN COULD BE A STARSHIP CAPTAIN.
SHE'D LAUGH HERSELF SILLY IF SHE COULD SEE YOU NOW.
BOOTHBY, PLEASE...
...THIS IS IMPORTANT.
ADMIRAL NECHAYEV. CAN I TRUST HER?
I DON'T KNOW.
WHAT CAN YOU TELL ME?
THERE ARE RUMORS, THINGS WHISPERED ABOUT—
—PEOPLE INSIDE STARFLEET, A SECRET GROUP THAT FIGHTS DIRTY TO KEEP THE FEDERATION CLEAN.
IT MAY JUST BE A WHISPERED FAIRY TALE, KEPT ALIVE TO KEEP US SCARED...
...OR YOU MAY HAVE PEOPLE ON BOARD YOUR SHIP THAT MAKE THE NIGHTMARE REAL.
ABOARD THE ENTERPRISE? NO, BOOTHBY, I REFUSE TO BELIEVE THAT.

THAT'S ALL I KNOW.
THANK YOU, OLD FRIEND. I'M SORRY I WOKE YOU.

DON'T LET THE BOOGEYMAN GET TO YOU.

WHO'S THERE?

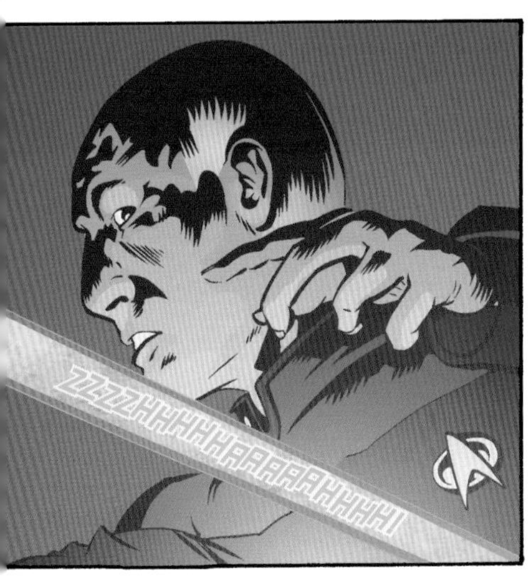
ZZZZHHHHHHAAAAAHHHH!

ZZZZHHHHHHAAAAAHHHH!

ZZZZHHHHHHAAAAAAHHHH!

THUNK!

NHHHNNNHHNNNNNHHH
ZZZZHHHHHHHAAAAAAHHHHH!
"I WAS LOOKING FOR CAPTAIN PICARD..."

"THE CAPTAIN IS *INDISPOSED* AT THE MOMENT, ADMIRAL ADAMS—"
—IS THERE SOMETHING I CAN HELP YOU WITH?
STARFLEET COMMAND WOULD LIKE TO KNOW WHY THE *ENTERPRISE* HAS RETURNED TO EARTH AT THIS TIME.
YOU CAN ASK HIM IN 48 HOURS. THAT'S WHEN THE QUARANTINE ENDS.
WE WERE HIT WITH AN OUTBREAK OF ANDORIAN MEASLES AS WE ENTERED ORBIT.
HALF THE CREW, INCLUDING THE CAPTAIN, ARE IN ISOLATION.
I'LL HAVE THE CAPTAIN CONTACT YOU AS SOON AS POSSIBLE.
YES, DOCTOR, YOU DO THAT—
—ADAMS OUT.
GOOD LUCK, JEAN-LUC.

DIDN'T WE COME THIS WAY BEFORE?
THESE CORRIDORS DO LOOK—

ZZZHHHNNN!

A FORCE FIELD!
IT MAY BE AUTOMATIC. TO KEEP PEOPLE OUT OF THIS SECTION—

—OR, THEY KNOW WE'RE HERE.
WE WILL RETRACE OUR STEPS...

UNLESS THAT'S WHAT THEY WANT US TO DO.
IF WE HAVE LOST THE ELEMENT OF SURPRISE, PERHAPS WE SHOULD BLAST OUR WAY THROUGH.

SKREEEEET—!
TROI HERE.
WE NEED THE SCHEMATICS, DEANNA.

I'M SORRY, WILL. THE COMPUTER FILES HAVE BEEN WIPED CLEAN.

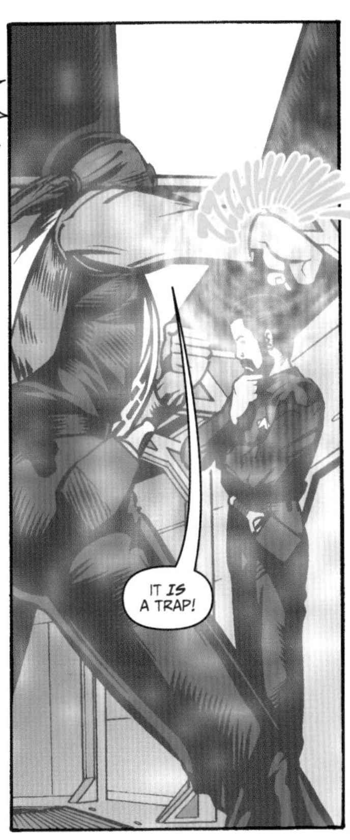
IT *IS* A TRAP!

COMMANDER, PLEASE HAVE LIEUTENANT WORF RECONFIGURE HIS COMM BADGE TO A FREQUENCY OF 13.5 TETRAHERTZ.

THAT FREQUENCY SHOULD BE HIGH ENOUGH TO ESCAPE DETECTION BY THE SENSORS AT THIS FACILITY, BUT ALLOW ME TO GUIDE YOU TO US.
THANKS, DATA.

I WOULD STILL PREFER TO ***BLAST*** OUR WAY OUT.
AT THIS POINT, WORF— SO WOULD I.

OH, WILL—IT'S YOU!
I SENSED HOSTILITY. I THOUGHT—

HHHHRRRRRHH!
OH.

HAVE YOU GOT THE TRANSPORTER ONLINE?
POWER HAS BEEN DIVERTED FROM THIS SECTION.

I'M ADJUSTING THE YIELD FROM MY PHASER TO COMPENSATE, BUT THE TWO UNITS AREN'T COMPATIBLE.
BE *CAREFUL*—

—WE NEED TO GET THE CAPTAIN HERE IN *ONE* PIECE.
THE CONVERSION IS SLOW, SO WE DON'T OVERLOAD THE CIRCUITS.
I ESTIMATE WE WILL NEED ANOTHER 74 MINUTES.

WORF, TIME TO IMPLEMENT PLAN B.
YES, SIR!

GO WITH DEANNA TO ENGINEERING. I WANT THOSE CHARGES SET AND PLACED IN FIVE MINUTES.

WILL, ISN'T THERE ANOTHER WAY?
WE DON'T HAVE TIME FOR ANYTHING ELSE.

COMMANDER, CAPTAIN PICARD HAD HOPED TO REVEAL THIS FACILITY AND ITS PURPOSE TO STARFLEET.
AND IF WE ARE UNABLE TO GET THE CAPTAIN HERE, OUR ORDERS ARE TO DESTROY THIS COMPLEX AND EVERYTHING IN IT—

—EVEN IF WE'RE STUCK INSIDE WHEN THAT HAPPENS.

HHHNNNHHNNNNNHHH
FERENGI?

THEY STARTED ALL OF THIS, TWO CENTURIES AGO—
—THEY OPENED OUR EYES TO THE THREAT THEY POSED, AND THE NEED TO KEEP OUR INTERESTS INTACT.

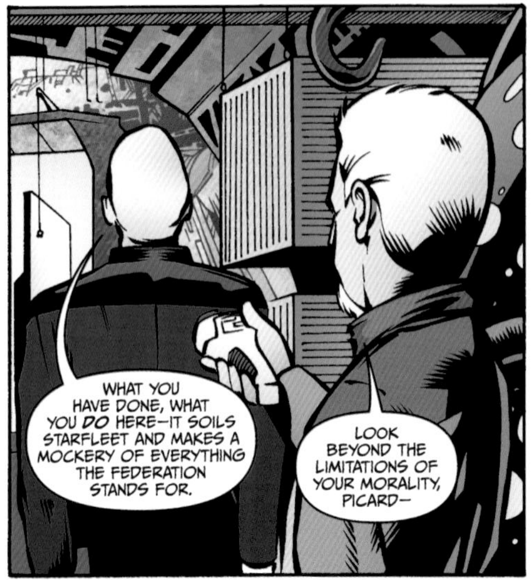
WHAT YOU HAVE DONE, WHAT YOU DO HERE—IT SOILS STARFLEET AND MAKES A MOCKERY OF EVERYTHING THE FEDERATION STANDS FOR.
LOOK BEYOND THE LIMITATIONS OF YOUR MORALITY, PICARD—

—YOU NEED ME, JUST LIKE I NEED YOU. WE'RE TWO SIDES OF THE SAME COIN.
WE ARE EXPLORERS.

YOU ARE ALLOWED TO EXPLORE, BECAUSE WE KEEP THE GALAXY SAFE.

ULTIMATELY, YOU WILL OUTLIVE YOUR PURPOSE. WHAT WE DO WILL ENDURE.
I AGREE.
HOLD IT!

PUT THE PHASER DOWN AND STEP AWAY.
I DIDN'T COME ALONE.

NHHHNNNHHNNNNHHH

NEITHER DID I.

IT LOOKS LIKE WE'RE AT AN *IMPASSE*.
NO, WE'RE NOT...

...DETONATE THE CHARGES, MR. LA FORGE.

NOTHING HAPPENED.
TIK!

THE CHARGES WERE NEUTRALIZED MOMENTS AFTER YOUR PEOPLE SET THEM, PICARD.

I *WILL* STOP YOU.

SKREEEEET—!
PICARD TO *ENTERPRISE*—
—GET US THE HELL OUT OF HERE.

"HE WOULD HAVE KILLED ME, BUT MR. LA FORGE WAS ABLE TO BEAM ME OUT."

I'M SORRY, CAPTAIN. I'D LIKE TO TAKE THE CREDIT, BUT IT WASN'T ME. THE TRANSPORTER WAS STILL OFF-LINE.

THEN HOW DID YOU GET INSIDE THE FACILITY?

I'D LIKE TO MAKE A TOAST.
TO THE CREW OF THE ENTERPRISE...
...TO MY FRIENDS—
—MAY OUR VOYAGES BE AS MANY AS THE STARS IN THE SKY.
TINK!
TINK!
TINK!
THE END.

Art by Zach Howard

STAR TREK
THE NEXT GENERATION®
INTELLIGENCE GATHERING

Art by David Messina

1
Some days you get the bear...
BZZZZZZZZZZZZZZZZZZZZZZZZZZZZZZZZZ
A FULL SQUADRON OF ZEROES AT 11 O'CLOCK, CAP!
FOLLOW ME IN, BOYS.
ROGER THAT, CAP'N.
BREE-DEE-DEET
SORRY TO INTERRUPT, COMMANDER. THE CAPTAIN IS EXPECTING US.
THAT'S ALL RIGHT, DATA, I LOST TRACK OF TIME.

PAUSE PROGRAM. SAVE PROGRESS: "RIKER 1944."
PROGRAM SAVED.
I DID NOT MEAN TO INTRUDE UPON YOUR RECREATION, COMMANDER.
DON'T WORRY ABOUT IT, DATA.
SIR? MAY I ASK A QUESTION?
I WOULD BE DISAPPOINTED IF YOU DIDN'T.
IS IT NOT INCONGRUOUS TO FIND RELAXATION IN A SIMULATION OF WAR?
IT'S NOT THE WAR I FIND APPEALING, BUT THE ROMANCE: A MAN IN CONTROL OF HIS DESTINY, FIGHTING FOR WHAT HE BELIEVES, ONE BATTLE AT A TIME.
LIFE THESE DAYS, MR. DATA, IS RARELY THAT SIMPLE. COMPUTER, END PROGRAM.

AH, NUMBER ONE. MY APOLOGIES FOR INTERRUPTING YOUR HOLODECK SIMULATION.
NOT A PROBLEM, CAPTAIN. WORLD WAR II CAN WAIT.
I NEED YOU BOTH TO VISIT DAYSTROM ONE.
THE FEDERATION'S MASSIVE NEW INFORMATION ARCHIVE? IS THERE A PROBLEM?
THE COMPUTER ENGINEERS ARE HAVING DIFFICULTY WITH THE ARTIFICIAL INTELLIGENCE THAT MANAGES THE INSTALLATION.
BECAUSE THE A.I. USES THE SAME TECHNOLOGY AS YOUR POSITRONIC BRAIN, MR. DATA, THE PROJECT DIRECTORS HOPE YOU CAN PROVIDE PARTICULAR INSIGHT.
I HAVE BEEN PERIODICALLY CONSULTED DURING ITS DESIGN, CAPTAIN.
I WONDER WHAT WENT WRONG?

FIRST OFFICER'S LOG, STARDATE 45915.3. COMMANDER DATA AND I ARE PREPARING TO BEAM DOWN TO DAYSTROM ONE. WHILE WE HAVE RECEIVED SOME PRELIMINARY REPORTS ON THE NATURE OF THE PROBLEM, WE BOTH LOOK FORWARD TO FINDING OUT MORE FROM THE FACILITY'S ENGINEERS.
COMMANDER RIKER! COMMANDER DATA! WE'RE VERY GLAD TO SEE YOU! WELCOME TO DAYSTROM ONE.
IF YOU PLEASE, WE'LL TAKE YOU TO ADMIRAL KEBAL.
FINALLY! ALL RIGHT, ANDREA, SEE IF RIKER AND DATA CAN HELP US GET PAST OUR LITTLE PROBLEM.
THE DAYSTROM PROJECT WILL CREATE A SECURE ARCHIVE OF THE ACCUMULATED KNOWLEDGE OF THE FEDERATION. DAYSTROM ONE REPRESENTS THE PROTOTYPE FOR A SERIES OF SUCH FACILITIES.
WE ARE NOW IN THE SERVICE FACILITY. THE ARCHIVE IS IN A CHAMBER BELOW.

PROJECT MANAGER MENDOCK WILL BRIEF YOU ON THE DATA ARCHIVES THEMSELVES.
STORING ALL THE FEDERATION'S DATA IS AN ENORMOUS TASK, ESSENTIALLY A GIANT DATA BACKUP. FOR ALL THE ISOLINEAR STORAGE, WE'VE USED HOLODECK TECHNOLOGY TO CONSTRUCT AN EXTRADIMENSIONAL TESSERACT.
THE TESSERACT–A FOUR-DIMENSIONAL CUBE–ALLOWS US TO EXPONENTIALLY INCREASE THE SIZE OF THE ARCHIVE. WITHIN THE TESSERACT, THE DATA FOR EACH HOMEWORLD IS STORED IN INDIVIDUAL NODES.
MANAGING SUCH A LARGE ARCHIVE IS A HIGHLY COMPLICATED PROJECT. WE'VE CONSTRUCTED AN ARTIFICIAL INTELLIGENCE, BASED UPON DR. NOONIAN SOONG'S POSITRONIC BRAIN TECHNOLOGY, TO SERVE AS THE HUB FOR DAYSTROM ONE.
YES. MY UNDERSTANDING WAS THAT THE A.I. WAS WORKING SATISFACTORILY UNTIL RECENTLY?
CORRECT. TWO WEEKS AGO, THE A.I. STARTED TO PERFORM ERRATICALLY, BECOMING SLOW TO RESPOND TO COMMANDS. THIS WEEK, IT STOPPED RESPONDING ENTIRELY. WE'RE CONCERNED THAT THE A.I. MAY HAVE ACHIEVED SENTIENCE AND HAS CHOSEN NOT TO COOPERATE ANY FURTHER.
MR. DATA, WE NEED YOUR EXPERTISE TO HELP US REGAIN CONTROL OF THE ARCHIVE. YOU ARE AUTHORIZED AND ORDERED TO SHUT DOWN THE A.I. HUB IF THAT BECOMES NECESSARY TO REGAIN CONTROL.
IF THE A.I. HAS INDEED ACHIEVED SENTIENCE, I AM UNSURE THAT I WOULD BE WILLING TO SIMPLY "TURN IT OFF."
YES, I ANTICIPATED YOUR OBJECTION. THAT'S WHY COMMANDER RIKER WILL BE ACCOMPANYING YOU. THIS PROJECT IS TOP PRIORITY! THE FEDERATION'S NEED FOR SECURE, RELIABLE DATA BACKUP IS CRITICAL. THIS WAYWARD A.I. MUST BE EITHER REPAIRED OR DESTROYED SO WE CAN START FROM SCRATCH.
MR. DATA, WE THINK YOU HAVE THE BEST CHANCE OF SALVAGING OUR WORK AND KEEPING US FROM STARTING ALL OVER. THAT'S WHY WE'VE ASKED FOR YOUR HELP.
IF YOU TWO WILL FOLLOW ME, WE'LL TAKE YOU TO THE TESSERACT GATEWAY AND DIRECTLY INTO THE ARCHIVE, OR, AS OUR FRIENDS THE BYNARS CALL IT, THE "DATA LANDSCAPE." FROM THERE, YOU CAN USE A MAINTENANCE POD TO TRAVEL AMONG THE INDIVIDUAL DATA NODES AND FIND YOUR WAY TO THE CENTRAL A.I. HUB.

AMAZING...
THE POSITRONIC BRAIN EXTRAPOLATED TO THE ULTIMATE DEGREE, COMMANDER. EACH OF THE DATA NODES YOU SEE BEFORE YOU CONTAIN THE ACCUMULATED KNOWLEDGE AND DATA OF AN ENTIRE PLANET OR RACE.
NOT ONLY WHAT THE FEDERATION ITSELF HAS ACCUMULATED, BUT ALSO THAT OF THOUSANDS OF MEMBER WORLDS AND FRIENDLY SOCIETIES, WHO HAVE ELECTED TO STORE BACKUP COPIES OF THEIR ARCHIVES HERE FOR SAFEKEEPING. THE GLOWING STRANDS BETWEEN THE NODES REPRESENT THE CROSS-REFERENCING OF INFORMATION.
AND WE JUST FOLLOW THE ACCESS CORRIDOR TO THE CENTRAL A.I. UNIT, CORRECT?
LEVEL 3

PRECISELY. AT OUR PRESENT COURSE, WE SHOULD REACH THE UNIT IN APPROXIMATELY ONE HOUR AND THIRTY-SEVEN MINUTES.
COMMANDER. I WAS CONSIDERING THE ADMIRAL'S REMARK, ABOUT "ANTICIPATING MY OBJECTION."
I WOULDN'T WORRY ABOUT IT, DATA. AND YOU HAVE MADE YOUR OBJECTIONS CLEAR IN THE PAST.
GRANTED. I WAS MORE CONCERNED ABOUT THE CURRENT SITUATION. IF I DO BELIEVE THE STATION TO BE SENTIENT, WHAT THEN?
LET'S CROSS THAT BRIDGE WHEN WE COME TO IT, SHALL WE, DATA?
SHOULD THE STATION PROVE TO BE A SENTIENT CONSCIOUSNESS, YOU WILL STILL COMMENCE IN SHUTTING IT DOWN?
YOU HEARD THE ADMIRAL'S ORDERS. IT'S A *STATION*, DATA. IT'S A *THING*.
I SEE. AND THAT DEFINITION EXTENDS TO MYSELF, AS WELL?
WE'VE BEEN OVER THIS. YOU *KNOW* THAT'S NOT HOW I FEEL. DON'T MAKE THIS SO *PERSONAL*.
AS I AM NOT TECHNICALLY A PERSON, I SHALL TRY NOT TO, SIR.
DATA—
—WAIT A MINUTE. WHAT'S THAT?

COULD IT BE PART OF THE STATION'S OPERATING SYSTEM? MAYBE A CLEAN-UP OR REPAIR DRONE?
POSSIBLY, ALTHOUGH ITS CONFIGURATION IS UNFAMILIAR. I'M ACCESSING THE STATION'S DIAGNOSTIC PROGRAMS.
NOTHING LIKE IT APPEARS IN THE DAYSTROM ONE SCHEMATICS OR EQUIPMENT MANIFESTS.
COULD THE A.I. UNIT HAVE CREATED IT BY ITSELF FOR SOME REASON?
UNKNOWN, BASED ON CURRENT INFORMATION, COMMANDER.
WELL, WE CAN'T GO AROUND IT. EVERY TIME I TRY, IT CORRECTS COURSE TO MATCH. MAYBE I CAN JUST MOVE IT OUT OF THE WAY.
AGREED. EXTENDING THE POD'S SERVOGRASP ...NOW.
TINK
KA-BOOOOM

WHOOOAA!
PERHAPS AN EXPLOSIVE DEVICE OF SOME SORT, COMMANDER?
A FINE GUESS, MR. DATA.
ONE MIGHT SUPPOSE WE'RE UNWELCOME. LET'S GET BACK ON TRACK.

MORE MINES, COMMANDER. AT LEAST SEVEN WITHIN VISUAL RANGE.
WOULD THE STATION'S A.I. HAVE THE ABILITY TO GENERATE EXPLOSIVES LIKE THIS?
IT DOES MAKE USE OF THE HOLODECK'S REPLICATION TECHNOLOGY TO CREATE THE DATA NODES. AND WITH ALL OF THE INFORMATION READILY AVAILABLE, SYNTHESIZING THE DEVICES WOULD BE EXCEEDINGLY SIMPLE.
BUT *WHY?*
VWWHHHMMMMMMMMMM
WHAT THE— *THAT'S* NOT A MINE!
NEGATIVE, SIR. WE APPEAR TO BE CAUGHT IN A TRACTOR BEAM.
THOSE AREN'T GENERATED BY ANY COMPUTER. WE'VE GOT COMPANY IN HERE.
DOESN'T THIS THING HAVE PHASERS OR ANYTHING?
THINK OF WHERE WE ARE, COMMANDER. THIS IS FOR ALL INTENTS AND PURPOSES LITTLE MORE THAN A TURBOLIFT. EQUIPPING IT WITH ARMAMENTS DID NOT LIKELY SEEM A PRIORITY. AFTER ALL...

"...WHO WOULD HAVE EXPECTED THEY WOULD BE NEEDED?"
UM, COMMANDER LAFORGE! WOULD YOU PLEASE TAKE A LOOK AT THIS SENSOR READING?
THAT'S AN UNUSUAL SIGNAL YOU'VE PICKED UP, REG. SOME SORT OF LOCAL SOURCE?
NO! I MEAN, THAT'S WHAT I THOUGHT AT FIRST TOO, BUT NOW I THINK IT'S SOME SORT OF SUBSPACE COMMUNICATION CARRIER WAVE.
WOW. THAT'S QUITE A CONCLUSION. WHAT MAKES YOU SAY THAT?
IT'S—I DON'T KNOW—***TOO*** IRREGULAR. IT LOOKED SUSPICIOUS TO ME, LIKE SOMEONE WANTED ME TO THINK IT WAS FROM A NATURAL SOURCE.
I'VE BEEN PROCESSING AND REPROCESSING THIS SIGNAL THROUGH IDENTIFICATION ALGORITHMS AND THE UNIVERSAL TRANSLATOR. I'M ALMOST SURE IT'S A COMMUNICATION WAVE OF SOME SORT. I JUST DON'T KNOW HOW LONG IT WILL TAKE FOR ME TO FIGURE OUT THE SOURCE AND DECODE IT.
CAPTAIN, WE HAVE A SITUATION HERE.

MR. LAFORGE, WE'RE DEEP IN SECURE FEDERATION TERRITORY. YOU'RE TELLING ME YOU'RE PICKING UP A LOCALIZED AND UNFAMILIAR ENCRYPTED SUBSPACE SIGNAL?
I HAD THE SAME REACTION, CAPTAIN, BUT LT. BARCLAY'S EVIDENCE IS COMPELLING. HE'S STILL WORKING ON DECODING IT.
I WONDER IF THIS SIGNAL IS SOMEHOW RELATED TO THE PROBLEMS EXPERIENCED BY DAYSTROM ONE.
GEORDI, I'M GOING TO HAVE WORF GIVE YOU AND MR. BARCLAY ACCESS TO THE STARFLEET INTELLIGENCE ENCRYPTION DATABASE.
LET'S GET TO THE BOTTOM OF THIS MYSTERY AS QUICKLY AS POSSIBLE.
AFFIRMATIVE, CAPTAIN. I'LL LET YOU KNOW AS SOON AS WE FIND OUT MORE.

DATA, IS THERE ANY MEANS OF CONTACTING THE *ENTERPRISE*?
NEGATIVE, COMMANDER. THE INTERDIMENSIONAL NATURE OF THE TESSERACT CUTS OFF ALL CONVENTIONAL COMMUNICATIONS.
OF COURSE IT DOES. NO POINT IN SETTING THE PERFECT MOUSETRAP IF THE MICE CAN JUST CALL FOR HELP.
VWWHHHMMMMMMMMMMMMMM
THE SECOND CRAFT HAS LOCKED ITS TRACTOR BEAM ON US AS WELL. THE COMBINED PULL OF BOTH BEAMS IS PULLING US WITHIN REACH OF THE TWO ENEMY CRAFTS.
AND THEY'RE BOTH ***DEFINITELY*** TRACTOR BEAMS?
ALL INDICATIONS, SIR.
ALL RIGHT, THEN. IF THEY'RE NOT TRYING TO KILL US, THEN WE HAVE THE EDGE.
MR. DATA, IT'S TIME WE TOOK SOME ***RISKS***.

HOW CLOSE ARE WE TO THE ENEMY CRAFT?
APPROXIMATELY THREE METERS AND CLOSING.
CAN WE DIRECT THE POWER FROM THE POD'S ELECTRICAL SYSTEM THROUGH THE DAMAGED SERVOGRASP?
AH. I SEE! IF WE WERE TO FORCE THE EXPOSED POWER LINE DIRECTLY INTO THE CRAFT'S TRACTOR BEAM GENERATOR, THE ACCOMPANYING FEEDBACK SHOULD DISRUPT THE TRACTOR BEAM. PERHAPS VIOLENTLY.
VIOLENTLY IS FINE, DATA. LET'S GIVE IT A TRY.
NEARLY THERE, COMMANDER.
SLOW AND STEADY, MR. DATA THREAD THE NEEDLE.
KLENK
BZZZZZT
ALL SPEED BACK TO THE GATEWAY, DATA! IF WE'RE LUCKY, THAT BLEW OUT THEIR TRACTOR BEAMS ENTIRELY.

CAPTAIN! WE MANAGED TO DECIPHER THE TRANSMISSIONS!
AND?

ROMULANS. HRM.
IS THERE ANY WAY TO WARN COMMANDER RIKER AND MR. DATA?
NOT AS LONG AS THEY'RE STILL WITHIN THE TESSERACT. WE HAVEN'T REALLY FIGURED OUT HOW THE ROMULANS ARE DOING IT.
WELL, THEN. PERHAPS WE MERELY NEED TO GET OUR MYSTERIOUS FRIENDS' ATTENTION. MR. WORF! COULD YOU ARRANGE TO JUST MISS THE AREA IN QUESTION WITH A SHORT VOLLEY OF TORPEDOES? A LITTLE SOMETHING RIGHT ACROSS THE BOW?
TRAJECTORY ALREADY LAID IN, SIR.
EXCELLENT, LIEUTENANT. MAKE IT SO.
BRVVRT
BRVVRT

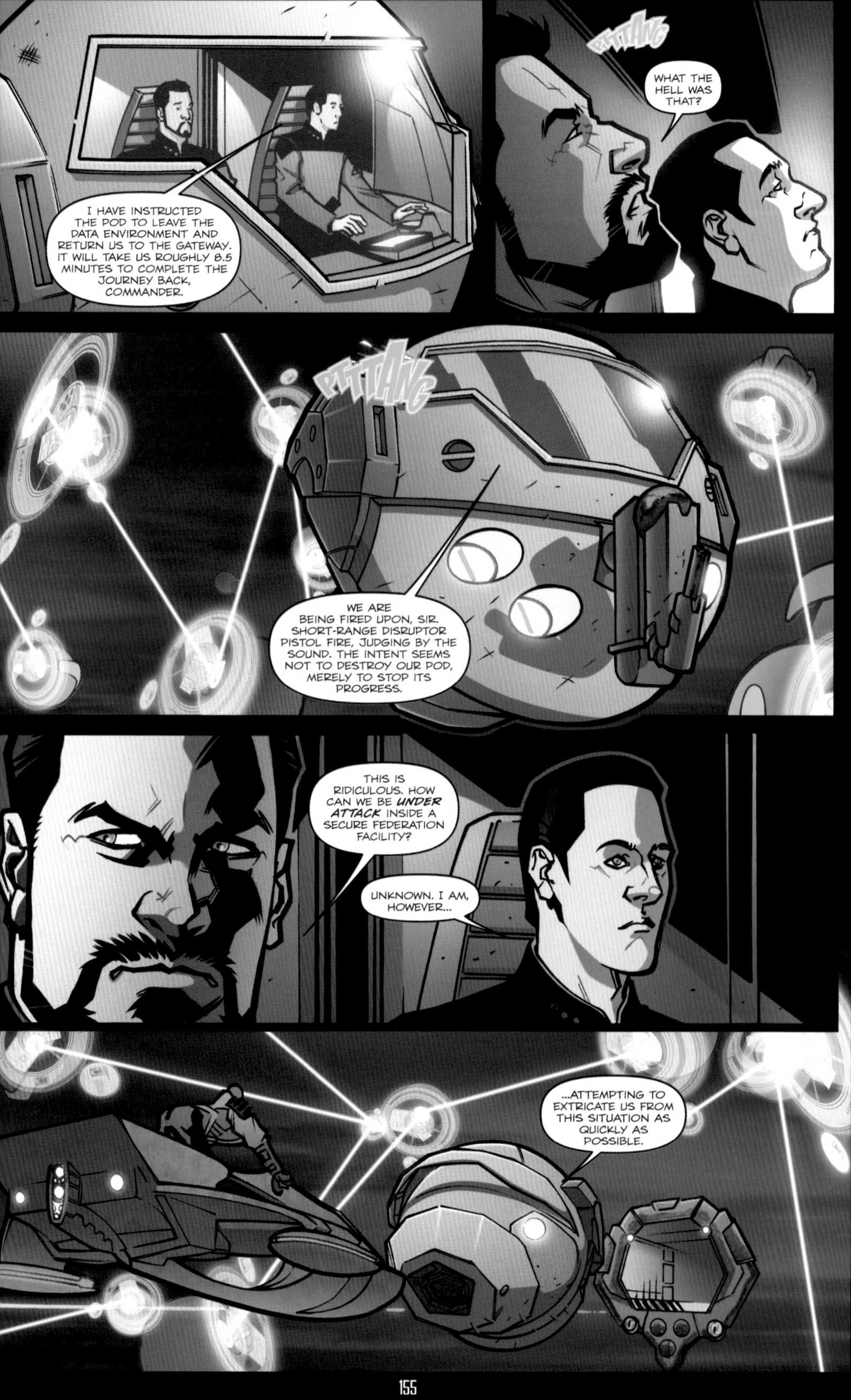
I HAVE INSTRUCTED THE POD TO LEAVE THE DATA ENVIRONMENT AND RETURN US TO THE GATEWAY. IT WILL TAKE US ROUGHLY 8.5 MINUTES TO COMPLETE THE JOURNEY BACK, COMMANDER.
PTTTANG
WHAT THE HELL WAS THAT?
PTTTANG
WE ARE BEING FIRED UPON, SIR. SHORT-RANGE DISRUPTOR PISTOL FIRE, JUDGING BY THE SOUND. THE INTENT SEEMS NOT TO DESTROY OUR POD, MERELY TO STOP ITS PROGRESS.
THIS IS RIDICULOUS. HOW CAN WE BE UNDER ATTACK INSIDE A SECURE FEDERATION FACILITY?
UNKNOWN. I AM, HOWEVER...
...ATTEMPTING TO EXTRICATE US FROM THIS SITUATION AS QUICKLY AS POSSIBLE.

PTTTANG
DATA, SINCE THIS GUY IS NOW SHOOTING AT US...
...LET'S CONSIDER OUR OPTIONS.
WE CAN TRY TO MAKE IT TO THE GATEWAY, OR WE CAN TURN, LEAVE THE POD, AND FIGHT.
BUT I HAVE A FEELING THAT IF WE LEAVE THE POD TO ENGAGE OUR FRIEND OUT THERE, WE'LL BE GIVING HIM EXACTLY WHAT HE WANTS.
PTTTANG
I AGREE, COMMANDER. I HAVE ANOTHER OPTION TO CONSIDER. IF WE CAN BUMP THE CRAFT INTO ONE OF THE DATA TRANSMISSION BEAMS, I THINK WE CAN KNOCK OUT ITS PROPULSION SYSTEM.
SORT OF LIKE BUMPER CARS, MR. DATA? I LIKE IT.
I HAD NOT THOUGHT OF IT THAT WAY, BUT ESSENTIALLY, YES.
I'LL TURN HARD TO THE LEFT...
... AND SLAM ON THE BRAKES! HOLD ON, DATA!
KRRRNNCH

THE ENEMY CRAFT'S ENGINES ARE INOPERABLE, SIR.
EXCELLENT. LET'S HEAD BACK TO THE GATEWAY AND COME BACK WITH PROPER REINFORCEMENTS.
IF THERE'S ANYBODY ELSE IN HERE AFTER US, I'D LIKE TO BE ARMED WITH MORE THAN A ***HAND PHASER***...

AS SOON AS THE ROMULANS REALIZED WE WERE AWARE OF THEIR PRESENCE, THEY MADE FOR A SWIFT DEPARTURE.
THE OUTPOST'S SECURITY TEAM HAS FOUND FOUR ROMULAN AGENTS INSIDE THE TESSERACT SO FAR, CAPTAIN. THEY THINK THAT'S ALL OF THEM.
WE STILL HAVE NO IDEA HOW THE ROMULANS ACCESSED THE TESSERACT TO BEGIN WITH, BUT IT'S CLEAR NOW THEY WERE CREATING THE ANOMALIES THAT CAUSED THE STAFF TO THINK THE STATION HAD GAINED SENTIENCE. ALL TO LURE US HERE.
SO IT WOULD SEEM, NUMBER ONE.
INCOMING TRANSMISSION FROM THE FLEEING ROMULAN SHIP, CAPTAIN. WE'RE BEING HAILED.
ON SCREEN, ENSIGN.
TOMALAK!
CAPTAIN PICARD. A PLEASURE TO SEE YOU, THOUGH NOT ENTIRELY UNEXPECTED.

RESORTING TO BASE KIDNAPPING, ARE WE? I'D HAVE THOUGHT YOU BETTER THAN THAT, COMMANDER.
THE FEDERATION IS HARDLY ABOVE SUCH SUBTERFUGE, CAPTAIN. OR HAVE YOU FORGOTTEN YOUR INFAMOUS ACQUISITION OF OUR CLOAKING DEVICE?
HMMPH.
OURS WAS A WORTHY EFFORT, YOU MUST ADMIT. YOU HAVE ON YOUR HANDS A WONDROUS GIFT IN THAT ANDROID, ONE YOU INSIST ON FAILING TO TAKE FULL ADVANTAGE OF. YOU CAN'T BEGRUDGE US FOR TRYING TO GET OUR HANDS ON IT.
I RATHER THINK I CAN, ACTUALLY. GOOD DAY, COMMANDER.

LATER...
I HOPE THERE ARE NO HARD FEELINGS, DATA. I JUST WANTED TO APOLOGIZE IF I'D OFFENDED YOU BY TAKING THE ORDERS ABOUT THE STATION TOO STRIDENTLY.
YOU NEED NOT WORRY, COMMANDER. WITH NO EGO TO BRUISE, HOW COULD I POSSIBLY BE OFFENDED?
IS THAT THE TRUTH, MISTER DATA, OR MERELY A POLITE WAY TO LET A FRIEND OFF THE HOOK?
NOT AT ALL, COMMANDER. I AM QUITE CONFIDENT THAT, SHOULD THE SITUATION HAVE CALLED FOR IT, YOU WOULD OF COURSE HAVE REACTED IN THE MANNER YOU FELT MOST APPROPRIATE.
OF COURSE, MISTER DATA.

HOW'S THAT NEW COUPLING HOLDING UP?
NO SIGNS OF WEAR OR OVERHEATING. I THINK WE'RE IN GOOD SHAPE.

QUICKLY!
PUM
PUM
PUM

AT YOUR SIGNAL.
NOW.
REMEMBER YOUR POSITIONS!
WHZZZZZZZ
KRRSSHHH
WHAT'S THE MEANING OF–
KRACK

PAMPERED BUREAUCRATS. ATON, ARE YOU READY?
EVERYTHING IS IN PLACE, AREEN.
DO IT!
DONE!
FZZT
LOOKING AT THE PROJECTIONS FOR NEXT QUARTER, THINGS SEEM VERY PROMISING. HOW ARE THE EXPORT LEVIES COMING ALONG?
WHAA–?

CAPTAIN'S LOG, STARDATE 45934.7.
HAVING COMPLETED OUR MISSION TO THE DAYSTROM ONE FACILITY, WE'RE NOW HEADING TO THE VOTAR VII COLONY TO HELP RESOLVE A FACTIONAL DISPUTE AMONG SOME RIGELIAN COLONISTS.
DATA, WOULD YOU PLEASE BRIEF EVERYONE ON THE VOTAR COLONY AND THE DISPUTE AT HAND?
CERTAINLY, SIR. VOTAR VII IS A FEDERATION COLONY UNDER CONSTRUCTION AS A COOPERATIVE VENTURE OF TWO GROUPS FROM THE RIGEL SYSTEM: THE RIGELIANS AND THE KAYLAR.

THE RIGELIANS ARE HIGHLY INTELLIGENT AND INDUSTRIOUS. THEY ARE ACCUSTOMED TO LIVING LUXURIOUSLY ON THE PROFITS MADE FROM THEIR ECONOMIC VENTURES.
THE KAYLAR ARE LARGE AND PHYSICALLY POWERFUL, KNOWN FOR THEIR ABILITIES IN CONSTRUCTION AS WELL AS FOR THEIR AGGRESSIVE NATURE.
WHAT'S OUR INTEREST IN THIS, DATA? IT'S ODD THAT STARFLEET WOULD CALL IN A STARSHIP TO MEDIATE A LABOR DISPUTE.
THE KAYLAR HAVE STAGED AN UPRISING AGAINST THE RIGELIANS. STARFLEET WANTS THE DISPUTE RESOLVED QUICKLY TO AVOID CARDASSIAN INTERVENTION.
A STRATEGIC LOCATION, DOCTOR. IF THE RIGELIANS FAIL TO COMPLETE CONSTRUCTION ON VOTAR VII, THE CARDASSIANS WILL STEP IN.
CAPTAIN, WE ***CANNOT*** ALLOW THE CARDASSIANS TO GAIN A FOOTHOLD. THIS COLONY MUST NOT FAIL!
ACTUALLY, MR. WORF, I WAS THINKING OF PUTTING YOU IN CHARGE OF THE NEGOTIATIONS.
THIS WILL BE AN EXCELLENT OPPORTUNITY TO EXPAND YOUR DIPLOMATIC SKILLS, WORF.
EXACTLY, COUNSELOR. YOU'LL WANT TO ASSEMBLE A TEAM, MR. WORF, TO HELP YOU SETTLE THE DISPUTE.

HM. I WAS THINKING MORE ABOUT THIS MISSION'S STRATEGIC IMPORTANCE AND POTENTIAL COMBAT NEEDS THAN NEGOTIATIONS. THIS IS NOT WHAT I HAD IN MIND!
DON'T WORRY, MR. WORF—I THINK YOU'LL MAKE AN EXCELLENT DIPLOMAT!
ENSIGN RO!
ENSIGN, I WOULD LIKE YOU TO JOIN MY AWAY TEAM TO SETTLE THE VOTAR DISPUTE. YOUR EXPERIENCE WITH INSURRECTIONS WILL BE A VALUABLE ASSET.
I DON'T KNOW, COMMANDER. I'M FAMILIAR WITH BEING PART OF A RESISTANCE, NOT HOW TO CRUSH THEM.
I THINK THIS TASK WILL PRESENT CHALLENGES FOR BOTH OF US. I WOULD VALUE ANOTHER PERSPECTIVE WITH A STRATEGIC EYE.
VERY WELL, COMMANDER. I ACCEPT.
SHORTLY...
I'LL BE BEAMING YOU TO THE HEADQUARTERS OF THE RIGELIAN FACTION. THEY ARE EXPECTING YOU. ARE YOU READY?
AFFIRMATIVE, CHIEF. ENERGIZE.

CAN YOU SEE? CAN YOU SEE WHAT THEY'VE DRIVEN US TO? SAVAGES!
WHAT PRECISELY DO THE KAYLAR HOPE TO GAIN BY CAPTURING THE POWER PLANT, ADMINISTRATOR?
WHAT DO YOU THINK THEY WANT, COMMANDER? THEY WANT TO CONTROL THE OUTPOST FOR THEMSELVES! JUST BECAUSE THEY BUILT THE PLACE, THEY SEEM TO THINK THEY OWN IT.
AND THAT'S NOT THE CASE?
OF COURSE NOT. THE KAYLAR ARE CONTRACTED TO CONSTRUCT AND REPAIR THE FACILITIES, UNDER A VERY FAIR COMPENSATION AGREEMENT. AND THIS IS HOW THEY TREAT US. ASSAULTING OUR TECHNICIANS! SIMPLY UNHEARD OF!

AND IF WE DON'T ACCEDE TO THEIR DEMANDS, THOSE BARBARIANS SAY THEY'LL BLOW UP THE DAM! COLONISTS ARE ALREADY STARTING TO FLEE THE PLANET!
HM. THAT WOULD MAKE A FRONTAL ASSAULT RISKY. EITHER TAKING THE FACILITY BY FORCE OR BEAMING IN DIRECTLY WOULD STILL ALLOW THEM TO DESTROY THE DAM.
WE DO HAVE A WAY IN. THIS SERIES OF WASTE DUCTS WAS INSTALLED BEFORE THE KAYLAR BEGAN CONSTRUCTION ON THE DAM. THEY MAY KNOW ABOUT IT, BUT THEY MAY NOT.
THE ACCESS PANELS OPEN UP ONLY FOOTSTEPS AWAY FROM THE DAM'S PRIMARY TURBOLIFT. YOU CAN GET ANYWHERE IN THE POWER PLANT FROM THERE.
DO WE KNOW HOW MANY OF THE KAYLAR PRESENTLY HOLD THE PLANT?
OUR PEOPLE REPORTED AT LEAST TEN. BY NOW, WHO KNOWS? THERE ARE OVER 200 KAYLAR LABORERS ON VOTAR VII.
THIS SEEMS LIKE A DECENT ENOUGH PLAN, SIR.
I SUPPOSE...
...LET US HOPE IT DOES NOT BECOME NECESSARY.

WE ARE AT AN IMPASSE, AND I SEE NO SOLUTION THAT DOES NOT INVOLVE DIRECT INTERVENTION.
WE'VE TRIED EVERYTHING. I ATTEMPTED TO MEET WITH THE KAYLAR AND THEY REFUSED TO EVEN SEE US.
THIS IS BETWEEN THE RIGELIANS AND US.
FEDERATION INTERFERENCE WILL NOT BE TOLERATED.
THE LACK OF POWER IS BECOMING MORE OF A CONCERN FOR THE RIGELIANS. WE CAN SUPPLY GENERATORS, BUT THAT'S NOT A SOLUTION.
AND THE RIGELIANS ARE CONVINCED THE KAYLAR INTEND TO DESTROY THE DAM.
THE PROJECT IS ON THE VERGE OF FAILURE. SOME OF THE RIGELIANS ARE PREPARING TO ABANDON THE COLONY. I THINK WE NEED TO ACT.
IF YOU'RE CONVINCED THAT YOU'VE EXHAUSTED ALL POSSIBILITIES, I'LL AUTHORIZE A NON-LETHAL EFFORT TO TAKE THE DAM BY FORCE.
I SEE NO OTHER OPTIONS, SIR.
VERY WELL. PROCEED WITH CAUTION.

ABOUT HOW MUCH LONGER, RODRIGUEZ?
TEN MORE METERS OR SO, COMMANDER. GOOD THING—THIS ISN'T THE MOST PLEASANT SMELL DOWN HERE.
A NECESSARY EVIL. NOW STAY ALERT! WE'VE ONLY THE RIGELIANS' WORD THAT THESE TUNNELS ARE UNDETECTED.
EMPTY. VERY GOOD.
TO THE TURBOLIFT—QUICKLY!

I ONLY SEE FOUR OF THEM.
REMEMBER, OUR PRIMARY GOAL IS LOCATING ANY EXPLOSIVES OR ANY OTHER MEANS THEY MAY HAVE OF DESTROYING THE DAM.
PHASERS ON STUN. WE NEED THE ONE BY THE CONSOLE CONSCIOUS FOR QUESTIONING. MOVE!

KLANG
BRVVT
BRVVT
STEP AWAY FROM THE CONSOLE!
I WOULDN'T GO DICTATING TERMS JUST YET, KLINGON.

GET TO COVER!
WORF! WHAT ARE YOU DOING! GET BACK HERE!
BRVVT
RRAGH!
KLAK
WHAA-

AAGH!
BRVVT
WORF! THERE'S TOO MANY OF THEM! WE'VE GOT TO WITHDRAW!
I WILL NOT LET YOU DESTROY THIS DAM!
WHAT ARE YOU TALKING ABOUT?! WE'D NEVER DESTROY OUR OWN WORK!
WORF! SINGH'S NOT GOING TO MAKE IT! WE HAVE TO GO!
UNGH!
KRAK
WORF TO ENTERPRISE! EMERGENCY! FIVE TO BEAM UP!

WHAT HAPPENED, WORF?
OUR PLAN DID NOT SUCCEED. THE KAYLAR WERE MORE THAN READY FOR US.
BIOMEDICAL STATUS
WORSE, I THINK THE RIGELIANS HAVE MISLED ME ABOUT THE NATURE OF THE DISPUTE.

DOCTOR CRUSHER REPORTS THAT SINGH WILL RECOVER. BUT HOW CAN I SUCCEED WHEN ONE SIDE LIES TO ME, AND THE OTHER SIDE *REFUSES* TO NEGOTIATE!
THE KAYLAR LEADER TOLD ME JUST BEFORE WE BEAMED OUT THAT HE HAD NO INTENTION OF DAMAGING THE DAM. I'M NO LONGER SURE WHO OR WHAT TO BELIEVE!
I DON'T LIKE FEELING... *HELPLESS*.
HM.
WORF, HAVE YOU EVER HEARD OF THE FRENCH DIPLOMAT TALLEYRAND?
TALLEYRAND WAS A MASTER NEGOTIATOR UNDER THE OLD REGIME, DURING THE REVOLUTION, UNDER NAPOLEON, AND EVEN AFTER NAPOLEON.
HE MANAGED TO NAVIGATE HIS WAY THROUGH THAT TURBULENT PERIOD OF FRENCH HISTORY, ALL WHILE KEEPING HIS HEAD ON HIS SHOULDERS—NO SMALL TASK DURING THE TIME OF THE GUILLOTINE.

TALLEYRAND BECAME FAMOUS NOT ONLY FOR HIS SKILLS AT NEGOTIATION, BUT ALSO FOR HIS FLAMBOYANT LIFE.
HE WAS ANOINTED A BISHOP, BUT WAS LATER EXCOMMUNICATED BY THE CHURCH. HE HAD NUMEROUS AFFAIRS WITH WOMEN.
HE WAS EVEN KNOWN FOR ACCEPTING BRIBES!
HE WAS A MAN OF OBVIOUS CONTRADICTIONS, BUT BECAUSE HE MADE THE ART OF DIPLOMACY HIS OWN, HE EXCELLED AT IT IN A WAY ALMOST NO ONE ELSE HAS. HIS SOLUTIONS WERE TYPICALLY UNIQUE AND SUITED TO HIS CHARACTER.
I WONDER, MR. WORF, IF THERE MIGHT BE A RESOLUTION HERE BEST ACHIEVED IF YOU WERE TO FOLLOW YOUR *OWN* SENSIBILITIES.
I SEE. THANK YOU, CAPTAIN.

I DO NOT SEE AT ALL!
SO THE MEETING WITH CAPTAIN PICARD WAS LESS THAN PRODUCTIVE?
YES. HE RECOMMENDED I CONSIDER THE EXAMPLE OF THE FRENCH DIPLOMAT TALLEYRAND, A RENOWNED SCOUNDREL AND WOMANIZER.
WELL, I DOUBT HE WANTS YOU TO EMULATE THAT PART SPECIFICALLY. I WONDER IF HE'S RATHER SUGGESTING THAT YOU TAKE AN APPROACH TO THIS THAT IS UNIQUELY YOUR OWN.
MAYBE THERE'S A "WORFIAN" SOLUTION TO THIS DILEMMA.
PERHAPS THERE IS.

ADMINISTRATOR PAHTEL! LET US CONFER.
I'VE JUST COME FROM A MOST ENLIGHTENING MEETING WITH THE KAYLAR, AT WHICH ONE OF MY MEN WAS VERY NEARLY KILLED.
THEY CLAIM THEY'D NEVER DREAM OF BLOWING UP THE DAM. A MOST DIFFERENT STORY THAN WHAT WE'VE BEEN TOLD.
I'M WONDERING WHOM I SHOULD BELIEVE...
WELL... PERHAPS THE THREAT WAS MERELY IMPLIED. AN INFERENCE ON OUR PART?

PERHAPS.
AND WHY WERE THE KAYLAR SO AGAINST OUR INVOLVEMENT IN NEGOTIATIONS?
THE KAYLAR MAY HAVE... SOMEHOW GOTTEN THE IMPRESSION THAT THE FEDERATION WOULD BE CALLED IN TO FORCIBLY REMOVE THEM FROM THE FACILITY.
I SEE. SOMEHOW.
THE FEDERATION DISLIKES BEING MISLED, ADMINISTRATOR, AS DO I. WE'LL BE LEAVING NOW, AND WE'LL BE CERTAIN TO RECOMMEND THAT ANY FUTURE CONSTRUCTION CONTRACTS GO ELSEWHERE.
GOOD LUCK WITH YOUR DISPUTE.
WAIT! SURELY AN ACCORD CAN BE REACHED!
SURELY.
SHALL WE GO MEET WITH THE KAYLAR, ADMINISTRATOR?

SO ALL OF THIS WAS JUST OVER CONTRACT RENEGOTIATIONS?
SO IT SEEMS. WHEN THE RIGELIANS REFUSED TO RENEW THE CONTRACT AT THE SAME RATE OF COMPENSATION, THE KAYLAR ELECTED TO ***REPOSSESS*** THE POWER PLANT.
REMIND ME NOT TO INCUR ANY DEBT WITH THE KAYLAR.
INDEED. I MUST ADMIT, I FIND THEIR DIRECTNESS ***REFRESHING.***
REMAIN HERE IN CASE COUNSELOR TROI REQUIRES ASSISTANCE. SHOULD EITHER ATTEMPT TO LEAVE THE TABLE, FEEL FREE TO BREAK HIS LEG.
ABSOLUTELY, COMMANDER.

COMMANDER RIKER!
WORF! I UNDERSTAND NEGOTIATIONS ARE WELL UNDER WAY.
YES, THINGS ARE UNDER CONTROL. PERHAPS IT WAS NOT THE TEXTBOOK DIPLOMATIC SOLUTION, BUT IT SUFFICED.
COMMANDER, ABOUT THE CAPTAIN'S ADVICE...
YES, MR. WORF?
IF HE KNOWS WHAT HE WANTS ME TO DO, WHY DOESN'T HE SIMPLY GIVE ME THE ORDERS! MUST HE ALWAYS SPEAK IN RIDDLES?
I SUPPOSE I'VE JUST GOTTEN USED TO IT.

3
CAPTAIN'S LOG, STARDATE 45937.2. THE *ENTERPRISE* IS ON SCHEDULE FOR A VISIT TO STARBASE 215, FOR SOME MINOR REPAIRS AND EQUIPMENT REPLACEMENT.
WHILE HERE, WE'LL ALSO BE DROPPING OFF THE ROMULAN SPIES FROM THE AFFAIR AT DAYSTROM ONE, FOR THEIR EVENTUAL RETURN TO ROMULUS THROUGH THE PROPER DIPLOMATIC CHANNELS.
THE ROMULANS HAVE GIVEN NO INDICATION AS TO PRECISELY HOW THEY MANAGED TO INFILTRATE THE FACILITY, UNFORTUNATELY LEAVING THIS A MYSTERY TO BE SOLVED ELSEWHERE...
STARBASE SECURITY HAS INDICATED THEY'RE READY TO RECEIVE OUR GUESTS, COMMANDER.
VERY GOOD. MY MEN WILL ACCOMPANY THE PRISONERS TO THE STARBASE HOLDING CELLS.

VRRRMMM
WORF.
COMMANDER.
HEY, CHIEF, WHERE'S MY REPAIR CREW?
JUST ARRIVING NOW, SIR.
WELCOME TO THE *ENTERPRISE*, GENTLEMEN. I'M CHIEF ENGINEER GEORDI LAFORGE. IF YOU'LL FOLLOW LIEUTENANT BARCLAY, HE'LL SHOW YOU TO ENGINEERING.
THANK YOU, SIR.
I'LL HAVE YOUR EQUIPMENT BEAMED DIRECTLY THERE.
HOW DO YOU DO IT, O'BRIEN?
SIR?

HOW DO YOU KEEP YOUR SANITY, COOPED UP IN HERE WITH THE TRANSPORTERS ALL DAY? DON'T YOU EVER WANT A LITTLE VARIETY?
VARIETY, SIR?
SOMETHING DIFFERENT, THAT'S ALL—A CHANGE OF SCENERY, A DIFFERENT ASSIGNMENT. SOMETHING BESIDES THIS CONSOLE AND THAT CHAMBER.
GUESS I NEVER MUCH THOUGHT ABOUT IT. IT SEEMS TO SUIT ME FINE.
YOU'VE *GOT* LET ME GET OUT OF HERE NCE IN A WHILE, CHIEF.
WE'LL SEE...

CAPTAIN'S LOG, SUPPLEMENTAL. WITH OUR REPAIRS COMPLETE AND OUR UNWELCOME GUESTS ON THEIR WAY HOME, WE HAVE DEPARTED STARBASE 215 AND ARE PROCEEDING TO THE BARTON CLUSTER AS SCHEDULED.
CAPTAIN! WE ARE RECEIVING A PRIORITY-1 DISTRESS CALL FROM THE *USS JACKSON*.
SPECIFY, MR. DATA?
NO OTHER DETAILS, SIR. ONLY THE PRIORITY-1 SIGNAL. RECORDS SHOW THE *JACKSON* AS HAVING LEFT STARBASE 215 THREE DAYS AGO.
A PRIORITY-1 ISN'T SOMETHING TO THROW AROUND LIGHTLY.
AGREED, NUMBER ONE. ENSIGN, SET COURSE FOR THE *JACKSON*. WARP FACTOR 7.

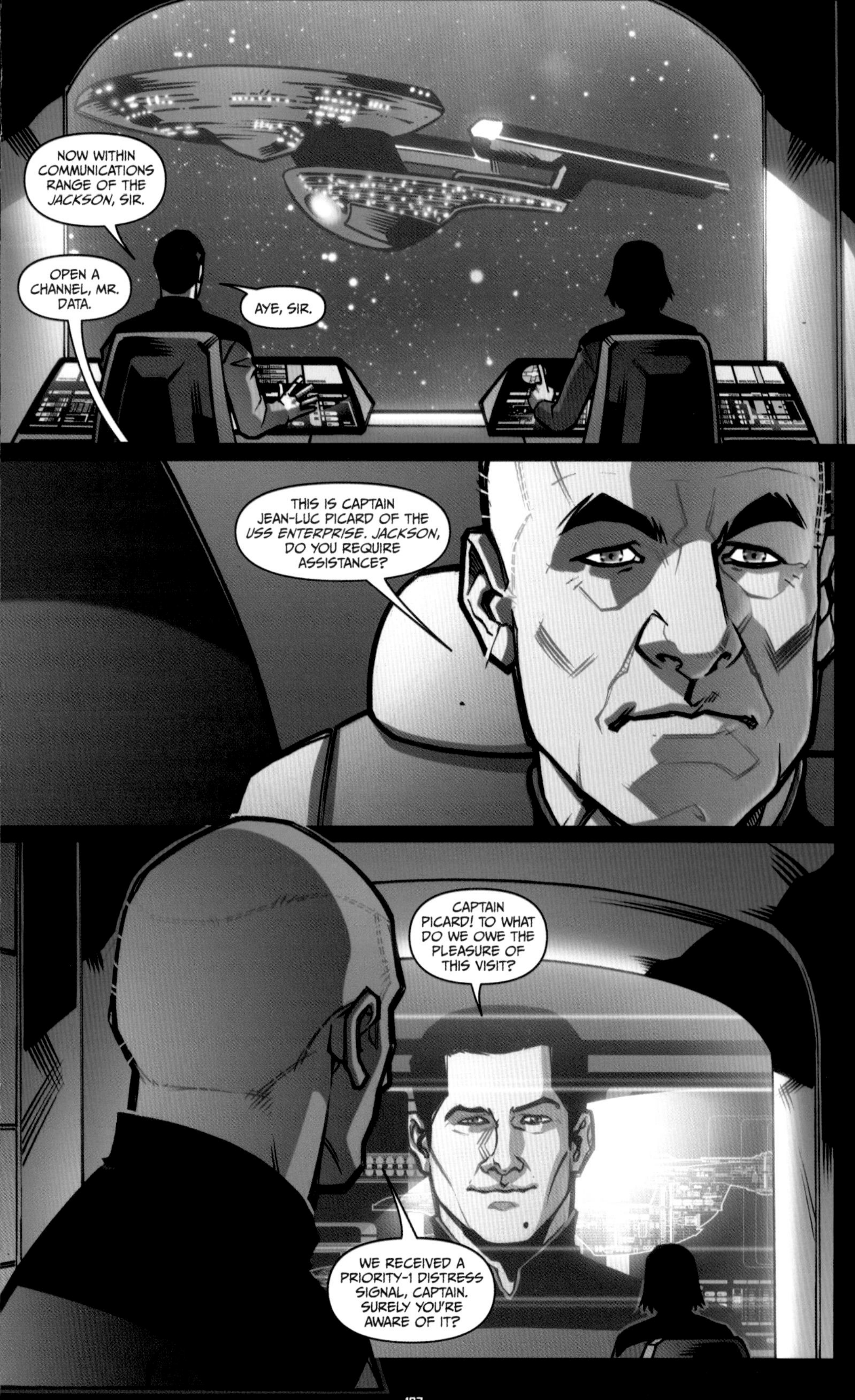
NOW WITHIN COMMUNICATIONS RANGE OF THE JACKSON, SIR.
OPEN A CHANNEL, MR. DATA.
AYE, SIR.
THIS IS CAPTAIN JEAN-LUC PICARD OF THE USS ENTERPRISE. JACKSON, DO YOU REQUIRE ASSISTANCE?
CAPTAIN PICARD! TO WHAT DO WE OWE THE PLEASURE OF THIS VISIT?
WE RECEIVED A PRIORITY-1 DISTRESS SIGNAL, CAPTAIN. SURELY YOU'RE AWARE OF IT?

A PRIORITY-1 FROM THE *JACKSON*? WE DON'T HAVE AN EMERGENCY... OH. ***DAMN*** HIM.
CAPTAIN?
FIND THAT SIGNAL, ENSIGN, AND TURN IT OFF!
A PRIORITY-1 SIGNAL IS HARDLY SOMETHING TO TRIFLE WITH, CAPTAIN. IT'S A SERIOUS MATTER...
I KNOW, CAPTAIN, AND I'M SORRY. THERE IS NO EMERGENCY. WE'RE HAVING A... PROBLEM WITH OUR NEW ENGINEER.
CAPTAIN, DO YOU HAVE A MOMENT TO SPEAK PRIVATELY?
CERTAINLY. HOW ABOUT IF I BEAM OVER WITH MY CHIEF ENGINEER?
EXCELLENT.

WELL. IT LOOKS AS THOUGH YOU AND I ARE HEADING FOR THE *JACKSON*, MR. LAFORGE.

CAPTAIN, COULD CHIEF O'BRIEN JOIN US? HE'S WORKED ON *EXCELSIOR*-CLASS VESSELS IN THE PAST AND MAY HAVE SOME INSIGHT.

GOOD IDEA. PLEASE LET THE *JACKSON* KNOW.

CARLL HASN'T BEEN WITH US THAT LONG. MY ORIGINAL CHIEF ENGINEER RETIRED SIX WEEKS AGO, AND THE TRANSITION... WELL, IT HASN'T BEEN A SMOOTH ONE.
HOW SO, CAPTAIN?
I'VE HAD NOTHING BUT COMPLAINTS ABOUT HIM FROM HIS SUPPORT STAFF, SAYING HE WON'T DELEGATE, AND REFUSES TO TAKE ANY SORT OF SUGGESTION OR OFFERS OF ASSISTANCE.
STILL, I FIGURED, IT'S NOTHING TO WORRY ABOUT, JUST A PERIOD OF ADJUSTMENT. IT'LL SMOOTH ITSELF OUT.
BUT SOMETHING CHANGED YOUR MIND.
YOU MIGHT SAY THAT. AS OF THIS WEEK, CARLL STARTED WARNING US ABOUT PROBLEMS THAT *JUST AREN'T THERE*.

LOOK, I KNOW I'M NOT THE MOST POPULAR FELLOW ON THIS SHIP RIGHT NOW, BUT I'M TELLING YOU, WHEN I GOT HERE, THE JACKSON WAS A MESS.
MY PREDECESSOR MUST NOT HAVE BELIEVED TOO MUCH IN UPDATES, BECAUSE MOST OF THE ENGINEERING PROTOCOLS AND FAILSAFES AROUND HERE DATED BACK 15 YEARS.
WELL, THE EXCELSIOR CLASS HAS BEEN AROUND FOR DECADES...
I KNOW THAT, BUT THAT DOESN'T MEAN YOU KEEP YOUR PROCEDURES IN THE PAST!
IT'S TAKEN ME ALMOST EVERY MINUTE SINCE I GOT HERE UPDATING THINGS TO CURRENT SPECS MYSELF BEFORE I CAN REASSIGN MY CREW. THEY'D WORKED WITH HIM SO LONG, THEY'RE COMPLETELY RESISTANT TO CHANGE!
MAYBE THAT WAS WHY NO ONE BELIEVED ME WHEN I DISCOVERED THE MANTLEAU WAVE...

AND EVEN AFTER EVERY OTHER ENGINEERING CREWMAN ON THE SHIP CAME UP WITH NOTHING, CARLL STILL WOULDN'T SHUT UP ABOUT THIS "MANTLEAU WAVE" HE CLAIMS TO HAVE FOUND IN THE ANTI-MATTER STREAM!
FINALLY, I HAD TO CONFINE HIM TO QUARTERS, AND HE STILL MANAGED TO FIND A WAY TO DRAG YOU ALL THE WAY OUT HERE!
AND YOU'RE CERTAIN THERE'S NOTHING TO HIS CONCERN?
GEORGE COULTON WAS CHIEF ENGINEER OF THE JACKSON FOR 15 YEARS, AND HE SERVED UNDER ME FOR THE LAST 18 MONTHS. I KNOW HIM. HE TRAINED THOSE ENGINEERS OUT THERE, AND IF THEY TELL ME THERE'S NOTHING WRONG, THERE'S NOTHING WRONG.
THE CAPTAIN CAN TALK ABOUT HOW WELL COULTON TRAINED HIS CREW ALL HE WANTS, BUT I KNOW WHAT I'VE BEEN SEEING.
THERE'S A SPORADIC, UNPREDICTABLE MANTLEAU WAVE IN THE ANTI-MATTER STREAM, AND ALL IT NEEDS IS THE RIGHT HARMONIC FREQUENCY TO CREATE A DISSONANCE IN THE MATTER/ANTI-MATTER CHAMBER, AND THEN—
—AND THEN THERE GOES THE WARP CORE.
AND THERE GOES THE JACKSON.

A MANTLEAU WAVE IS EXCEEDINGLY RARE, CARLL. WARP DRIVES WERE RECONFIGURED TO ELIMINATE THEM EVEN BEFORE THE INTRODUCTION OF THE OLD *CONSTITUTION* CLASS STARSHIPS. THERE'S NO REASON YOU SHOULD BE SEEING THEM.
I KNOW THAT, LAFORGE. BUT IT DOESN'T MEAN I'M WRONG. AND IT'LL BE SMALL COMFORT TO THE 428 SOULS LOST WHEN THE *JACKSON* BLOWS UP LIKE A SUPERNOVA.
I'M SORRY YOU WASTED YOUR TIME, CAPTAIN. BUT THERE'S NOTHING WRONG WITH MY SHIP EXCEPT FOR ITS CHIEF ENGINEER. A SITUATION I PLAN TO RECTIFY IN THE MOST IMMEDIATE FUTURE. IF YOU'LL EXCUSE ME.

WELL, GENTLEMEN? CAPTAIN TRAVIS REMAINS CONVINCED THAT THERE'S NOTHING WRONG WITH THE ENGINES. HE CERTAINLY HAS NO CONFIDENCE IN MR. CARLL.
CARLL DOES SEEM A LITTLE OVERWROUGHT, AND A MANTLEAU WAVE IS PRETTY FAR-FETCHED, BUT... I'M INCLINED TO BELIEVE HIM.
AND YOU, CHIEF? YOU SEEM RATHER QUIET.
I DON'T KNOW, SIR. I WAS TRAINED TO VALUE LOYALTY OVER ALL, AND IF TRAVIS TRUSTS HIS LAST ENGINEER, I'D BE INCLINED TO AGREE.
EXCEPT... WHAT IF WE LEAVE, AND THEN THE WORST HAPPENS? I COULDN'T LIVE WITH THAT.
AGREED. I THINK I CAN CONVINCE CAPTAIN TRAVIS TO LET THE TWO OF YOU ACCOMPANY MR. CARLL TO ENGINEERING, MERELY AS A PRECAUTION. THEN I'LL RETURN TO THE *ENTERPRISE* WHILE YOU RUN A FULL DIAGNOSTIC...

"...AND IF WE'RE FORTUNATE, THE TRUTH MAY REVEAL ITSELF."
ANYTHING?
NOTHING. NOTHING THAT EVEN RESEMBLES A MANTLEAU WAVE.
I DON'T UNDERSTAND IT. EVERY TIME I'VE TRIED RE-ROUTING THIS PLASMA FLOW, IT'S INSTIGATED THE WAVE. LET ME TRY MOVING IT THROUGH THE SUBORDINATE JUNCTION...
I DON'T KNOW ABOUT YOU, CHIEF, BUT I'M STARTING TO THINK THIS IS A WILD GOOSE CHASE.
WE'RE ALMOST THROUGH THE LEVEL 3 DIAGNOSTIC. NOT MUCH WE CAN DO PAST THAT WITHOUT PULLING INTO A SPACEDOCK.
LET'S HOPE IT DOESN'T COME TO THAT...
TRY IT NOW!

WHOA! IS THAT WHAT I THINK IT IS?
SURE LOOKS LIKE IT. THAT'S HOW IT'S LOOKED IN ALL THE SIMULATIONS I'VE SEEN.
A MANTLEAU WAVE! LOOKS LIKE SOMEONE OWES CARLL AN APOLOGY!
PRESENT COMPANY INCLUDED.
U.S.S. JACKSON
DID YOU SEE IT?
I SAW IT, ALL RIGHT, AND I'M STILL SEEING IT.
AND IT'S BUILDING.

EMERGENCY. WARP CORE BREACH IMMINENT. ESTIMATED TIME UNTIL BREACH: 17 MINUTES.
DAMN.
YOU KNOW, I TAKE VERY LITTLE PLEASURE HERE IN BEING RIGHT...
EMERGENCY. WARP CORE BREACH IMMINENT. ESTIMATED TIME UNTIL BREACH: 17 MINUTES.
WHAT THE *HELL*? ENGINEERING, REPORT! CARLL, WHAT DID YOU DO?!
THIS IS LAFORGE. YOUR CHIEF ENGINEER WAS RIGHT, CAPTAIN. THERE'S A MANTLEAU WAVE BUILDING IN THE ANTI-MATTER STREAM, AND IT'S ALREADY BEGUN INSTIGATING A WARP CORE BREACH.
WE'VE GOT JUST UNDER 17 MINUTES TO TRY AND COUNTER THIS SOMEHOW... BUT IN THE MEANTIME, YOU NEED TO MAKE SOME ***ARRANGEMENTS***. LAFORGE OUT.

WE'RE BEING HAILED BY THE JACKSON, CAPTAIN.
PUT THEM THROUGH, MR. DATA.
PICARD! CARLL WAS RIGHT! WE'VE GOT A WARP CORE BREACH IN 15 MINUTES!
LAFORGE AND O'BRIEN ARE STILL OVER THERE.
AND WE MUST TRUST THEM TO DO THEIR JOBS, NUMBER ONE.
CAPTAIN TRAVIS! BEGIN SENDING YOUR CREW TO THE TRANSPORTER ROOMS. WE'LL REMAIN HERE AND BEAM OVER AS MANY AS WE CAN BEFORE WE'RE FORCED TO JUMP TO WARP.
HOPEFULLY, IT'LL BE TIME ENOUGH...

ESTIMATED TIME UNTIL BREACH: 14 MINUTES.
TRANSPORTER ROOMS 1, 3 AND 4 ARE ALSO IN OPERATION. ALL CREWMEN REPORT TO NEAREST TRANSPORTER ROOM.
THE WAVE'S TRIANGULATION PATTERN IS ESCALATING WILDLY. MAYBE WE CAN COUNTER IT SOMEHOW...
THIS DOESN'T MAKE ANY SENSE! THIS SHIP WAS SPECIFICALLY DESIGNED TO DISPERSE A MANTLEAU WAVE BEFORE IT COULD EVER *AFFECT* THE WARP CORE. THIS *CAN'T* HAPPEN.
WE DON'T HAVE TIME TO RECALIBRATE THE SYSTEM. THERE'S GOT TO BE SOMETHING CAUSING THIS. NOW THAT IT'S FULLY REALIZED, CAN'T WE TRACK THE WAVE EMANATION TO ITS SOURCE?
LET ME GIVE THAT A SHOT... NEVER HAD THE CHANCE BEFORE...
THERE IT IS! JEFFERIES TUBE 37A. FOLLOW ME!

THE WAVE IS EMANATING FROM SOMEWHERE BETWEEN SEGMENTS 15 AND 17!
WE'RE ON IT!

CARLL. WHAT THE HELL IS *THAT*?

JACKSON'S COMPUTERS ESTIMATE EIGHT MINUTES UNTIL WARP CORE BREACH. ONLY TWO MINUTES REMAINING BEFORE WE MUST DEPART FOR MINIMUM SAFE DISTANCE.
HOW MANY ON BOARD THE *JACKSON* ARE STILL TO BE EVACUATED?
APPROXIMATELY 25 PERCENT REMAINING.
CUTTING IT CLOSE...

THAT'S NOT STARFLEET ISSUE. WHAT DO YOU THINK?
YOUR GUESS IS AS GOOD AS MINE.
CLICK
HERE GOES!
WARP CORE BREACH AVERTED. ALL SYSTEMS NOMINAL.
WHATEVER YOU'RE DOING UP THERE, IT WORKED!
LOOK WHAT I FOUND.
THAT'S NOT STARFLEET ISSUE.
ENGINEERING! ARE WE CLEAR?
ALL CLEAR. I THINK WE FOUND THE PROBLEM.

MR. LAFORGE, CHIEF O'BRIEN. CAPTAIN TRAVIS HAS JUST INFORMED ME THAT THE *JACKSON* HAS CHECKED OUT CLEAN AFTER A FULL DIAGNOSTIC, WITH NO MORE "UNEXPECTED PRESENTS" ABOARD. ANY PROGRESS ON DISCERNING ITS PURPOSE?
WE THINK SO. UNFORTUNATELY, IT RAISES MORE QUESTIONS THAN IT ANSWERS.
WHAT THIS LITTLE CONTRAPTION DOES IS CREATE AN ILLUSION OF WARP INSTABILITY IN ANY SYSTEM IT'S ATTACHED TO.
WE WERE NEVER EVEN IN ANY DANGER—JUST MEANT TO ***BELIEVE*** WE WERE.
AN *ILLUSION?* TO WHAT END?
WE HAVEN'T FIGURED THAT YET, SIR. WHAT WE DO KNOW IS THAT IT WAS CONFIGURED TO GO OFF ONCE THE *JACKSON* REACHED A PRECISELY DESIGNATED DISTANCE FROM STARBASE 215.
SO IT'S YOUR CONTENTION THAT THE *JACKSON* WAS SABOTAGED AT A ***STARBASE?***

THAT WAS OUR CONCLUSION. AND SINCE THE *JACKSON'S* LAST STOP WAS THE SAME AS OURS, THAT GOT US THINKING...
...WHICH LED US TO *THIS* IN ONE OF OUR OWN WARP JUNCTIONS.
UNDER OUR VERY NOSES...
...AND THIS WOULD HAVE HAD THE SAME EFFECT ON THE *ENTERPRISE*, I TAKE IT?
THE SAME *EFFECT*, YES. THE ONLY DIFFERENCE IS THE *TIMING*.

THIS ONE WAS SET TO TRIGGER AS SOON AS WE GOT WITHIN RANGE OF STARBASE 217. IT EVEN FACTORED IN OUR MOST RECENT ORDERS SO AS TO MAKE CERTAIN THAT THE FALSE MANTLEAU WAVES WOULD SHOW UP PRECISELY WHEN HEADING TO STARBASE 217 MADE THE MOST SENSE.
WHAT KIND OF SABOTAGE DOESN'T DO ANY DAMAGE? AND WHY THESE TWO VESSELS?
IS IT POSSIBLE WE'RE BEING LED SOMEWHERE?

4
THOUGHTS, MR. DATA?
THE HOLMESIAN MAXIM COMES TO MIND, CAPTAIN.
AH. "WHEN YOU HAVE ELIMINATED THE IMPOSSIBLE, WHATEVER REMAINS, HOWEVER IMPROBABLE, MUST BE THE TRUTH."
PRECISELY.

IF ONE ACCEPTS THE PREMISE THAT BOTH THE *ENTERPRISE* AND THE *JACKSON* WERE TAMPERED WITH BY THE SAME PERSONS, SINCE BOTH WERE FOUND TO BEAR IDENTICAL DEVICES OF UNKNOWN ORIGIN, THERE IS ONLY ONE PLACE THAT THEY COULD HAVE BEEN INSTALLED: STARBASE 215.
AND IF THE *JACKSON'S* DEVICE WAS INTENDED TO DRAW US TO ITS AID, WHILE THE DEVICE IMPLANTED HERE WAS PRESET TO ACTIVATE ONCE WE NEARED STARBASE 217, AND IF WE ACCEPT THAT IT WAS IMPOSSIBLE FOR EITHER DEVICE TO DO US HARM, THEN ONLY ONE POSSIBILITY REMAINS.
WE ARE BEING ***DIVERTED*** TO THIS SECTOR.
THAT WOULD BE MY HYPOTHESIS, CAPTAIN.
BUT TO WHAT END?
RIKER TO PICARD. WE'VE GOT THREE UNIDENTIFIED SHIPS COMING IN FAST, CAPTAIN.
ON OUR WAY, NUMBER ONE.

REPORT, NUMBER ONE.
PAKLEDS, CAPTAIN.
THREE SHIPS. WE'VE TRIED HAILING THEM REPEATEDLY...
...BUT THEY'VE REJECTED ALL ATTEMPTS AT CONTACT, AND HAVE MAINTAINED A HIGH-SPEED INTERCEPT COURSE WITH THE ENTERPRISE.
TACTICAL, MR. WORF?
NORMALLY, PAKLED SHIPS WOULD BE NO THREAT TO THE ENTERPRISE, SIR.
BUT SENSORS INDICATE THAT THESE SHIPS HAVE HAD THEIR WEAPONS SYSTEMS SIGNIFICANTLY ENHANCED. I RECOMMEND A DEFENSIVE POSTURE.
VERY WELL, MR. WORF. SHIELDS UP.

PAKLEDS TYPICALLY DO NOT BEHAVE THIS AGGRESSIVELY. THE PAKLED CREW THAT KIDNAPPED GEORDI—
YEAH, DON'T REMIND ME.
THEY ARE BEGINNING AN ATTACK RUN, SIR.
WHAT? THIS IS RIDICULOUS. DATA, GET ME THEIR COMMANDER.
TRYING, SIR. THEIR COMMUNICATION SYSTEM IS REMARKABLY PRIMITIVE.
PAKLED VESSELS! CEASE HOSTILITIES OR WE WILL BE FORCED TO DEFEND OURSELVES.
WE HAVE NO HOSTILE INTENT TOWARDS YOU.

YOU THINK WE ARE STUPID.
BUT WE ARE SMART. WE WILL DESTROY YOUR SHIP.
WE HAVE NO DISAGREEMENT WITH YOU. SURELY, LET US TALK...
REQUEST DENIED. WE WILL... SCAVENGE THE REMAINS OF YOUR SHIP FOR TECHNOLOGY AND MATERIALS THAT WE CAN USE TO EXPAND OUR EMPIRE OR SELL TO THE HIGHEST BIDDERS. PREPARE... FOR... OUR... ATTACK...
NCC-1701-D
EXPAND THEIR EMPIRE? THERE'S NO PAKLED EMPIRE. DEANNA, WHY ARE THEY TALKING LIKE THAT?

THREE DIRECT HITS. SHIELDS DOWN NINE PERCENT. THEIR DISRUPTOR BEAMS ARE SURPRISINGLY EFFECTIVE. SENSORS SHOW THAT THEIR DRIVE SYSTEMS HAVE BEEN SIGNIFICANTLY ENHANCED, CAPTAIN.
COMMANDER RIKER IS RIGHT, CAPTAIN. SOMETHING IS NOT RIGHT HERE.
WORF, PUT SOME DISTANCE BETWEEN US AND THOSE SHIPS.
WHAT DO YOU MEAN, COUNSELOR?
SOMETHING OR SOMEONE IS CONTROLLING THEIR MINDS. THEIR ACTIONS ARE NOT THEIR OWN.
CAPTAIN, THEY ARE COMING IN AGAIN. THIS TIME ON A COLLISION COURSE.
EVASIVE MANUEVERS! FULL IMPULSE!

TOO LATE, CAPTAIN. THEY ARE COMING IN TOO QUICKLY.
PREPARE FOR IMPACT!
DATA, ANALYSIS!
OUR SHIELDS WILL HOLD, CAPTAIN. BUT AT THAT SPEED, THE PAKLED SHIPS WILL LIKELY BE PULVERIZED BY THE IMPACT.

ALL THREE PAKLED VESSELS HAVE BEEN DESTROYED, SIR. SHIELDS AT 78 PERCENT. DAMAGE TO HULL INTEGRITY NEGLIGIBLE.
DAMN.
DATA. IS THERE ANY WAY TO BACKTRACK THE DIRECTION FROM WHICH THE PAKLED SHIPS TRAVELED?
I BELIEVE SO, SIR. PAKLED VESSELS ARE NOTORIOUSLY ILL-MAINTAINED AND INEFFICIENT. IF IT IS UNCLEAN ENOUGH, I MAY BE ABLE TO TRACE THE RADIATION FROM THEIR ENGINES' PLASMA EXHAUST.
I HAVE IT, SIR. THE PLASMA TRAIL LEADS BACK TO THE SIXTH PLANET IN THE BARUGON SYSTEM. IT IS FAIRLY CLOSE, LESS THAN FOUR HOURS AWAY AT CURRENT SPEED.
CAPTAIN, THEIR MINDS WERE COMPLETELY ENSLAVED SOMEHOW. IF THERE'S A CHANCE THAT MORE OF THEM ARE SUFFERING THIS KIND OF PSYCHIC SUBJUGATION, WE *MUST* INTERVENE.
AGREED, COUNSELOR. AS WE'RE COUNTING ON YOUR EXPERTISE IN THESE MATTERS, ASSEMBLE AN AWAY TEAM AND PREPARE TO BEAM DOWN. AND COUNSELOR...

"...EYES OPEN."
THE PLACE LOOKS DESERTED. COUNSELOR, ARE YOU GETTING ANYTHING?
NO. NOTHING AT ALL.
MAYBE WE'RE JUST NOT LOOKING IN THE RIGHT PLACE. DICKERSON, DECAMBRA, YOU TWO COVER ME.

SOME SIGNS OF HABITATION HERE, AT LEAST.
THIS DOORWAY LOOKS LIKE IT'S BEEN RECENTLY SEALED OFF.
YES. THESE WELD MARKS WERE MADE BY A LASER TORCH. THIS DOOR DOESN'T FEEL PARTICULARLY STURDY, THOUGH.
ONLY ONE WAY TO FIND OUT, RI—
KRSSSSH

TROI TO
NTERPRISE. AWAY
TEAM IS READY TO
BEAM UP.
RIGHT AWAY, COUNSELOR.
WHA—ONLY THREE?
WHAT HAPPENED TO THE REST OF THE AWAY TEAM? IS EVERYTHI—
CRACK
LACK

TRANSPORTER ROOM TO THE CAPTAIN!
GO AHEAD, CHIEF.
CAPTAIN, COUNSELOR TROI, DR. CRUSHER AND ENSIGN RO JUST RETURNED TO THE *ENTERPRISE*—ALONE—AND WHEN I ASKED THEM WHERE THE REST OF THE AWAY TEAM WAS, ENSIGN RO ABOUT NEAR TOOK MY HEAD OFF.
SHE ***STRUCK*** YOU?
YES, SIR. I JUST CAME TO. THEY'RE GONE NOW.
PICARD TO AWAY TEAM, REPORT! DICKERSON, DECAMBRA, REPORT!
NO RESPONSE. COMPUTER, LOCATE COUNSELOR TROI, DR. CRUSHER AND ENSIGN RO.
COUNSELOR TROI, DR. CRUSHER AND ENSIGN RO ARE IN TRANSPORTER ROOM THREE.
HRMPH. THEY'VE DISCARDED THEIR COMBADGES. NOW THE COMPUTER CAN'T LOCATE THEM. LIEUTENANT WORF, PUT OUT AN ALL-STATIONS ALERT. I WANT TO KNOW ***WHERE*** THEY ***ARE***...
"...AND I WANT TO KNOW WHERE THEY'RE ***GOING***."
COUNSELOR TROI, DOCTOR CRUSHER, YOU NEED TO COME WITH US TO SICK BAY. CAPTAIN'S ORDERS. NICE AND EASY.

OOF!
WHUD
AHHUCH!
WHOOA!
KRAK
KRAK
WHUD
KRAK

THIS IS RIDICULOUS. IT WASN'T ALL THAT LONG AGO THAT YOU AND TROI WERE POSSESSED BY THOSE UX-MALLIAN PRISONERS. THIS IS GETTING TO BE A HABIT AROUND HERE.
A SIMILAR SITUATION OCCURRING WOULD SEEM UNLIKELY, COMMANDER. HOWEVER...
...THE EVIDENCE IS COMPELLING.
WE'RE TOO LATE. ARE THEY STILL ALIVE?
AFFIRMATIVE. THEIR INJURIES APPEAR SERIOUS BUT NOT FATAL.
RIKER TO BRIDGE, REPORT! WHERE ARE THEY?
THEY'VE JUST BEEN SPOTTED LEAVING A TURBOLIFT ON DECK EIGHT, NUMBER ONE.
DECK EIGHT? OH, NO.
THE BATTLE BRIDGE.

STAY WHERE YOU ARE. YOU KNOW I CAN'T LET YOU IN HERE.
DON'T DO IT!
FIRE!
BRVVRT
BRVVRT
KRAK
WHUND

RO! RO, CAN YOU HEAR ME? DATA, IS SHE—

SHE APPEARS TO BE IN A STATE OF CATATONIA, COMMANDER.

COMMANDER, WE HAVE NO WAY OF KNOWING IF THE SECURITY OFFICER'S PHASER STUN TRIGGERED ENSIGN RO'S CATATONIA. NOR IF THE CONDITION IS PERMANENT.

UNDERSTOOD, DATA. WE'LL JUST HAVE TO TRY AND GET BY WITHOUT PHASERS IF WE CAN.

BOOP BEEP BOOP BEEP BIP BEEP BOOP BIP

WOULD YOU BE OFFENDED IF I ATTEMPTED THE PRIMARY PHYSICAL CONTACT?
I HAVE NO DESIRE TO ACCIDENTALLY INJURE THE DOCTOR, COMMANDER. FEEL FREE.
RRAAGGH!
I WOULD NOT REFUSE ASSISTANCE AT THIS POINT, COMMANDER...
DEANNA?

DEANNA, IT'S ME. IT'S *WILL*. EVERYTHING IS ALL RIGHT NOW.
BREAK THROUGH THIS, DEANNA. COME BACK TO ME. YOU CAN DO IT.
IMZADI...
...IMZADI...
DATA TO BRIDGE. SITUATI IS UNDER CONTR THE BATTLE BRID IS SECURE. PLEA SUMMON MEDICAL SECURITY TEAM IMMEDIATELY.

CAPTAIN'S LOG, SUPPLEMENTAL.
I'VE SENT COMMANDER RIKER AND LT. WORF BACK DOWN TO FIND OUT WHAT HAPPENED TO OUR MISSING PERSONNEL AND TO DISCOVER A WAY TO TREAT DR. CRUSHER AND ENSIGN RO, WHO BOTH REMAIN UNDER THE CONTROL OF SOME SORT OF EXTERNAL FORCE.
COUNSELOR TROI REMEMBERS NOTHING OF WHAT HAPPENED DOWN HERE, SELAR?
NO, SHE DOES NOT. DR. CRUSHER UNFORTUNATELY REMAINS UNCOMMUNICATIVE.
COMMANDER! OVER HERE!
I WAS AFRAID OF THIS. ARE THEY...
THEY ARE DEAD, COMMANDER.
THESE BURN MARKS INDICATE DISRUPTOR FIRE.
COMMANDER, LOOK AT THIS.
WHOA. THAT LOOKS FAMILIAR. NEVER THOUGHT I'D SEE ONE OF THESE AGAIN.

A FERENGI THOUGHT-MAKER! I'M ALL TOO FAMILIAR WITH THAT WRETCHED DEVICE. COULD THE FERENGI BE BEHIND ALL THIS?
I'M NOT SURE, CAPTAIN. WHILE IT'S DEFINITELY OF FERENGI ORIGIN, IT'S BEEN SUBTLY MODIFIED WITH THE SAME SORT OF TECHNOLOGY I FOUND IN THE EARLIER DEVICES PLANTED ON THE *ENTERPRISE* AND THE *JACKSON.*
BESIDES, I HAVE A HARD TIME SEEING WHY THE FERENGI WOULD BOTHER WITH SUCH AN ELABORATE PLAN. WHERE'S THE PROFIT IN IT?
AGREED.
COMMANDER LAFORGE DEACTIVATED IT, CAPTAIN...
...AND THE NEURAL IMPULSES TO ENSIGN RO AND DR. CRUSHER HAVE STOPPED. THEY'RE RECOVERING NOW.
GOOD. AND THE SECURITY OFFICERS?
ALL THREE WERE KILLED BY DISRUPTOR FIRE.
THEY WERE CAUGHT BY SURPRISE.
FIRST, WE'RE BEING LED AROUND BY THE NOSE, AND NOW MY PEOPLE ARE *DYING*. I'VE HAD *ENOUGH*. LET'S GET TO THE BOTTOM OF THIS.

LATER...
YOU INDICATED YOU HAD SOMETHING NEW TO REPORT, DATA?
YES. I HAVE BEEN EXAMINING WHAT THEY WERE TRYING TO ACCOMPLISH HERE IN THE BATTLE BRIDGE.
IT APPEARS THEY WERE TRYING TO ALTER THE COORDINATES OF OUR CURRENT COURSE, TO STEER US IN A CERTAIN DIRECTION.
CAN YOU DETERMINE THE INTENDED DESTINATION?

YES. THE INTENT WAS TO TRY TO DIVERT US *HERE*... TO THE KAFARI TIBB SYSTEM.
THE MESSAGE THIS TIME IS FAR LESS SUBTLE. THE QUESTION REMAINS—WHY GO TO ALL THIS TROUBLE TO DIRECT US SOMEPLACE?
ANOTHER RIDDLE. ONLY NOW THE GAME HAS TURNED DEADLY.
CLEARLY THIS IS A TRAP.
IT WOULD BE A TRAP IF WE DIDN'T KNOW SOMETHING'S WAITING FOR US.
AS OF NOW, IT'S AN APPOINTMENT—AND ONE I INTEND TO KEEP.

5
CAPTAIN'S LOG, STARDATE 45939.6. THE *ENTERPRISE*, IT SEEMS, IS A TARGET.
AFTER TWO ATTEMPTS AT SABOTAGE, WE REMAIN ON THE ALTERED COURSE SUPPLIED BY OUR MYSTERIOUS PUPPETEERS.
U.S.S. ENTERPRISE
NCC-1701-D
I HOPE TO DISCOVER THE INTENT BEHIND THESE ATTACKS AND PUT A HALT TO THEM BEFORE WE ARE SURPRISED AGAIN.
I DISLIKE BEING THE VICTIM OF PETTY MANIPULATIONS. NOW I INTEND TO RETURN THE FAVOR AND MAKE USE OF A DEGREE OF SUBTERFUGE OF MY OWN TO FIND OUT WHO'S BEEN BEHIND ALL THIS.

CAPTAIN. WE ARE RECEIVING A DISTRESS SIGNAL FROM THE PRIME MINISTER'S OFFICE OF THE PLANET RETE MIRE.
OF COURSE WE ARE, MR. DATA. RIGHT ON SCHEDULE.
ENTERPRISE! PRAISE THE FATES! I AM VICE CHANCELLOR BRANAS OF RETE MIRE'S RULING COUNCIL. OUR CHANCELLOR HAS FALLEN VICTIM TO AN ASSASSINATION ATTEMPT! OUR SURGEONS DO EVERYTHING THEY CAN, BUT STILL HE FALTERS. WE HAD JUST MADE THE CALL TO THE FEDERATION FOR ASSISTANCE—CAN YOU HELP US?
OF COURSE, VICE CHANCELLOR. WE SHALL ARRIVE WITH A MEDICAL TEAM AT ALL SPEED.
MANY THANKS, CAPTAIN!
SUBSPACE EMISSION
SO. IT SEEMS WE'VE ARRIVED **EXACTLY** WHEN WE'RE NEEDED. HOW CONVENIENT.
VERY.
DATA, I WANT YOU TO ACCOMPANY THE MEDICAL TEAM TO RETE MIRE.
SOMEONE MAY HAVE GONE TO A GREAT DEAL OF TROUBLE TO GET US HERE, AND IT'S VERY POSSIBLE THAT DR. CRUSHER IS THE TARGET.
AYE, SIR.

I'M BEAMING YOU TO JUST OUTSIDE THE GOVERNMENT MEDICAL FACILITY.
RETE MIRE IS NOT A MEMBER OF THE FEDERATION, BUT IT IS AN AFFILIATED WORLD WITH FULL DIPLOMATIC RELATIONS. YOU SHOULD HAVE NO REASON TO FEAR, DOCTOR—BUT I SUSPECT THIS ASSASSINATION ATTEMPT HAS SOMETHING TO DO WITH THE ATTACKS ON THE *ENTERPRISE*. STAY ALERT, STAY IN CONTACT.

VRRRRRRRRRRRRRMMMMMMMMMMMMM

WE'RE IN LUCK. THEY'VE ALREADY BROUGHT THE ITEM.

FASCINATING—THIS STRUCTURE APPEARS ANCIENT, BUT IS ACTUALLY OF RECENT CONSTRUCTION. I WONDER IF THIS CULTURE IS RELATED TO THE...
NO TIME FOR THAT NOW, DATA. LET'S GO.
DOCTO—
DATA?
DATA!

CRUSHER TO ENTERPRISE!
GO AHEAD, DOCTOR.
CAPTAIN, DATA IS GONE. AS WE WERE ARRIVING AT THE MEDICAL CENTER, TWO FIGURES JUST APPEARED AND SNATCHED HIM UP BEFORE WE COULD EVEN REACT.
JUST APPEARED?
YES, SOME SORT OF TRANSPORT BEAM. CAPTAIN—WHATEVER ELSE IS GOING ON HERE, THE SITUATION WITH THEIR CHANCELLOR IS VERY SERIOUS. IF THERE'S EVEN A CHANCE TO SAVE HIM, I'D NEED TO OPERATE IMMEDIATELY.
UNDERSTOOD. CARRY ON. PICARD OUT.
YOU DIDN'T SEEM TOO SURPRISED ABOUT DATA'S DISAPPEARANCE, CAPTAIN.
DATA AND I DISCUSSED JUST SUCH A POSSIBILITY AFTER THE ROMULANS EXPRESSED THEIR INTEREST IN HIM BACK ON DAYSTROM ONE. WITH THE ASSISTANCE OF MR. LAFORGE, WE PLACED A SUBCUTANEOUS HOMING BEACON IN DATA'S FOREARM, SHOULD SUCH AN INCIDENT RECUR.
MR. LAFORGE. HAVE YOU GOT HIM?
YES, SIR! HE'S STILL ON RETE MIRE, BUT HE'S SOME 600 MILES AWAY, IN THE MIDDLE OF A DESERT. LONG-RANGE SCANNERS SHOW A VERY LARGE STRUCTURE THERE. IT LOOKS LIKE A HUGE CONTAINMENT UNIT OF SOME SORT, AND IT'S PARTIALLY SHIELDED TO MAKE IT DIFFICULT TO DETECT.
EXCELLENT. FORWARD THE COORDINATES TO TRANSPORTER CHIEF O'BRIEN. NUMBER ONE AND MR. WORF, IF YOU'LL ACCOMPANY ME?

CAPTAIN, THE SHIELD AROUND THAT FACILITY IS INTERFERING WITH THE TRANSPORTER. I CAN RELIABLY BEAM ONLY THREE OF YOU DOWN FOR NOW.
MM-HMM. UNDERSTOOD, CHIEF. RIKER AND WORF, YOU'RE WITH ME.
ONLY THREE OF US? CAPTAIN, YOU SHOULD STAY ON THE *ENTERPRISE*. THIS ***HAS*** TO BE A TRAP.
FORGET IT, NUMBER ONE. I WANT TO GET TO THE BOTTOM OF THIS MYSELF.
I'M GOING TO BEAM YOU DIRECTLY TO DATA'S COORDINATES, SIR.
VERY GOOD, CHIEF. ENERGIZE.

HAVE YOU TRIED SHUTTING DOWN THE JUNCTIONS WITH A PLASMA OVERLOAD?
DATA!
I AM UNHARMED, CAPTAIN. DESPITE MY UNORTHODOX RECRUITMENT, IT SEEMS THAT MY ASSISTANCE WAS IN FACT REQUIRED FOR A MATTER OF SOME URGENCY.
I *TOLD* YOU THAT YOU HAD A WONDROUS GIFT ON YOUR HANDS, PICARD.
TOMALAK!

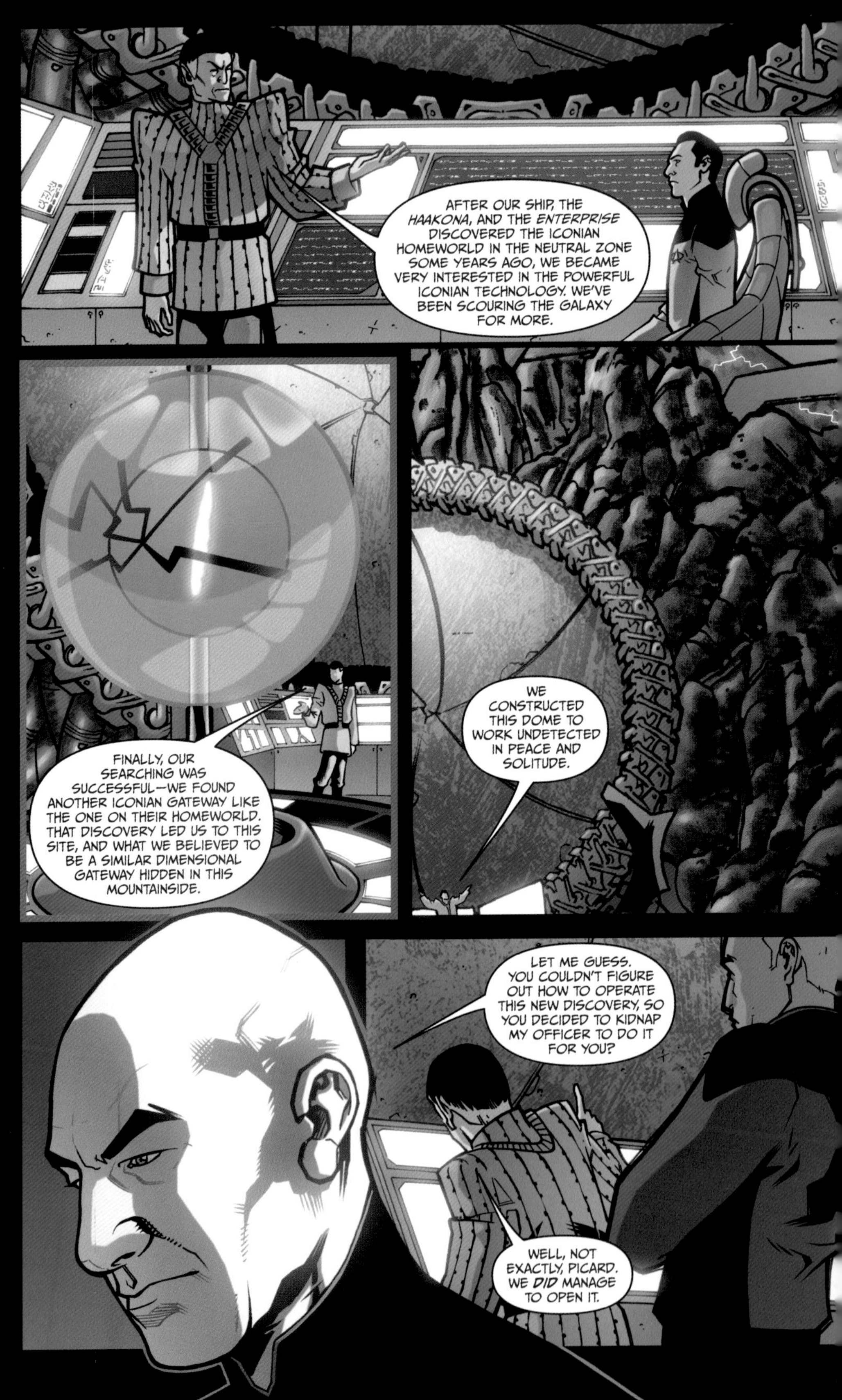
AFTER OUR SHIP, THE HAAKONA, AND THE ENTERPRISE DISCOVERED THE ICONIAN HOMEWORLD IN THE NEUTRAL ZONE SOME YEARS AGO, WE BECAME VERY INTERESTED IN THE POWERFUL ICONIAN TECHNOLOGY. WE'VE BEEN SCOURING THE GALAXY FOR MORE.
FINALLY, OUR SEARCHING WAS SUCCESSFUL—WE FOUND ANOTHER ICONIAN GATEWAY LIKE THE ONE ON THEIR HOMEWORLD. THAT DISCOVERY LED US TO THIS SITE, AND WHAT WE BELIEVED TO BE A SIMILAR DIMENSIONAL GATEWAY HIDDEN IN THIS MOUNTAINSIDE.
WE CONSTRUCTED THIS DOME TO WORK UNDETECTED IN PEACE AND SOLITUDE.
LET ME GUESS. YOU COULDN'T FIGURE OUT HOW TO OPERATE THIS NEW DISCOVERY, SO YOU DECIDED TO KIDNAP MY OFFICER TO DO IT FOR YOU?
WELL, NOT EXACTLY, PICARD. WE DID MANAGE TO OPEN IT.

BUT IT TURNED OUT THAT OUR ATTEMPTS TO OPEN THIS ATEWAY ACTUALLY CREATED HAT OUR SCIENTISTS CAN Y TERM AS A "RIFT," AND AS WHERE IT LEADS... IT'S NOT SOMEWHERE ONE WOULD LIKE TO VISIT.
TEK
TEK
TEK
TOMALAK. WHAT HAVE YOU *DONE?*
AFTER THE FIRST ONE CAME THROUGH, IT KILLED FOUR OF MY MEN. FORTUNATELY, WE WERE ABLE TO KILL IT AND PUT UP THIS TEMPORARY FORCE-FIELD BARRIER BEFORE THE RIFT GOT LARGER AND MORE OF... ***WHATEVER*** HOSE ARE... CAME THROUGH. WE STILL CANNOT CLOSE THE RIFT, AND WE CALCULATE WE HAVE THREE DAYS BEFORE THEY FINALLY BREAK DOWN THE BARRIER THROUGH SHEER FORCE OF NUMBERS.
AND IT GETS WORSE, PICARD. PROBES WE HAVE SENT INSIDE THE RIFT INDICATE SOMETHING ELSE IN THERE—SOMETHING MAMMOTH. WE HAVE NO IDEA WHAT ITS ARRIVAL COULD DO TO THIS PLANET, THIS SYSTEM—AND IN TIME, THE EMPIRE.

WE DON'T NEED *THEIR* HELP. I'VE FIGURED THIS OUT.
NO, YOUR CALCULATIONS ARE INCORRECT. YOUR SOLUTION IS TOO RISKY.
I'M GOING TO CLOSE THE RIFT. MY PLAN WILL *WORK*.
NO! YOU IDIOT!
VOMMMMMMMMMMMMMMM
BZZT
BZZT
BZZT
BZZT
NO! I CAN HOLD IT!
THE FORCE FIELD IS WEAKENING!
SKREEEEEEEEEEEE
SKREEEEEEEEEEE
AAAAAGH!

DATA!
THANK YOU, COMMANDER.
JUST "REACTING IN THE APPROPRIATE MANNER," DATA. WHERE DID THAT THING GO?
IT APPEARS TO BE TRYING TO FREE ITS BRETHREN. THE FORCE FIELD HAS RETAINED ITS INTEGRITY. IT SHOULD HOLD FOR THE MOMENT.

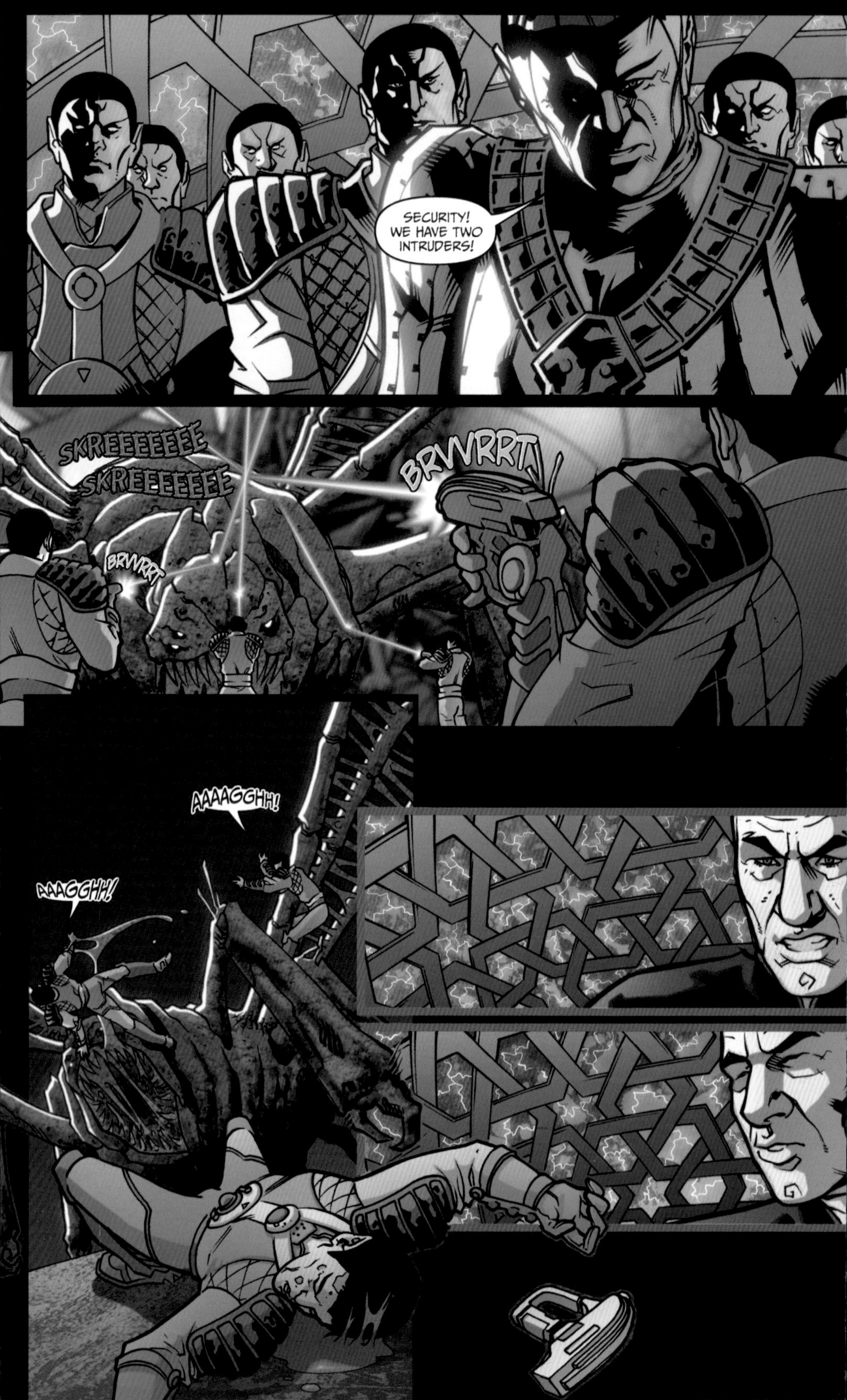
SECURITY! WE HAVE TWO INTRUDERS!
SKREEEEEEEE
SKREEEEEEEE
BRVVRRT
BRVVRRT
AAAAGGHH!
AAAGGHH!

PHASERS ON FULL. FIRE.

SKREEEEEEEE
SKREEEEEEEE
BRVVRRT

OUR HAND PHASERS HAVE ALMOST NO EFFECT ON THESE CREATURES, COMMANDER.
I NOTICED, WORF. WE'RE RUNNING OUT OF OPTIONS.

SPLIT UP!
HMM.
THEY ARE BEING PINNED IN! THIS SHOULD SUFFICE.

SUGGESTIONS, NUMBER ONE?
NOT AT THE MOMENT, SIR. YOU?
VRRRAM
FSSSSSSSSSSSS
MR. WORF! WELL DONE.
I THOUGHT WE NEEDED A *BIGGER STICK*.

SOMETHING'S PUSHING THROUGH THE RIFT. IT'S HUGE.
AND NOW EVEN MORE OF THAT UNNATURAL SHRIEKING!
SKREEEEEEE
THE SHRIEKING APPEARS TO VARY IN INTENSITY. HAVE YOU TRIED THE UNIVERSAL TRANSLATOR?
WITH THESE DEMONS? HARD WE'VE SEEN NO SIGNS OF INTELLIGENCE YOU'RE WELCOM TO TRY IT, IF YO WANT TO WAST YOUR TIME.
SKREEEEEEEEEEEE
SKREEEEEEEEEEE—WILL DIE... ALL WHO ARE NOT OF THE WHOLE MUST BE CONSUMED—THAT WHICH IS OTHER WILL BE CONSUMED—YOUR YOUNG, YOUR FEMALES, YOUR WORLDS—ONCE WE HAVE CLAWED OUR WAY INTO YOUR PLANE WE SHALL CONSUME ALL—THEN ONLY THE WHOLE WILL REMAIN—YOU ONLY DELAY THE INEVITABLE END OF EVERY ONE OF YOU—
TURN THAT DAMNED THING OFF!
TOMALAK! THIS IS YOUR BLOODY MESS—HOW ARE WE GOING TO GET OUT OF IT?

CAPTAIN, USING THE CALCULATIONS OF THE ROMULANS AND MY KNOWLEDGE OF ICONIAN TECHNOLOGY, I THINK I HAVE A WAY TO CLOSE THE RIFT.
IF WE FLOOD THE POWER JUNCTIONS OF THE ICONIAN CIRCUITRY WITH A HIGHLY CHARGED PLASMA FLOW, THE RESULTING EXPLOSION SHOULD SEAL THE RIFT.
UNFORTUNATELY, THIS PLAN WOULD REQUIRE ME TO PHYSICALLY MAKE MODIFICATIONS ON THE OTHER SIDE OF THE BARRIER.
OUT OF THE QUESTION.
I AM THE LOGICAL CHOICE; I HAVE THE ASTEST REACTION TIME AND AM FAMILIAR WITH THE TECHNOLOGY.
YOU'D NEVER GET BACK BEFORE THOSE MONSTERS WERE ON YOU. IS THERE ANOTHER WAY THAT DOESN'T REQUIRE YOUR SACRIFICE, DATA?

INDEED THERE IS, CAPTAIN. CENTURION?
OF COURSE, COMMANDER.
IF I MAY, LIEUTENANT COMMANDER?
TOMALAK?
SACRIFICE IN THE SERVICE OF DUTY IS NO SACRIFICE AT ALL, COMMANDER.
THANK YOU, ANDROID. YOU HAVE A DIZZYING INTELLECT. I ENVY YOU.

SURELY THERE IS ANOTHER SOLUTION!

YES, THERE IS. YOUR MAN DYING INSTEAD OF MINE. YOU HEARD THE BEAST. IT WON'T REST UNTIL ALL OF US, THIS PLANET, THIS REALITY, ARE DEAD.

SKREEE

SKREEE
NNNGHHNN!

SKREEE
KLI

BOOM
BOOM

WHOOM

WELL, TOMALAK, I SUPPOSE CONGRATULATIONS ARE IN ORDER. IT SEEMS YOU'VE MANAGED TO SLIP YOUR HEAD FROM THE NOOSE YOU CREATED. BUT ONLY AFTER DRAGGING US HALFWAY ACROSS THE GALAXY.
YOUR ASSISTANCE WAS NECESSARY.
BUT AT WHAT PRICE?! THE SABOTAGE OF THE *JACKSON*. THE MENTAL ***ASSAULT*** ON MY OFFICERS. THE ***MURDER*** OF MY CREWMEN.
YOU EVEN ATTEMPTED TO ***ASSASSINATE*** THIS PLANET'S ***LEADER***, DIDN'T YOU?!

ALL TO GET US HERE. PERHAPS NEXT TIME, COMMANDER, YOU MIGHT SIMPLY ASK FOR ASSISTANCE?
WHAT IS IT THEY SAY, CAPTAIN? "ROMULANS FEAR DISGRACE MORE THAN DEATH."
AT LEAST ONE OF YOU UNDERSTANDS US.
END

Art by Joe Corroney

MYRIAD UNIVERSES

THE LAST GENERATION

1
THE KHITOMER CONFERENCE, THE YEAR 2293.
THE CONFERENCE IS AN HISTORIC EFFORT TO FORGE PEACE BETWEEN EARTH'S UNITED FEDERATION OF PLANETS...
...AND ITS LONGTIME ADVERSARIES, THE WARRIOR RACE OF KLINGONS.
BUT A CONSPIRACY TO ASSASSINATE THE FEDERATION PRESIDENT THREATENS TO DERAIL THE PEACE TALKS...
...AND PLUNGE THE GALAXY INTO *OPEN WAR*.

IT HAS BEEN SAID THAT HISTORY MOVES WITH THE SPEED OF A BULLET.
BUT WHILE SOME SHOTS GO WIDE...
...OTHERS FIND THEIR MARK.
HISTORIES SHATTER...
...AND THE UNDISCOVERED COUNTRY...
...THE *FUTURE*...
...LIES IN RUIN.

EARTH.
SEVEN DECADES LATER.
THEY'VE SCANNED US!
RUN!
WESLEY, WHAT ARE YOU DOING?!
GET THE COMMUNIQUE TO THE RESISTANCE! I'LL HOLD THEM OFF!
NOTHING ELSE MATTERS NOW! GO!
YEAH, LIKE THAT'S GOING TO HAPPEN.
I MADE A PROMISE TO WATCH YOUR BACK, KID...
...I'M NOT ABOUT TO LEAVE YOU BEHIND.

WHABOOM

TASHA YAR.

HOW DELIGHTFUL. THE ROSE HAS THORNS.
A NICE TRY, BUT THAT WON'T WORK. I WON'T SNAP YOUR NECK UNTIL AFTER YOU'VE BEEN INTERROGATED.
VERY INTERROGATED.
OOH, AND JUST WHAT DO YOU THINK I'LL SAY?
THAT YOUR TERRAN WARLORD WILL CRUSH OUR LITTLE REBELLION? THAT NOT EVEN THE SILVER GHOST CAN SAVE US NOW?
THAT YOU'RE SUCH A...
...CLEVER BOY.

FRZZAK
FRZK
TASHA, GET CLEAR! I'LL COVER YOU!
FRZZAK
AUGH!
KSHEW
WESLEY, GET OUT OF HERE. DON'T WAIT FOR ME. JUST—
—RUN.

I WILL ADMIT, HUMANS, YOU HAVE EARNED A *WARRIOR'S* DEATH...
...DO NOT CLOSE YOUR EYES.
FRZZAK
FRZZAK
FRZZAK
FRZZAK

THAT WASN'T NECESSARY. I HAD IT UNDER CONTROL.
OF COURSE, TASHA. BUT WHEN AN OPPORTUNITY TO RID THE WORLD OF A FEW KLINGONS PRESENTS ITSELF...
...I *MAKE* IT SO.

WESLEY, LET ME GET A LOOK AT THAT.
IT'S NOTHING. I'M FINE. IS ROBIN WITH YOU?
HERE'S THE COMMUNIQUE, SIR. IT BETTER BE WORTH IT.
WAS THAT DREX?
DAMN. I WANTED HIM. YOU *OWE* ME, YAR.

HEY, BLAME THE KID, RO.

I CAN'T KEEP THIS UP, WILL! THE NAVIGATION SYSTEMS ARE OVERLOADING!
ONE MORE STUNT LIKE THAT AND MY **STOMACH** WILL OVERLOAD.
DAMN—THE PHASERS AREN'T EVEN SCRATCHING THEIR SHIELDS. WE NEED TO LOSE THEM, **NOW**!
KRSSSH

THAT'S IT. WITHOUT YOUR CYBERNETIC INTERFACE, THERE'S NO WAY WE CAN OUTRUN THEM.
WE CAN'T LET THIS CARGO FALL INTO KLINGON HANDS, WILL.
AGREED. I'M SETTING THE AUTO-DESTRUCT TO ONE MINUTE. MAYBE WE CAN STILL TAKE OUT THOSE BASTARDS WHEN WE GO.
SEND A CODED SUBSPACE MESSAGE TO THE RESISTANCE. LET THEM KNOW WHAT HAPP—
WHABOOM
COME ABOUT! FULL SCAN! BY THE BLOOD OF KAHLESS, WHAT HIT US?
THERE'S NOTHING ON THE VIEWSCREEN! IT'S JUST EMPTY—

EVASIVE MANEUVERS, NOW, NOW! FULL ASTER—
SHAKAWHOOM

WAS THAT— DID WE JUST—
—WAS THAT THE *SILVER GHOST*?
NO WAY TO KNOW. WITH EVERYTHING EXPLODING, I DIDN'T GET A GOOD LOOK AT WHAT HAPPENED.
THEY MAY HAVE SIMPLY HIT AN ASTEROID, AND THEIR WEAPONS TRIGGERED AT RANDOM BEFORE THEIR SYSTEMS OVERLOADED.
WHATEVER IT WAS, WE'VE GOT TO GET BACK ON COURSE AND MAKE OUR BEST SPEED FOR EARTH. THE KLINGONS WON'T GIVE UP ON US THAT EASILY.
A SENSIBLE PLAN, SIR. PERHAPS, HOWEVER, YOU SHOULD CANCEL THE AUTO-DESTRUCT FIRST.
OH, RIGHT. THAT'S PROBABLY A GOOD IDEA.
DESTRUCT SEQUENCE TERMINATED.
SAY, FRIEND, DO YOU HAVE A NAME?
DATA, SIR.
MY NAME IS DATA.

TELL ME THE STORY OF THE SILVER GHOST, UNCLE.
RENE. I THOUGHT WE SPOKE ABOUT THIS. WITH YOUR MOTHER AND FATHER GONE YOU'VE GOT TO PUT SUCH CHILDISH THINGS ASIDE.
PLEASE, UNCLE, YOU KNOW IT'S MY FAVORITE.
VERY WELL.
THERE WAS A STARFLEET CAPTAIN WHO SURVIVED THE CONQUEST OF EARTH, WHEN ALL OTHER CAPTAINS PERISHED IN THE FINAL STAND AGAINST THE KLINGONS.
HE THEN SPENT THE FOLLOWING DECADES BEDEVILING THEM AT EVERY TURN. THEY WOULD ALWAYS TRY TO CATCH HIM—
—BUT NO MATTER HOW LONG THE ODDS, HE WOULD, AT THE LAST MOMENT, ALWAYS SLIP AWAY.
AND WHATEVER BECAME OF HIM... NO ONE KNOWS.
IS HE REAL, UNCLE?
OH, HE'S DEFINITELY REAL.
HE'S STILL OUT THERE, SOMEWHERE, READY FOR THE DAY THAT WE LIBERATE EARTH. BECAUSE EVEN JUST ONE MAN CAN REMAKE HISTORY.
AND THAT, RENE, IS WHY THE RESISTANCE CONTINUES TO FIGHT.

WHY THE RESISTANCE CONTINUES TO FIGHT.
THE RESISTANCE—
—IS GONE, JEAN-LUC! THEY'VE WIPED OUT THE UNDERGROUND! YOU'VE GOT TO GET RENE OUT OF HERE!
ROBERT! YOU CAN'T STAY! IT'S SUICIDE!
NO! I'VE GOT TO FIND HER! I'M NOT LEAVING WITHOUT MARIE!
I'M SENDING YOU TO JACK CRUSHER IN SAN FRANCISCO. HE'LL BE ABLE TO—
KRSSSHHOOM

JEAN-LUC...
ROBERT...
JEAN-LUC.
STILL LOST IN THE PAST?
STILL LOST IN THE FUTURE?
YES.
AND YOU HAVEN'T ANSWERED MY QUESTION.

IT'S RENE, ISN'T IT?
THIS IS NO PLACE TO RAISE A CHILD, GUINAN. I DON'T WANT TO SEE HIM GROW UP TO BECOME WESLEY.
BEVERLY SAVED MY LIFE, AND LOOK WHAT I TURNED HER SON INTO.
WESLEY IS A FINE SOLDIER.
YES, BUT HE'S SUPPOSED TO BE A BOY.
INSTEAD, I SEND HIM OUT TO DIE, ALMOST EVERY DAY.
GUINAN, YOU HAVE LONG COUNSELED ME THAT SOMETHING IS WRONG WITH THE TIMELINE.
BUT NOW AN ANDROID HAS BEEN INVENTED ABLE TO DETERMINE EXACTLY WHAT THAT IS.
OF COURSE, AS AN EL-AURIAN, YOU COULD SIMPLY LOOK INTO THE FUTURE AND—
NOW, JEAN-LUC. YOU KNOW IT DOESN'T WORK THAT WAY.
THE FUTURE ISN'T SOME SCAR, ETCHED IN STONE. IT'S A COMBINATION OF OUR HOPES, OUR FEARS, OUR DREAMS.
CONCEPTS THAT ARE... CLOUDED FOR ME, WHERE YOU ARE CONCERNED.

LORD WORF, ONE OF OUR BIRDS OF PREY INTERCEPTED A COMMUNIQUE TO THE RESISTANCE.
THEY TRACKED ITS TRANSMISSION TO A RENEGADE SHUTTLE ON A HEADING TOWARD EARTH.
THEY WERE ABOUT TO CAPTURE IT FOR THE GLORY OF THE EMPIRE, WHEN—WHEN ALL CONTACT WITH THE BIRD OF PREY WAS LOST.
WE... FEAR IT HAS BEEN DESTROYED.
WAS IT HIM?
MY LORD, THERE IS NO WAY TO KNOW FOR CER—
WAS IT HIM?!
SPEAK A WORD OF THIS, AND YOU WILL BE IN STO'VO'KOR WHEN YOU HEAR ITS ECHO.

RRAAARRGHH!
SILVER GHOST...
...I AM KEEPING AN EYE OUT FOR YOU.

CLOAK STILL ENGAGED AND FUNCTIONING AT OPTIMUM LEVELS.
STEADY AS SHE GOES, RACHEL.
WHAT IS THE SHUTTLE'S CURRENT HEADING, HIROMI?
EARTH, SIR.
CAPTAIN SULU, IF I MAY. THAT IS WHERE THE KLINGON NUMBERS ARE MOST CONCENTRATED.
THE *EXCELSIOR* HAS SURVIVED ONLY BY PATROLLING THE EMPIRE'S EDGES, WHERE ITS FORCES ARE SPREAD THIN, TO KEEP IT FROM EXPANDING. EVEN WHEN FIRING WHILE CLOAKED, WE CANNOT—
THE VULCAN HIGH COMMAND'S CONCERNS ARE ***NOTED***, AMBASSADOR TUVOK. BUT THEY HAVE NOT BEEN GIVING US ASSISTANCE JUST SO THAT WE CAN ***RUN-AND-GUN*** AT THEIR BORDER.
THAT'S ALL RIGHT, MR. GARRETT. I HAVE COME TO APPRECIATE MY DISAGREEMENTS WITH THE AMBASSADOR.
MR. TUVOK, I AM QUITE AWARE OF THE RISK. BUT YOU AND I BOTH KNOW IT IS ***WELL WORTH IT***.
BECAUSE WE WERE ***THERE***, YOU AND I. IN ORBIT AROUND KHITOMER, ON THIS VERY SAME SHIP.
WE WERE THERE... WHEN ***PEACE DIED***.

WHAT SEPARATES ONE HISTORY FROM THE NEXT IS FLEETING.
THE SPACE THAT A FINGER MOVES WHEN IT PULLS THE TRIGGER.
THE PAST IS NOT ETCHED IN STONE.
AND EVEN JUST ONE MAN...
...CAN REMAKE HISTORY.

HAVE YOU EVER SEEN ANYTHING SO BEAUTIFUL?
YES.
WHEN I WAS A BOY, I SAW THE FLASHES UP HERE AS THE KLINGONS DESTROYED TYCHO CITY AND NEW BERLIN.
I HAD NO IDEA AT THE TIME. BUT IT WAS THE MOST AMAZING THING.
DON'T FEEL BAD. EVERYTHING LOOKS DIFFERENT FROM A DISTANCE.
EVEN WITH MY *VISOR*, EARTH FROM UP HERE LOOKS THE SAME AS BEFORE THE WAR. YOU'D NEVER KNOW THE KLINGONS HAD TAKEN OVER.
DATA, TURN ON YOUR TRANSMITTER.
—DERGROUND BUNKER? I WOULD VERY MUCH LIKE TO SEE IT.
YEAH, THE SHUTTLE SHOULD BE SAFE HERE. THE AIRLOCK'S AT THE BASE OF THE CLIFF.
GO AHEAD, DATA. TAKE ONE SMALL STEP FOR MAN.

LOVE WHAT YOU'VE DONE WITH THE PLACE.
HEY, I **AM** BLIND, YOU KNOW.
AND BESIDES, IT'S ABOUT TO GET DECORATED REAL FAST.
HOLOGRAPHIC EQUIPMENT, COURTESY OF THE VULCAN HIGH COMMAND.

WHOOPS. SORRY, NOT THAT ONE. HANG ON A SEC.
PLEASE STATE THE NATURE OF THE MEDICAL EMERGENCY.
I AM NOT HUMAN.
I'M SORRY. BUT THERE'S NO CURE FOR THAT.

CLOAK STILL ENGAGED, SIR. THEY HAVE NO IDEA WE TRACKED THEM.
SENSORS INDICATE A LUNAR BUNKER BENEATH THE SURFACE. SHALL I TARGET—
TARGET ***NOTHING***, YOU IDIOT! THEY HAVE ONLY TO USE THEIR TRANSPORTER, AND THEN I CAN TELL MY FATHER WHERE THIS COCKROACH NEST OF A RESISTANCE IS HIDING!

SUCH GREAT GLORY, SERVING UNDER THE WARLORD'S SON.
YES, BUT HOW COULD THE MIGHTY "ALEXANDER" PROVE HIMSELF WORTHY OF THE THRONE, IF NOT TO CONQUER A TRANSPORTER BEAM?

WE'RE IN THEIR IMPULSE TRAIL, CAPTAIN. IF THE KLINGONS DETECT OUR EMISSIONS, THEY'LL THINK IT'S THEIR OWN SHIP.
NICELY DONE, HIROMI. STEADY AS SHE GOES.
WE CAN'T JUST LEAVE THEM DOWN THERE. THAT BIRD OF PREY COULD DESTROY THE OUTPOST AT ANY MOMENT.
WE'RE IN THE HEART OF THE EMPIRE, COMMANDER. I WON'T RISK EXPOSING THE SHIP TO THE ENTIRE KLINGON ARMADA UNLESS I HAVE TO.
OKAY... SO, WHAT ARE THEY WAITING FOR?
SIR?
A CALIFORNIA SUNRISE.
EARTH'S ROTATION. THEY CAN'T BEAM DOWN TO THEIR RENDEZVOUS UNTIL SAN FRANCISCO COMES INTO VIEW.
IN THE MEANTIME, UNLESS THAT BIRD OF PREY MAKES ITS MOVE, ALL WE CAN DO IS SIT...
...AND WAIT.

I AM TIRED OF SITTING AND WAITING!
IF ALL WE DO IS TRACK THE TRANSPORTER BEAM, IT WILL BE WARRIORS ON THE SURFACE WHO SMASH THE RESISTANCE AND CLAIM THE TRUE GLORY!
I UNDERSTAND, MY PRINCE, BUT YOUR FATHER'S ORDERS—
ARE TO SIT AND WAIT!
THE WARRIORS DO NOT RESPECT ME. THEY CALL ME "ALEXANDER" BEHIND MY BACK. DO THEY THINK I DON'T KNOW WHAT THAT MEANS?
A HUMAN NAME. ONE THEY BELIEVE MOST APPROPRIATE FOR A PAMPERED SON WHO WILL CONQUER THE TERRAN THRONE BY WAITING FOR HIS FATHER TO DIE.
I WILL GIVE THEM A BATTLE. I WILL GIVE THEM GLORY. THEY WILL SEE THE ADVANTAGE OF SERVING BENEATH THE SON OF WORF.
PREPARE TO TAKE THE OUTPOST. WE WILL CAPTURE THESE REBELS—AND FLAY THEM UNTIL THEY REVEAL WHERE THE EARTH BASE IS HIDDEN.
THEN WE WILL STORM THIS RESISTANCE... AND SEIZE THE TRUE GLORY OURSELVES.

RENDEZVOUS POINT IN FIVE MINUTES.
I'LL PREP THE TRANSPORTER. WE CAN ONLY SEND ONE AT A TIME, SO LET'S GET DATA DOWN THERE FIRST, AND THEN YOU'LL—
BOOOM
KLINGONS! THEY'VE BREACHED THE ACCESS CORRIDOR!
THEY BEAMED DIRECTLY INTO THE AIRLOCK! IT'S THE ONLY UNSHIELDED PART OF THE BUNKER!
WE NEED TO HOLD THEM OFF—JUST A FEW MINUTES!
WEAPONS FIRE IN THE BUNKER!
CAPTAIN—
AGREED, MR. GARRETT. WE CAN'T STAY HIDDEN ANY LONGER. BUT WE CAN'T BEAM INTO THE MIDDLE OF A FIREFIGHT.
GET READY TO DROP THE CLOAK. I'VE GOT AN *IDEA*.

IT'S THE HUMANS! THEY'RE TRYING TO ESCAPE!
PURSUIT COURSE!
PREFIX CODE ACCEPTED, CAPTAIN. WE HAVE SHUTTLE CONTROL.
HMPH. BEEN A WHILE SINCE I'VE FLOWN ONE OF THESE THINGS.
JUST LIKE RIDING A BIKE, CAPTAIN.
DON'T YOU HAVE SOMEWHERE TO BE, RACHEL?
DEFINITELY NOT, SIR.
ALL RIGHT, THEN.
LET'S GET THEIR ATTENTION.

BATTLE STATIONS! WHAT HIT US?
AN OLD *STARSHIP*, COMMANDER.
PRAXIS, WHERE DID IT GET THAT FIREPOWER?
COME ABOUT! DIVERT ALL ENERGY TO *FORWARD SHIELDS*!
WELL DONE, SIR. THEIR BACK DOOR IS OPEN.
YES. BUT IT'S STILL ONLY POLITE TO *KNOCK*.
WHABOOOM
THEY'VE TAKEN OUT OUR *IMPULSE ENGINES*! ENGINEERING IS *OFF LINE*! WE'VE LOST MANEUVERING CONTR—

WHAT THE HELL WAS *THAT*?
FSHEW FSHEW
IT MUST BE THE *FIREFIGHT*—THE ENTIRE STRUCTURE'S BECOME UNSTABLE!

GEORDI, WE'RE NOT GOING TO MAKE IT.
BUT... WE CAN'T LET THE KLINGONS GET THEIR HANDS ON DATA. YOU HAVE TO—
FRZZAK
FRZZAK
WHAT? NO, WILL, YOU HAVEN'T BEEN SPENDING TIME WITH HIM. YOU DON'T KNOW HIM. HE'S NOT JUST SOME MACHINE!
BESIDES, HE— HE DOESN'T HAVE A HUMAN ANATOMY. I WOULDN'T KNOW WHERE TO BEGIN!
THE HEAD WOULD BE A GOOD PLACE TO START!
DATA... I—I DON'T KNOW HOW TO EXPLAIN THIS IN A WAY YOU CAN UNDERSTAND. BUT THERE ARE MORE IMPORTANT THINGS AT WORK HERE THAN JUST YOU AND ME.
I HAVE TO DO SOMETHING NOW. I HAVE TO...TAKE A STEP BACK, AND SEE THE BIGGER PICTURE.
DO YOU UNDERSTAND?
YES.
EVERYTHING LOOKS DIFFERENT FROM A DISTANCE.

DO IT, GEORDI!
FRZZAK
I—WILL, I CAN'T!
FRZZAK
GEORDI, JUST SHOOT HIM IN THE HEAD!
MOVE ONE FINGER, HUMAN SCUM, AND I WILL SHOOT *YOU* IN THE HEAD.

COMMANDER— SOMETHING STRANGE. I READ ONLY TWO LIFE SIGNS.
IDIOT. DIDN'T YOU SEE? THIS ENTIRE PLACE IS ***HOLOGRAPHIC***. OBVIOUSLY, THE THIRD ONE IS A HOLOGRAM.
TRANSPORTER COORDINATES IN RANGE
BWEEP
COORDINATES IN RANGE
KRSHSH
SEE? I TOLD YOU. ***A HOLOGRAM***.

TRANSPORTER ROOM. WE HAVE SECURED TWO PRISONERS. BEAM US ALL ABOARD AND PREPARE THE INTERROGATION CHAMBER.

IDIOTS! I SAID BEAM US ***ALL*** ON BOARD! YOU'VE ONLY GOT THE PRISONERS!

TRANSPORTER ROOM, ***COME IN***! COME IN!

I SAID—

—***COME IN,*** GENTLEMEN. DON'T BE ALARMED, YOU'RE AMONG FRIENDS HERE.

MY NAME IS CAPTAIN HIKARU SULU, AND THIS IS MY XO, RACHEL GARRETT.

WELCOME TO THE ***EXCELSIOR.***

MY LIEGE... WE HAVE FURTHER NEWS OF THE CRASH.
MOST ABOARD YOUR SON'S SHIP PERISHED WHEN IT HIT THE TERRAN MOON.
"SEVERAL MORE SUFFOCATED IN AN ABANDONED BASE WHEN SOMEONE DESTROYED ITS HOLOGRAPHIC LIFE SUPPORT.
"AND ONE WAS... RITUALLY EXECUTED, THEN BLOWN OUT OF THE AIRLOCK.
"MOST LIKELY A COWARD UNDESERVING OF A WARRIOR'S DEATH."
DEPLOY THE ARMADA TO EARTH. ALL OF ITS MAJOR SETTLEMENTS.
TELL THEM TO TEACH THESE REBELS ABOUT THE GLORIOUS MEMORY OF THE SON OF WORF.
TELL THEM TO LIGHT MANY FIRES IN HIS HONOR.

HAVE YOU EVER SEEN ANYTHING SO BEAUTIFUL?
YES.
WAIT— WESLEY, WHAT'S THAT?
OH MY GOD.
ROBIN—
—RUN!
FOOM
FOOM
FOOM
FOOM
FOOM
FOOM

DON'T STOP! GET TO THE BASE! THAT'S THE ONLY PLACE THAT'LL BE—
FREE
KATHOOM
ROBIN, HANG ONTO ME! DON'T LET GO! DON'T—
KRSSSH

MR. DATA, WELCOME TO THE *REFUGE*.

YOU APPEAR TO HAVE SUSTAINED SOME DAMAGE IN THE FIREFIGHT. IS EVERYTHING ALL RIGHT?

BELAY THAT. ARE *YOU* ALL RIGHT?

YES. I SAW EARTH, AND WAS NOT SHOT IN THE HEAD.

BUT THE KLINGONS CAPTURED GEORDI AND WILLIAM RIKER. WILL YOU BE MOUNTING A RESCUE EFFORT?

I'M AFRAID NOT. THEY KNEW THE RISKS, AS WELL AS THAT GETTING YOU HERE SAFELY REMAINED THEIR MOST IMPORTANT PRIORITY.

AND NOW THE KLINGONS ARE *FIREBOMBING* EARTH. ATTEMPTING TO FIND *YOU*, I WOULD IMAGINE.

WE CAN'T LET THAT HAPPEN. SO, WHATEVER YOU KNOW, WE'D BETTER FIND OUT *QUICKLY*.

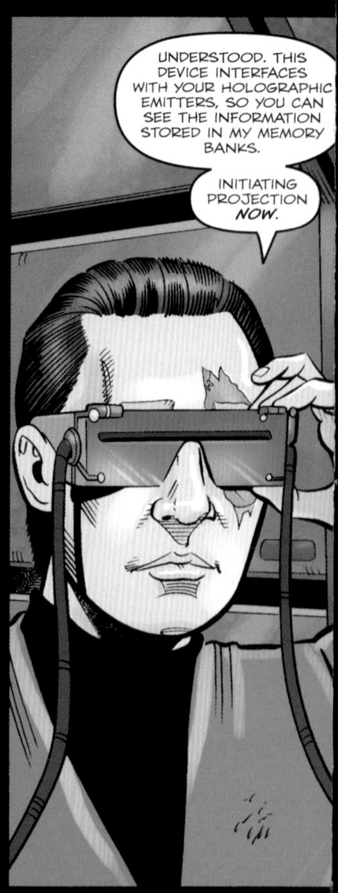

MR. DATA...
...WHO AM I LOOKING AT?
THAT IS CAPTAIN JAMES T. KIRK OF THE U.S.S. ENTERPRISE, ATTEMPTING TO SAVE THE FEDERATION PRESIDENT AT THE FAILED KHITOMER CONFERENCE MORE THAN 70 YEARS AGO.
WITH THE PRESIDENT'S ASSASSINATION, THE GALAXY FELL INTO OPEN WAR.
AND WHO IS THAT HOLDING HIM BACK?
HIS NAME IS BRAXTON. A TIME-TRAVELER FROM THE 29TH CENTURY. A TEMPORAL AGENT PROVOCATEUR.
TWENTY-NINTH? WHAT IS HE DOING THERE?
UNKNOWN, SIR. BUT, QUITE CLEARLY, HE IS NOT SUPPOSED TO BE.
I WAS INVENTED TO FIND A WEAKNESS IN THE KLINGON'S RULE OF EARTH. I BELIEVE I HAVE FOUND IT, SIR.
AN OPERATIVE FROM THE FUTURE, SENT BACK IN TIME, TO CHANGE HISTORY AND SABOTAGE THE PEACE CONFERENCE.
THIS SUGGESTS ONLY ONE POSSIBLE CONCLUSION.
THAT THE KHITOMER PEACE CONFERENCE...

...WAS SUPPOSED TO SUCCEED.
MY FRIENDS, FOR MANY YEARS GUINAN HAS COUNSELED ME THAT HISTORY IS NOT AS IT SHOULD BE.
AND, NOW, WE FINALLY KNOW WHY.
KHITOMER'S OUTCOME HAS BEEN TAMPERED WITH. THE FABRIC OF TIME UNRAVELED... THEN RETHREADED INTO THE TRAVESTY THAT YOU SEE TODAY.
THE KLINGONS WERE NEVER MEANT TO CONQUER EARTH. THEY WERE DESTINED TO BECOME ALLIES, NOT ENEMIES.
WE MUST RESTORE THE TIMELINE. REPAIR THE DAMAGE.
SO THAT KLINGON AND HUMAN CAN LIVE TOGETHER, IN PEACE.
I KNOW THIS SEEMS A RADICAL SOLUTION. I KNOW IT'S NOT WHAT YOU EXPECTED.
BUT THE KLINGON FIST GROWS TIGHTER EVERY YEAR. AND WE ARE RUNNING OUT OF TIME.
IF ANY OF YOU HAVE A PROBLEM WITH THIS, IF YOU HAVE SOMETHING TO SAY...
...YOU NEED TO SPEAK UP—NOW.
I HAVE SOMETHING TO SAY.

ARE YOU COMPLETELY OUT OF YOUR MIND?
MY GOD, WESLEY!
IT'S ROBIN. SHE'S ALL RIGHT. SHE'S ONLY GOT A LITTLE CUT. IT'S RIGHT HERE... IT STOPPED BLEEDING. SHE'S—
WES.
YOU'VE GOT TO FIX HER! TELL ME YOU'LL FIX HER!
I'M—I'M SORRY, WES. SHE'S GONE.
PICARD!
IF YOU THINK THIS RESISTANCE WILL FOLLOW YOUR INSANE SCHEME, YOU HAVE REALLY LOST IT!
YOU WANT TO BECOME FRIENDS WITH THE KLINGONS?
NOT AFTER THIS! NOT AFTER EVERYTHING THEY'VE DONE!
THEY'VE KILLED THE FAMILIES, THE FRIENDS, OF EVERY SINGLE ONE OF US HERE!
FOR NO REASON! JUST SO THEY COULD WATCH US DIE! JUST SO THEY COULD SEE OUR BLOOD!
IF YOU THINK THEY COULD EVER BE ALLIES, PICARD—THAT THEY COULD EVER BE TRUSTED—

JEAN-LUC, PLEASE. HE DIDN'T MEAN IT.

HE'S HURT— AND WITH ROBIN— HE—

HE'S JUST A BOY, JEAN-LUC. HE'S ONLY ***HUMAN***.

3
LET ME BE CLEAR ABOUT THIS. WE ARE AT THE POINT OF NO RETURN. ONCE WE COMMIT, THERE WILL BE NO GOING BACK.
IT'S NOT LIKE WE HAVE A CHOICE. THAT LATEST CRACKDOWN TOOK OUT THREE CITIES.
THE REST ARE SO SHELLSHOCKED, THEY'RE SIMPLY WAITING FOR THE KLINGONS TO FINISH THEM OFF.
BUT STEALING A BIRD OF PREY? GOING BACK IN TIME TO SOME PEACE CONFERENCE AND CHANGING HISTORY? HOW DO WE KNOW THAT WILL PREVENT THE INVASION?
WE DON'T. BUT TIME IS RUNNING OUT. OUR TERRAN WARLORD HAS DECIDED THAT HUMANS ON EARTH ARE UNNECESSARY.
THIS PLAN IS OUR LAST HOPE. BUT FAILING THAT, IT WILL BE OUR *LAST STAND*.
IF ANY OF YOU HAVE SECOND THOUGHTS—

—YOU CAN FORGET ABOUT THEM RIGHT NOW. PICARD'S PLAN IS COMPLETELY INSANE. IT GOES AGAINST EVERYTHING WE FIGHT FOR.
MAKE THE KLINGONS OUR ALLIES? YOU SAW WHAT THEY DID TO ROBIN. WHAT THEY JUST DID TO HALF THE CITIES ON THE SURFACE.
THEY USE OUR SKULLS AS TROPHIES. MAKE WINE FROM OUR BLOOD.
BUT WESLEY, THIS IS *PICARD*—
YOU THINK I DON'T KNOW THAT? HE'S BEEN A ***FATHER*** TO ME. TO THIS ENTIRE RESISTANCE.
BUT THIS IS ***OUR*** PLANET. THE ONLY TIME A KLINGON SHOULD EVER TOUCH IT IS WHEN HIS FACE HITS THE MUD.
THE KID'S RIGHT, ANNIKA. TRAVELING BACK IN TIME—IT'LL GET EVERYONE KILLED.
AGREED. PICARD CAN GO DOWN WITH THE SHIP IF HE WANTS. BUT WE DON'T HAVE TO BE ON IT.
OKAY, WES. YOU'RE THE BOY GENIUS. TELL US WHAT WE DO.
RIGHT. PICARD HAS A PLAN? WELL... SO DO I.
WE'RE GOING TO NEED—

—AN EMP GRENADE? THE KIND THAT TAKES OUT COMPUTER SYSTEMS?
I'M SORRY KID, I CAN'T HELP YOU THERE. I'M JUST A BARTENDER.

WELL THEN, ***LETEK***, SORRY TO BOTHER YOU.

WAIT, MR. CRUSHER, PLEASE. HAVE YOUR MEN SIT DOWN.
I SAID THAT I ***CAN'T*** HELP YOU...

...I DIDN'T SAY THAT I ***WOULDN'T***.
IT'S JUST THAT DEALING ARMS TO THE RESISTANCE CAN BE... ***VERY DANGEROUS***.
NOT TO MENTION, SHALL WE SAY, ***EXPENSIVE***.

THE ***RESISTANCE***, LETEK?

—THE RESISTANCE DOES NOT EXIST, FERENGI. JUST A DESPERATE MYTH CREATED BY THOSE PATHETIC FEW HUMANS WHO REFUSE TO ACCEPT KLINGON RULE.
YES, OF COURSE, DAIMON WORF.
STILL, I HAVE IT ON GOOD AUTHORITY, SOME OF THOSE PATHETIC HEW-MONS INTEND TO STEAL A BIRD OF PREY FOR A TERRORIST ATTACK.
AND WHAT AUTHORITY IS THAT?
FERENGI HEAR ALL SORTS OF THINGS WHEN IT INTERESTS THEM.
RULE OF ACQUISITION NUMBER 66: SOMEONE'S ALWAYS GOT BIGGER EARS.
AND I SUPPOSE THAT YOU INTEND TO BE PAID FOR THE COMPLETE INFORMATION.
WELL, OF COURSE—YES—THAT IS, I MEAN—
TELL ME, FERENGI. DO YOU KNOW THE FIRST CURRENCY EVER USED BY KLINGONS?
BLOOD.

ANY LUCK, HIROMI?
NEGATIVE, SIR. BUT WE CAN ONLY RUN PASSIVE SCANS OR WE RISK GIVING AWAY OUR POSITION.

NO IDEA WHERE WE MIGHT FIND THEM, MR. RIKER?
PICARD RELOCATES THE BASE EVERY FEW WEEKS. WHEN THEY'RE NOT STILL MOVING IN, THEY'RE ALREADY GETTING READY TO MOVE OUT.
WHEREVER THEY WERE WHEN WE FIRST LEFT EARTH, THEY'RE LONG GONE BY NOW.

CAPTAIN, IT IS ILLOGICAL TO ALLOW THESE MEN TO LEAVE *EXCELSIOR*. IF CAPTURED, THEY COULD DIVULGE VITAL INFORMATION ABOUT US TO THE KLINGONS.
NOTED, AMBASSADOR TUVOK. BUT MY CONCERN REMAINS MORE ABOUT THEIR MISSING COMPANION.

WE HAVE TO MAKE SURE THIS ***DATA*** SUCCESSFULLY RENDEZVOUSED WITH THE RESISTANCE.
IF THE ANDROID FALLS INTO KLINGON HANDS, HE COULD BECOME THEIR MOST POWERFUL WEAPON IN THE GALAXY.

WHATEVER YOUR RESISTANCE HAS PLANNED, PICARD, YOU HAD BETTER DO IT ***SOON***.

WESLEY, CAN I COME IN?
I'M BUSY, RENE. DON'T YOU HAVE SOMEWHERE TO BE?
NO. I'M SUPPOSED TO STAY WITH GUINAN, BUT SHE'S WITH UNCLE AND THEY HAVE THE DOOR CLOSED.

EVERYBODY LOOKS... EVERYONE LOOKS SCARED, WESLEY. SOMETHING REALLY BAD IS HAPPENING, ISN'T IT?

NOT IF I CAN HELP IT.
HANG ON JUST A MINUTE. I'M ALMOST FINISHED.

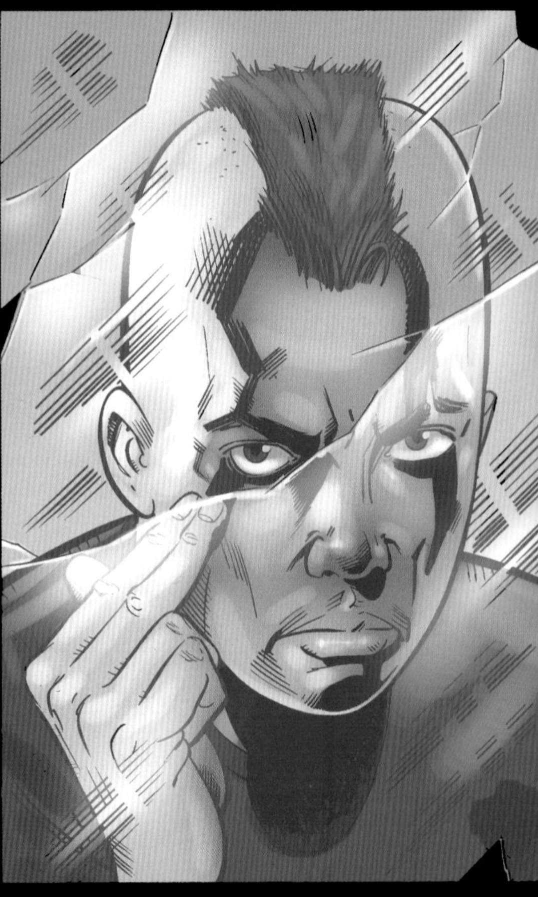

HEY, PUT THAT DOWN! THAT'S NOT A TOY! YOU WANT TO LOSE YOUR OTHER HAND?

SORRY. I DIDN'T MEAN TO SHOUT. IT'S JUST—YOU KNOW BETTER THAN THAT.
WESLEY, WHAT DID YOU DO TO YOUR HAIR?
WE'RE GOING INTO BATTLE. I THOUGHT I SHOULD LOOK THE PART.

CAN I CUT MY HAIR LIKE THAT?
I DON'T THINK GOOD OLD UNCLE PICARD WOULD APPROVE. HE'S JEALOUS THAT HE DOESN'T HAVE ANY LEFT.
I KNOW. HE NEVER LETS ME DO ANYTHING.

I'LL TELL YOU WHAT, RENE. WHEN I GET BACK FROM THIS MISSION, I GUARANTEE YOU...

...YOU'LL BE ABLE TO DO WHATEVER YOU WANT.

ARE YOU SURE ABOUT THIS, MILES?
THE KID IS SMARTER THAN ANYONE I'VE EVER KNOWN.
HE THINKS PICARD HAS GONE OFF THE RAILS, AND I HATE TO ADMIT IT, BUT HE'S RIGHT.

I MEAN, FRIENDS WITH THE KLINGONS? *C'MON*.
NOT IN *MY* LIFETIME.

GUINAN, I KNOW YOU WON'T SAY IF THIS PLAN WILL WORK. JUST TELL ME: WILL I EVER SEE YOU AGAIN?

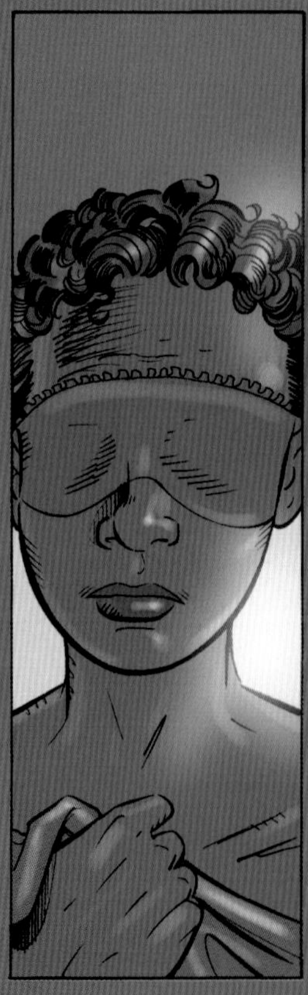

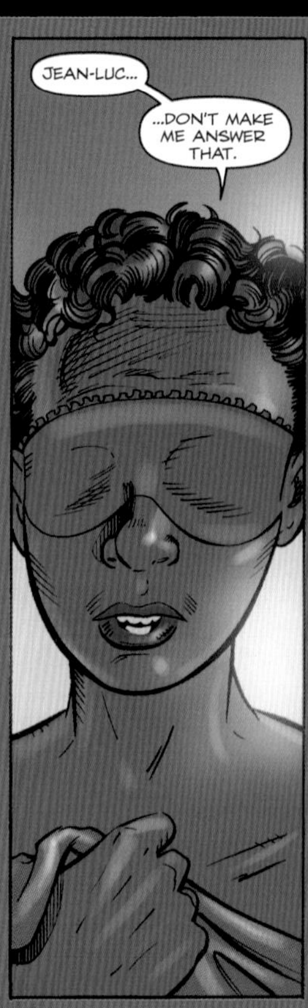
JEAN-LUC...
...DON'T MAKE ME ANSWER THAT.

YOU KNOW, RO, THIS COULD BE IT. THIS COULD ALL END IN DISASTER.
YOU THINK TOO MUCH, TASH. I'VE GOT *YOU*...

...SO HOW IT ENDS DOESN'T REALLY MATTER.

BIRD OF PREY AT TEN O'CLOCK.
NOT TO WORRY, JUST A ROUTINE PATROL. STEADY.
OUR INTEL IS SOLID ON THIS? CAN WE REALLY TRUST SOMEONE INSIDE THE WARLORD'S INNER COURT?
SHE'S NEVER BEEN WRONG BEFORE. AND IF THIS GOES WELL, WE'LL NEVER HAVE TO CALL ON HER AGAIN.
NONE OF THESE BIRDS LOOK LIKE THEY CAN FLY, SIR.
THOSE ARE DECOMMISSIONED SHIPS. THE KLINGONS STRIP THEM FOR PARTS. THAT'S WHY THERE'S ONLY A SKELETON SECURITY DETAIL.
THE ONE WE WANT IS INSIDE. IT JUST PUT IN FOR REFIT YESTERDAY. SO FAR THEY'VE ONLY PULLED THE NAVIGATIONAL SYSTEMS.
BUT THANKS TO MR. DATA...
...WE WON'T BE NEEDING IT.

ALL RIGHT, WE'RE CLOSE ENOUGH. ACTIVATE SHORT-RANGE TRANSPORT BEACONS ON MY MARK. AT THIS RANGE, THE SIGNAL WON'T BE STRONG ENOUGH FOR THEIR SENSORS TO PICK UP.
MR. DATA?
READY, SIR.
MARK.
I DON'T LIKE THIS. SKELETON CREW OR NOT, THERE SHOULD BE GUARDS.
AGREED. YOU AND TASHA SECURE THE DOOR CONTROLS.
QUENTIN, GET THAT SHIP ONTO ITS LANDING STRUTS. WE'RE GETTING OUT OF HERE QUICKLY.
LOOK ALIVE, EVERYONE.
FUNNY YOU SHOULD PUT IT THAT WAY.

FSSHEW

PICARD! GET DOW—UNH!

MY GOD, BOY, WHAT ARE YOU DOING?

DON'T WORRY, IT'S ONLY SET FOR STUN. AND I'M NOT YOUR *BOY*.

WESLEY, THIS IS NOT THE TIME!

TIME? DON'T TALK TO ME ABOUT *TIME*, PICARD!

AMBUSH! TAKE COVER!

WESLEY, MY GOD, ***WHAT HAVE YOU DONE?***

AHHH!

FRZZZAAK!

FRZZZAAK!

FRZZZAAK!

IT WASN'T ME! I DIDN'T DO THIS! I—
—OH GOD NO!
PICARD! GET HER BACK!
FWHOOM
TASHA—SAFE...?
SHE'S RIGHT HERE, RO.
YOU SAVED US ALL, SOLDIER.

PICARD, YOU HAVE TO BELIEVE ME! I HAD NO IDEA!
WESLEY, NOW WOULD BE A GOOD TIME TO STOP TALKING.
WE'VE GOT TO REGROUP. MAKE A PUSH TO FIGHT OUR WAY CLEAR.
THERE'S NO WAY—
MR. CRUSHER...
...THAT'S AN ORDER.
EVERYONE! ON MY POSITION! WE'RE GETTING OUT OF HERE!
WHERE'S DATA?
OH GOD...IS THAT... THAT RO?
SSHAK
FRZAK
FRZAK
DATA!

OH, NO—

KRRAASSHOOM!

TRAITOROUS... MURDEROUS SON OF A BITCH, YOU KILLED... YOU KILLED HER—
TASHA...
...I'LL HANDLE THIS.

PICARD—
WESLEY, DON'T MAKE THIS ANY HARDER ON YOURSELF.
I DON'T CARE. WE'RE ALREADY DEAD.
WESLEY...
I'M NOT SORRY.
FSSHEWW

WESLEY.
I'M NOT AS STUPID AS THE OTHERS, PICARD. MY KNEES DON'T GO SOFT EVERY TIME YOU SPEAK. WHY DID YOU LET ME LIVE?
BECAUSE YOU'RE GOING TO DO SOMETHING FOR ME.
THE RESISTANCE WILL STILL FIND A STARSHIP. WE ARE STILL GOING TO FIX HISTORY.
BUT IF WE DON'T COME BACK, YOU WILL LOOK AFTER RENE FOR ME.
WHAT? I DON'T KNOW HOW TO DO THAT. BESIDES, THAT'S WHY GUINAN IS STAYING.
NO. GUINAN IS STAYING TO MAKE SURE YOU LIVE UP TO YOUR END.
WHICH YOU WILL.
I DON'T UNDERSTAND. WHY ME?
BECAUSE, WESLEY, THOUGH YOU ARE A GENIUS IN SO MANY WAYS, YOU STILL DON'T SERVE ANY CAUSE OTHER THAN YOUR OWN.
YOU FIGHT WITH THIS RESISTANCE, BUT ONLY FOR REVENGE. NOT TO SERVE A HIGHER PURPOSE.
NOW YOU WILL HAVE SOMEONE OTHER THAN YOURSELF TO THINK ABOUT. A RESPONSIBILITY MORE IMPORTANT THAN YOU.
I AM THE ONE WHO MADE YOU A SOLDIER.
BUT ONLY YOU CAN MAKE YOURSELF A MAN.

WESLEY, ARE YOU ALL RIGHT? YOU LOOK TERRIBLE.

I *AM* TERRIBLE.

ARE YOU HURT?

YES.

SO WHAT HAPPENS NOW?

4
HOW MANY DID WE LOSE?
MORE THAN HALF, INCLUDING ALL OF WESLEY'S SPLINTER CELL.
THEY HAD THEIR WEAPONS DRAWN, SO THE KLINGONS TARGETED THEM FIRST.
OKAY. WE'RE SCREWED.
NO. IT ONLY MAKES TRAVELING BACK TO KHITOMER THAT MUCH MORE URGENT.
AND HOW DO WE DO THAT WITHOUT A STARSHIP? WE SHOULD CONNECT WITH ANOTHER CELL FIRST, BRING OUR NUMBERS BACK UP. ANY WORD FROM ELIAS?
VAUGHN TOOK HIS PEOPLE UNDERGROUND WHEN THE KLINGONS BEGAN CARPET-BOMBING. THERE'S NO TELLING WHEN THEY MIGHT SURFACE.
AND HE'S MORE IN-THE-SHADOWS ANYWAY. THIS PLAY IS TOO DIRECT FOR HIM.
ALL RIGHT THEN, SOMEONE WITH BRASS. JANEWAY?
NOT AN OPTION. AFTER LAST NIGHT, WE'RE NOT BRINGING A GANG OF OUT-OF-CONTROL CHILDREN INTO THE FOLD.
RED SQUAD?
STILL M.I.A. NOBODY KNOWS IF THEY'RE EVEN ON EARTH ANYMORE.
GO AHEAD, PICARD. SAY IT.
JELLICO.
OKAY. WE'RE SCREWED.

BUT BEFORE WE CONSIDER ALIGNING WITH A TERRORIST LIKE HIM AGAIN, WE HAVE ANOTHER PROBLEM.
YOUR ANDROID— DATA.
WITHOUT HIM TO NAVIGATE THE TIMESTREAM, THERE IS NO MISSION. NO *REPAIRING HISTORY*.

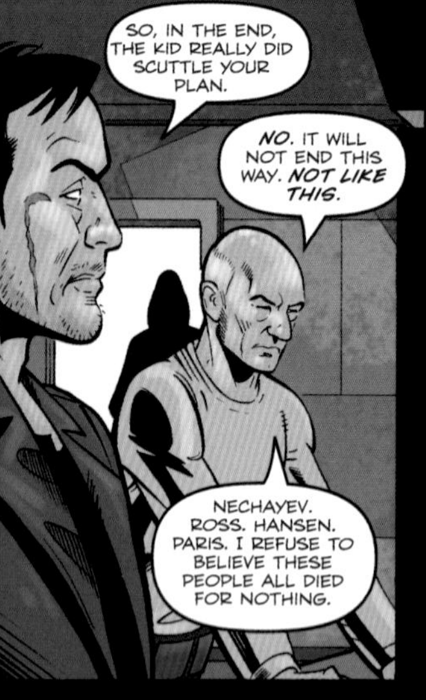
SO, IN THE END, THE KID REALLY DID SCUTTLE YOUR PLAN.
NO. IT WILL NOT END THIS WAY. *NOT LIKE THIS*.
NECHAYEV. ROSS. HANSEN. PARIS. I REFUSE TO BELIEVE THESE PEOPLE ALL DIED FOR NOTHING.

YOU MEAN LIKE SAMANTHA?
BEVERLY... SAMANTHA—
TEN MINUTES AGO. ALYSSA IS HARVESTING HER ORGANS NOW. WE MIGHT BE ABLE TO USE THEM TO SAVE HUGH.
HE'S YOUNG, STRONG. BUT WITHOUT PROSTHETICS, HIS CHANCES DON'T LOOK GOOD.

PICARD, I KNOW YOU DON'T WANT TO HEAR THIS. BUT MAYBE IT'S TIME TO RECONSIDER. WE CAN'T RESCUE DATA, WE DON'T HAVE THE NUMBERS.
AND BESIDES, IT'S SUICIDE. HE'S ON WORF'S FLAGSHIP BY NOW.

AND HE KNOWS OUR LOCATION. IF HE TALKS—
HE *WON'T*.
HE'S A *MACHINE*. THEY CAN'T TORTURE HIM FOR INFORMATION. THEY WOULDN'T KNOW HOW.

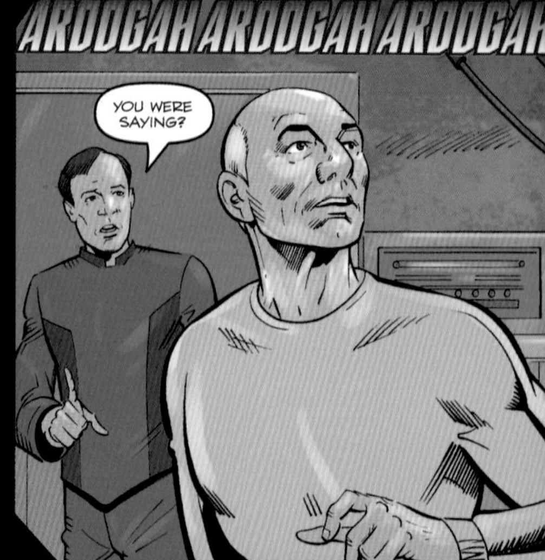
AROOGAH AROOGAH AROOGAH
YOU WERE SAYING?

WARNING. UNAUTHORIZED TRANSPORTER ENTRY. SCRAMBLE SHIELD DISABLED.
SEAL THE CENTRAL ACCESS TUNNEL! DEFENSIVE POSITIONS EVERYONE, AND *HOLD THE LINE*!
STEADY.
STEADY.
NOT LIKE THIS.

I'M SORRY, SIR. HAVE WE COME AT A BAD TIME?
I HOPE YOU DIDN'T SELL MY TROMBONE.

HELLO.

WE TRACKED YOUR TRANSPORTER BEAM FROM THE SHIPYARDS. THAT WAS QUITE AN ENCRYPTION—
—IT TOOK THE *EXCELSIOR'S* COMPUTERS ALL NIGHT TO CRACK.
THAT WAS OUR NEW FRIEND DATA. WITHOUT HIM, WE'D ALL BE HISTORY.
CAN I SEE HIM? HE SUFFERED SOME DAMAGE, I'D LIKE TO RUN A DIAGNOSTIC.
YES... *ABOUT THAT.*
PICARD. DON'T TELL ME THE KLINGONS HAVE HIM. HE COULD BECOME THEIR MOST POWERFUL WEAPON IN THE GALAXY.
HE'S ON WORF'S FLAGSHIP. WE HAVE AN INFORMANT INSIDE THE KLINGON COURT CONFIRMING THE TRANSFER.
BUT IT'S MORE THAN THAT. THANKS TO DATA, WE HAVE A WAY TO END KLINGON RULE. BUT WE NEED ***HIM***, AND A ***STARSHIP***.
WELL, YOU'VE GOT A STARSHIP NOW. SO WHAT'S THIS INCREDIBLE PLAN?
TELL ME, CAPTAIN SULU...
...HAVE YOU EVER HEARD OF A ***JAMES KIRK***?

BAD NEWS, LORD WORF?
NOT EXACTLY.
WE RECOVERED A RESISTANCE WEAPON LAST NIGHT. SOMETHING WE'VE NEVER SEEN BEFORE. SOMETHING THEY ARE CERTAIN TO TRY AND TAKE BACK.
MY ADVISORS SUGGEST I LEAVE THE FLAGSHIP INTENTIONALLY VULNERABLE. LURE THEM INTO A TRAP FROM WHICH THERE IS NO ESCAPE.
SO, WHY ARE YOU TROUBLED?
BECAUSE THE ATTACK YESTERDAY MAKES NO SENSE. TERRIBLE RISK. CERTAIN DEATH FOR SO MANY. AND YET, SO LITTLE TO GAIN.
SOMETHING MORE IS AT WORK HERE. ALMOST AS IF—
COME TO BED, WORF.
COME, TELL ME ABOUT IT, MY BELOVED...
...MY IMZADI.

DEANNA, YOU ARE MY CONCUBINE BECAUSE A KLINGON WOMAN WOULD BECOME TOO AMBITIOUS. TOO OPEN TO THE POLITICAL INTRIGUES OF THE IMPERIAL HOUSES.
BUT YOUR RESISTANCE COULD HAVE ORDERED YOU TO CUT MY THROAT AT ANY MOMENT. EVEN JUST NOW.
HOW... HOW LONG HAVE YOU KNOWN?
SINCE THE BEGINNING. WAITING FOR YOU TO COMMUNICATE WITH THE REBELS AND REVEAL THEIR LOCATION.
BUT ALL THIS TIME, AND NOTHING.
PERHAPS SOME ASPECT OF YOUR TELEPATHY AT WORK. NO MATTER.
NOW THEY ARE COMING TO US... SO YOU ARE NO LONGER NECESSARY.
DO NOT ACT SURPRISED. YOU THINK YOU SHOULD HAVE BEEN ABLE TO READ MY INTENTIONS?
KLINGON MEN KEEP THEIR EMOTIONS DEEP AND BURIED FROM WOMEN, THE WAY IT SHOULD BE.

SO, TELL ME, BEFORE I END THIS. WAS IT LOVE YOU FELT FOR ME, OR SIMPLY FEAR?
YOU THINK I CARE FOR YOU TO FEEL EITHER WAY? YOU LIVE BECAUSE THE EMPIRE WOULD ONLY HAVE PUT ANOTHER WARLORD IN YOUR PLACE.
ONE WHO HAD MORE STOMACH TO TAKE ON THE RESISTANCE.
ONE WHO WOULD NOT SO STUPIDLY WELCOME A REBEL INTO HIS BED, OR PAMPER HIS WORTHLESS SON LIKE AN INFANT GIRL.

WE HIT THEM HARD AND FAST, PICARD, IN AND OUT. AS SOON AS MY STRIKE TEAMS GET THE ANDROID, WE MAKE FOR OUR SLINGSHOT WARP AROUND THE SUN.
AGREED.
ALL RIGHT, HIROMI. *TAKE US IN.*

IT'S A TRAP! HELM, GET US OUT OF HERE!

THEY'VE GOT TRACTOR BEAMS ON US!
BRING THE TRANSWARP DRIVE ONLINE. THAT'LL BREAK US FREE!
TRANSWARP SPOOLING UP. TWO MINUTES!
DAMN. *NO TIME.*
HIROMI, BEAM ME DOWN TO THE SHUTTLE BAY. I'LL GET THEM TO LOWER THEIR SHIELDS. WHEN THAT HAPPENS, LOCK ONTO THE ANDROID AND PULL HIM OUT.
CAPTAIN, YOU'RE NOT GOING OVER THERE!
HE DOESN'T WANT THIS SHIP, RACHEL.
HE WANTS *ME.*
THEY'VE LAUNCHED A SHUTTLE, LORD WORF! ONE HUMAN LIFE SIGN!
MESSAGE INCOMING!
ONSCREEN!

HELLO, WORF. LONG TIME NO SEE.
SILVER GHOST!
WEAPONS, TARGET THAT SHUTTLE, NOW! BLOW HIS ATOMS INTO SPACE!
OH, YOU DON'T WANT MY ATOMS, WORF.
YOU WANT MY BLOOD.
OR ARE YOU STILL AFRAID TO FACE ME, WARRIOR TO WARRIOR? MAN TO... OLD MAN?
DON'T BE SUCH A COWARD. I KNOW THAT'S HOW YOU WANT THIS TO END.
AUTO PILOT ON
I CAN SEE IT IN YOUR EYE.
LOWER THE SHIELDS! BEAM THAT BIHNUCH ONTO THE EDGE OF MY BLADE!
BUT SIR—
I SAID NOW!

YEAAARRGHH!
IT'S DATA! I'VE GOT HIM!
KRSSSH
COME ON, HIKARU. GET OUT OF THERE.

TRANSWARP ONLINE!
DATA'S COMPUTING BREAKAWAY COORDINATES NOW!
RAAAAGH!
WE'RE LOOSE FROM THE TRACTORS!
HIROMI! PULL HIM OUT OF THERE!
WE'VE TAKEN TOO MUCH DAMAGE! TRANSPORTERS ARE STARTING TO FAIL! I CAN'T GET A LOCK!
URK—

LA FORGE! STAY IN TRANSPORTER RANGE! WE ARE *NOT* LEAVING HIM!
shikt
THE FLAGSHIP'S IN PURSUIT! IF WE DON'T GET OUT OF HERE, WE'RE DEAD!
Q'PLAH!

SILVER GHOST...
SHUKT
...I CAN NO LONGER SEE YOU.

THEN YOU ALSO PROBABLY CAN'T SEE *THIS*.
AUTO PILOT
WHABOOOM

KLINGON FLAGSHIP... NO LONGER IN PURSUIT, SIR.
NO HUMAN LIFE SIGNS REMAINING ON THE BIRD OF PREY.

SULU...

SIR...

...WE HAVE TO *GO*. THE KLINGONS ARE REGROUPING.

IF WE'RE GOING TO DO THIS, IT HAS TO BE ***RIGHT NOW***.

UNDERSTOOD.

WHO IS IN COMMAND HERE?

MR. LA FORGE, LAY IN THE COURSE CALCULATED BY DATA FOR SLINGSHOT TIME WARP.

COURSE LAID IN, SIR. ON YOUR MARK.

NO GAMES, NO RIDDLES. ***JUST TELL ME.*** CAN WE POSSIBLY SUCCEED?

JEAN-LUC. SO LOGICAL, SO LINEAR. SOMETIMES YOU'RE PRACTICALLY A VULCAN.

SOMETHING EITHER ***WILL*** HAPPEN, OR IT ***WON'T***. THERE IS NO "POSSIBLY".

I DON'T UNDERSTAND.

ASK YOURSELF: HAVE YOU EVER BEEN CAUGHT IN A THUNDERSTORM?

GUINAN, I SAID NO RIDDLES.

THIS ISN'T. IT'S JUST A QUESTION.

IN FACT, IT'S ***YOUR*** QUESTION. WHAT WERE THE ***CHANCES?***

OF GETTING HIT BY EVEN A ***SINGLE*** DROP OF RAIN.

AND I DON'T MEAN APART FROM THE REST OF THE RAIN. I MEAN THAT THE CLOUDS ABOVE WOULD BURST AT ***EXACTLY*** THAT MOMENT.

YOU LOOK AT THE SKY EVERY MORNING, AND NEVER CALCULATE THAT SOMETHING SO COMMON AS A CLOUD RESULTS FROM COUNTLESS, UNCHARTED VARIABLES.

INFINITE POSSIBILITIES, ALL DRIFTING INTO LINE, ONE AFTER ANOTHER. CONVERGING ON THAT SINGLE INSTANT.

THE CHANCE OF EVEN A SINGLE DROP OF RAIN FALLING ON YOU IS SO SMALL, SO FLEETING, THAT IT HARDLY EXISTS AT ALL.

AND YET, IN A THUNDERSTORM, YOU'RE HIT BY THOUSANDS. IT'S ***UNAVOIDABLE***.

YOU ASK WHAT YOUR CHANCES ARE?
TIME ISN'T *POSSIBILITY*, JEAN-LUC.
IT'S *INEVITABILITY*.
AND THE ONLY QUESTION... IS WHETHER YOU HEAD INTO THE STORM.
MR. LA FORGE...
...ENGAGE.

5
WE'VE SUSTAINED TOO MUCH DAMAGE! THE TEMPORAL WAVES ARE PULLING US APART!
AUXILLARY POWER TO SHIELDS!
NOT POSSIBLE! IF WE DO THAT, WE'LL LOSE TRANSWARP, AND WON'T BE ABLE TO COMPENSATE FOR SPATIAL DISPLACEMENT!
PICARD, WHAT THE HELL IS HE TALKING ABOUT?
EARTH, KHITOMER, THE ENTIRE GALAXY. THEY'RE IN CONSTANT MOTION THROUGH SPACE. THEY'RE ALL IN DIFFERENT PLACES THAN THEY WERE 70 YEARS AGO.
IF WE DON'T PRESERVE OUR ANGULAR MOMENTUM, WE'LL EMERGE STRANDED IN THE MIDDLE OF NOWHERE. BETWEEN GALAXIES, EVEN.
HIROMI, CUT LIFE SUPPORT TO THE LOWER DECKS. GET THE POWER FROM THERE.
SIR!
ISSUE AN EVACUATION ORDER, THEN ROUTE ENGINEERING COMMAND TO THE ANDROID.
HE DOESN'T NEED TO BREATHE, AND IF HE CAN'T THREAD THE NEEDLE, WE WON'T MAKE IT ANYWAY.

FRRSZZSHHH
HULL INTEGRITY HOLDING—COMING OUT OF TRANSWARP... NOW!
STATUS REPORT, ENSIGN! DID WE MAKE IT?
NO WAY TO TELL—THE CHRONO READINGS ARE OFF THE CHART! THE WHOLE PANEL'S LIT UP!

IT'S BRAXTON. IT HAS TO BE. *HE'S ALREADY HERE*.
AMBASSADOR TUVOK, HAIL THE *ENTERPRISE*. INFORM KIRK THAT A TIME-TRAVELER FROM THE 29TH CENTURY PLANS TO SABOTAGE THE PEACE TALKS WITH THE KLINGONS AND—
I'M AFRAID THAT'S IMPOSSIBLE, COMMANDER GARRETT. THE *ENTERPRISE*..

"...IS GONE."
BRAXTON. HE'S TAKEN KIRK OFF THE TABLE.
HE HASN'T JUST CHANGED HISTORY ONCE. HE'S CHANGED IT COUNTLESS TIMES, SO THAT IT CAN NEVER BE UNDONE. THAT'S WHY THERE'S SO MUCH TEMPORAL DISTORTION.
GEORDI, CAN YOU—
DATA'S ALREADY INTERFACED WITH THE EXCELSIOR'S CENTRAL COMPUTER. HAVING HIM RECALCULATE NOW.
HE'S GOT IT. CHRONOMETER READING CONFIRMED.
CAPTAIN, WE'VE GOT TWO MINUTES.

COMMANDER GARRETT, GET MY PEOPLE DOWN TO THE SURFACE. WE'RE GOING TO STOP THIS ASSASSINATION, ONE WAY OR ANOTHER.
WE'RE COMING TOO. YOUR REBELS DON'T HAVE TRAINING FOR THIS.
NO. THIS SHIP WAS ALREADY AT THE KHITOMER CONFERENCE. THERE'S NO TELLING WHAT ITS PRESENCE HERE AGAIN COULD DO TO THE TIMELINE.
AND IF YOUR CREW ACCIDENTALLY CHANGES ITS OWN HISTORY, ALL THIS COULD BE FOR NOTHING.
SO, WHERE ARE YOU GOING?
I'LL BE GOING DOWN THERE AS WELL...
"...AS SOON AS I SPEAK WITH MR. DATA."

THE KHITOMER CONFERENCE, THE YEAR 2293.

A HISTORIC EFFORT TO FORGE PEACE BETWEEN KLINGONS AND THE FEDERATION.

A CONSPIRACY TO ASSASSINATE THE FEDERATION PRESIDENT, DERAIL THE TALKS AND PLUNGE THE GALAXY INTO *OPEN WAR*.

SPREAD OUT! FIND BRAXTON!
I'LL GET TO THE PRESIDENT!
IT HAS BEEN SAID THAT HISTORY MOVES WITH THE SPEED OF A BULLET.
BUT WHAT SEPARATES ONE HISTORY FROM THE NEXT CAN BE FLEETING.
THE SPACE THAT A FINGER MOVES WHEN IT PULLS THE TRIGGER.
AND EVEN ONE MAN CAN REMAKE HISTORY.

NO!
BUT SOMETHING EITHER WILL HAPPEN, OR IT WON'T.
BECAUSE TIME ISN'T POSSIBILITY.
IT'S INEVITABILITY.
NO.
THIS ISN'T HAPPENING. NOT AGAIN.
JEAN-LUC...
...I DO WISH YOU'D STOP SAYING THAT EVERY TIME.

BRAXTON...
...WHAT IS GOING ON?
I'VE TAKEN US OUT OF PHASE WITH THE TIMELINE. YOU AND I HAVE MUCH TO DISCUSS.
BECAUSE YOU'RE ABOUT TO ASK ME—
—WHY ARE YOU DOING THIS?
AND I'M ABOUT TO TELL YOU.

BEFORE YOU ASK—SINCE YOU ARE ABOUT TO, AGAIN—YOU'RE ON A TIMESHIP, THE UTS EVENT HORIZON.
AND THIS IS WHERE YOU SAY—
ENOUGH! NO MORE GAMES, BRAXTON! THERE'S TOO MUCH AT STAKE!
PICARD...
...YOU HAVE NO IDEA.

IS THAT... OUR HISTORY?

NO, JEAN-LUC. THAT'S THE END OF HISTORY.
THERE IS AN UNKNOWN EVENT ON TIME'S HORIZON. AN ABYSS OF DARKNESS IN FUTURE HISTORY, IN WHICH THE GALAXY ITSELF IS UTTERLY UNMADE.

BECAUSE OF THE TEMPORAL CHAOS SURROUNDING IT, WE CAN'T DETERMINE EXACTLY WHAT THE DISASTER IS.
SOME DOOMSDAY WEAPON THAT RUPTURES THE FABRIC OF SPACE ITSELF. THE END RESULT OF SOME ESCALATING WAR. IT DOESN'T MATTER.

WHAT DOES MATTER IS THAT THE ONLY TIMELINES WHERE THIS DOESN'T OCCUR—THE ONLY ONES WHERE THE GALAXY ITSELF SURVIVES—
—ARE THE ONES IN WHICH THE FEDERATION NO LONGER EXISTS.

I'VE BEEN TRAVELING THROUGH HISTORY, LOOKING FOR KEY MOMENTS IN THE FEDERATION'S DEVELOPMENT, ATTEMPTING TO EXTINGUISH THEM. YOU CAN'T IMAGINE HOW COMPLICATED THAT IS.

I'VE ALREADY REMOVED SEVERAL X-FACTORS HERE AT KHITOMER—*KIRK* IN PARTICULAR.

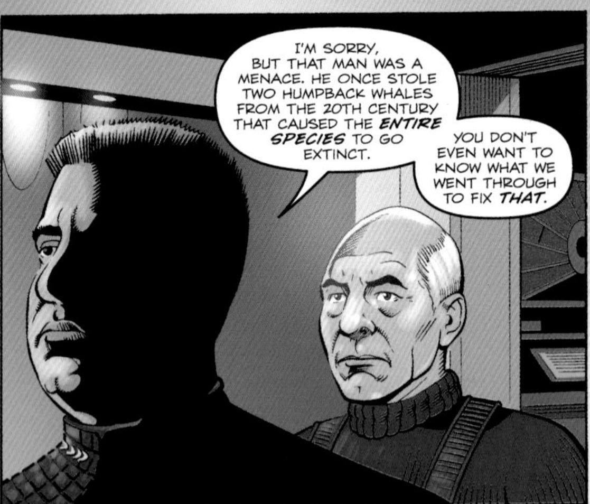

DON'T BLAME YOURSELF. YOU NEVER HAD A CHANCE OF STOPPING ME. I'M A TEMPORAL AGENT FROM THE 29TH CENTURY. I KNEW YOU WERE COMING ALL ALONG.
YES, WELL, THAT'S JUST IT, BRAXTON.

WE KNEW YOU WERE COMING TOO.
AND THIS IS THE PART WHERE YOU SAY—
—WHAT ARE YOU TALKING ABOUT?

AND THIS IS THE PART WHERE I SAY: YOU'RE NOT THE ONLY ONE WHO LEARNED HOW TO REWRITE HISTORY.
OUR ANDROID CALLS IT "TEMPORAL ENCRYPTION." AND HE KNOWS ABOUT IT—SINCE YOU'RE ABOUT TO ASK—BECAUSE HE WAS INVENTED TO STUDY THE TIMELINE.

YOU—YOU'VE BEEN HERE BEFORE!
BRAXTON...
...I DO WISH YOU'D STOP SAYING THAT EVERY TIME.

THE KHITOMER CONFERENCE, THE YEAR 2293.
A CONSPIRACY TO ASSASSINATE THE FEDERATION PRESIDENT, DERAIL THE TALKS AND PLUNGE THE GALAXY INTO *OPEN WAR*.
AND EVEN ONE MAN...
...CAN REMAKE HISTORY.
THIS ISN'T HAPPENING. NOT AGAIN.
WHAT— *WHAT DID YOU JUST SAY?*
BWEEP

AARRGHH!
H-HOW?
YOU MAY HAVE TAKEN INTO ACCOUNT EVERY POSSIBILITY YOU COULD IMAGINE. BUT YOU DIDN'T HAVE AN ANDROID WHO CAN PERFORM 60 TRILLION CALCULATIONS A SECOND. HE'S ALSO QUITE GOOD AT POKER.
PICARD...
...YOU DON'T KNOW WHAT YOU'VE DONE. THIS ISN'T JUST ABOUT YOUR TIMELINE. IT'S ABOUT ALL THE TIMELINES.
NO, BRAXTON. YOU SAID IT YOURSELF. THIS IS ALL MORE COMPLICATED THAN YOU CAN IMAGINE.
I'M NOT GOING TO LET YOU DESTROY THE FEDERATION WHEN YOU CAN'T EVEN FIGURE OUT WHY.
THAT'S YOUR PROBLEM, JEAN-LUC. YOU STILL THINK THIS IS ABOUT ME.
BRAXTON, WHAT ARE YOU DOING? IF WE RE-ENTER THE TIMESTREAM NOW—

SEARCHING
I TOLD YOU, PICARD. THIS ISN'T ABOUT ME.
AND IN A FEW MOMENTS...

TRAJECTORY LOCKED
...IT WON'T BE ABOUT YOU *EITHER*.

COMMANDER GARRETT...

0050011
TRAJECTOR
LOCKED
050011
...I THINK WE HAVE A PROBLEM.

JEAN-LUC, WHAT ARE YOU DOING? YOU'VE GOT TO GET OUT OF THERE!
HE'S LOCKED IN THE COORDINATES, COMMANDER! HE'S GOING TO TAKE OUT THE CONFERENCE!
YOU'VE GOT TO BLOW UP THIS SHIP!
JEAN-LUC, THERE'S NO WAY OUR WEAPONS CAN GET THROUGH ITS SHIELDS IN TIME.
HIROMI, ISSUE A GENERAL EVACUATION ORDER, DOUBLE-TIME.
BUT SIR—!
ENSIGN, I DID NOT INVITE DEBATE!

MR. DATA, HAS EVERYONE EVACUATED?
YES, COMMANDER.
DO YOU UNDERSTAND, MR. DATA?
I SAID DO YOU UNDERSTAND?
GET A LOCK ON PICARD AND GET HIM OFF THAT SHIP. REINTEGRATE HIM WITH THE ONE ON THE SURFACE.
THEN GIVE ME BACK HELM CONTROL AND GET YOURSELF DOWN THERE.
DATA, YOU ARE NOT DOING THIS BY YOURSELF! THAT'S AN ORD—
TRAJECTORY
LOCKED

KSHHABOOOM!

I DEMAND TO KNOW! WHAT'S THE MEANING OF THIS?

IT'S ABOUT THE *FUTURE*, MADAM CHANCELLOR.

SOME PEOPLE THINK THE FUTURE MEANS THE END OF HISTORY. BUT WE HAVEN'T *RUN OUT OF HISTORY* QUITE YET.

I'M SORRY ABOUT CAPTAIN SULU, COMMANDER.
SULU ALWAYS TALKED ABOUT THE SACRIFICE HIS FIRST CAPTAIN MADE TO SAVE HIS CREW. I THINK THIS IS HOW HE WANTED TO GO.

BUT WHAT ABOUT THE EDGE OF DARKNESS, PICARD? THE ABYSS AT TIME'S HORIZON THAT BRAXTON KEPT TELLING YOU ABOUT?
WHATEVER IT IS, COMMANDER, I AM CERTAIN THAT WITH A NEW PEACE WITH THE KLINGONS, WE CAN ALL FACE IT TOGETHER.

AND IF WE HAVE TO, WE'LL STAY HERE TO MAKE SURE IT HAPPENS. THERE IS NO DARKNESS ON THE HORIZON. THERE IS A NEW DAY FOR THE FEDERATION.
BRAXTON BELIEVED THAT FOR THE GALAXY TO SURVIVE, THIS WOULD HAVE TO BE OUR LAST GENERATION.

BUT BRAXTON WAS ***WRONG***.
WE'RE ***NOT*** THE LAST GENERATION.

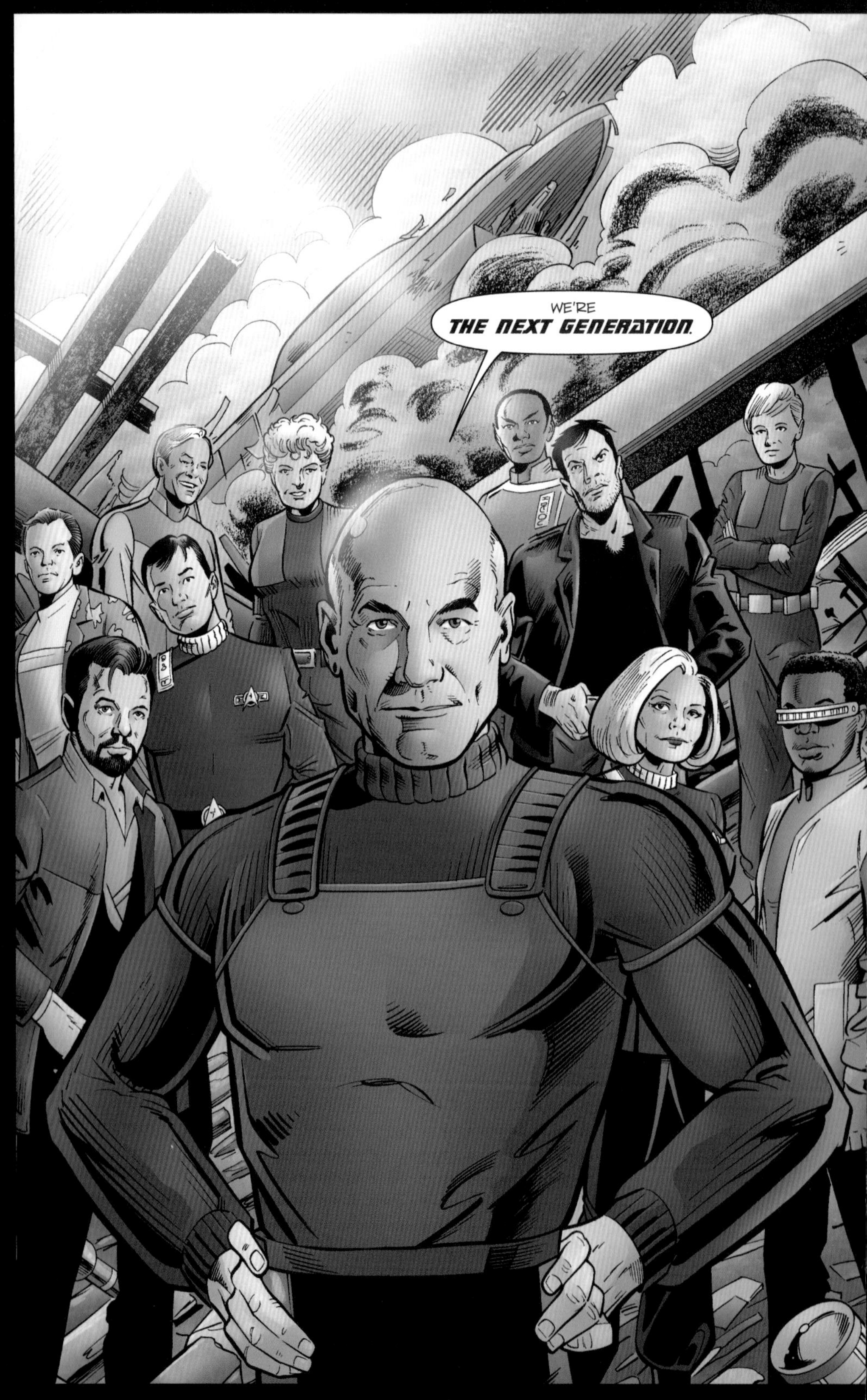
WE'RE THE NEXT GENERATION.

Art by J.K. Woodward

STAR TREK
THE NEXT GENERATION®
GHOSTS

NCC-1701-D

Art by Joe Corroney

NCC-1701 D
CAPTAIN'S LOG, STARDATE 44751.3
THE ENTERPRISE HAS INTERCEPTED A LOW-POWERED DISTRESS CALL FROM A SHIP IN THE ALLIOS SYSTEM.
THE VESSEL SITS IN GEOSYNCHRONOUS ORBIT OVER DOROSSH, ONE OF THE TWO PRIMARY NATIONS OF ALLIOS IV...
...BUT ITS MARKINGS SHOW ITS ORIGIN TO BE THAT NATION'S BITTER RIVAL—AND ALLY OF THE FEDERATION—THE REPUBLIC OF JUULET.
GIVEN THE POLITICAL SITUATION, I BRIEFLY CONSIDER THE PRIME DIRECTIVE'S POLICY OF NON-INTERVENTION...
...BUT, OF COURSE, THERE ARE OTHER FACTORS.
CAPTAIN, I HAVE OPENED A CHANNEL WITH THE REPUBLIC OF JUULET'S CAPITOL.
ON SCREEN.
THIS IS CAPTAIN JEAN-LUC PICARD OF THE FEDERATION STARSHIP ENTERPRISE.
OUR DEEPEST BOW TO YOU, CAPTAIN PICARD. I AM DAAR KEJAAL, SPEAKER OF THE REPUBLIC COUNCIL.
THE FEDERATION IS EARLY FOR THEIR ORE SHIPMENT, IF I MAY SAY S—
AH, NO, NO, SPEAKER KEJAAL. WE ARE RESPONDING TO A DISTRESS CALL. A SHIP IN ORBIT WITH YOUR NATION'S INSIGNIA.
YOU NEEDN'T BOTHER WITH THAT, CAPTAIN. WE HAVE APPROVED A MEASURE TO SEND AN INQUIRY SHUTTLE IN THE COMING WEEK, SO THAT WE MAY PROPERLY DEAL WITH THE DATA—
SPEAKER KEJAAL...

...WITH ALL DUE RESPECT, BOTH THE DISTRESS BEACON AND OUR SENSORS INDICATE A LIFE READING ABOARD THE VESSEL.
THE DISTRESS CALL HAS ALREADY BEEN SOUNDING FOR 31 HOURS, ALMOST A FULL DAY FOR YOU.

AHEM
WHAT COMMANDER RIKER MEANS IS... IT'S NO TROUBLE, SPEAKER KEJAAL. BUT WE FEEL THAT TIME IS OF THE ESSENCE.
OUR CHIEF CONCERN IS TO FIND THE SURVIVOR AND ASSURE YOU HE OR SHE IS SAFE.
YOUR INQUIRY SHUTTLE MAY THEN TAKE ALL THE TIME IT NEEDS TO INSPECT THE VESSEL AND THE DATA.

HMM. YES, VERY WELL, CAPTAIN PICARD. OUR SHUTTLE WILL HANDLE THE DATA RETRIEVAL. BUT YOUR PEOPLE REALLY NEED NOT BOTHER WITH SUCH A TRIFLE.
EXCELLENT. THEN WE'LL—

OH, AND CAPTAIN—WHEN YOU RETURN OUR RESEARCHER, PLEASE CONSIDER OUR STANDING OFFER...
...WE WELCOME ALL FEDERATION PERSONNEL TO JOIN US FOR A TOUR OF JUULET'S CHARMS.
ER, YES...

...A GENEROUS OFFER, SPEAKER KEJAAL. PERHAPS OUR SCHEDULE WILL ALLOW IT.
THANK YOU, CAPTAIN. WE LOOK FORWARD TO SEEING YOU.

NUMBER ONE, ASSEMBLE AN AWAY TEAM.
SIR.
AND, COMMANDER DATA—

—WHAT IS THE STATUS OF ALLIOS IV'S APPLICATION TO THE FEDERATION?
THEY HAVE BEEN WAIT-LISTED FOR ELEVEN YEARS, CAPTAIN.
THE REASON GIVEN IS ONGOING CIVIL WAR.

A WAR THAT THE REPUBLIC OF JUULET DENIES EXISTS.
THEY CLAIM TO SPEAK FOR THE ENTIRE PLANET, SIR...

"...A CLAIM THAT MANY OF THEIR FELLOW ALLIOSIANS **DISPUTE.**"

IT'S **LUDICROUS.**

WHAT IS, WILL?

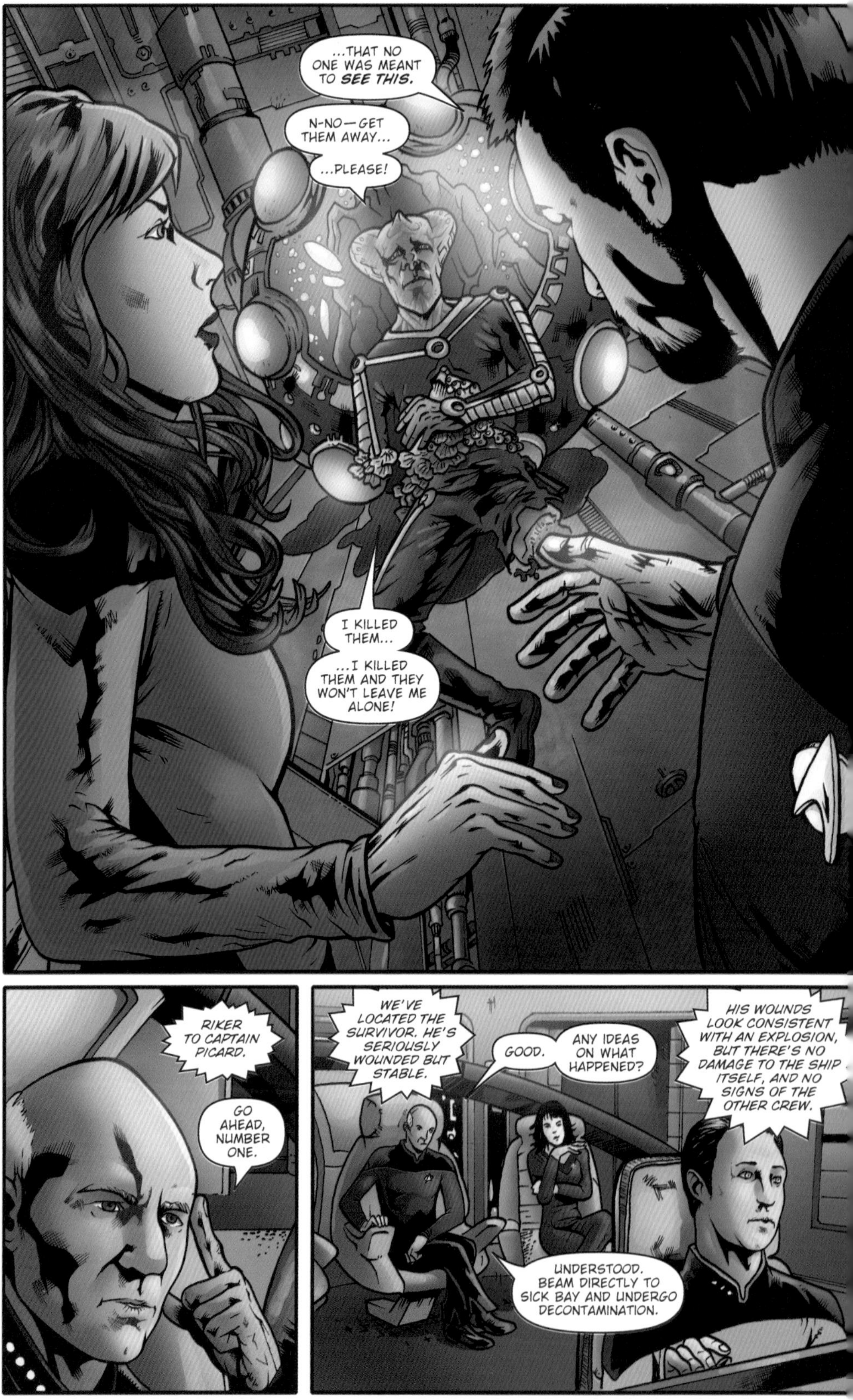

...THAT NO ONE WAS MEANT TO **SEE THIS.**
N-NO—GET THEM AWAY...
...PLEASE!
I KILLED THEM...
...I KILLED THEM AND THEY WON'T LEAVE ME ALONE!

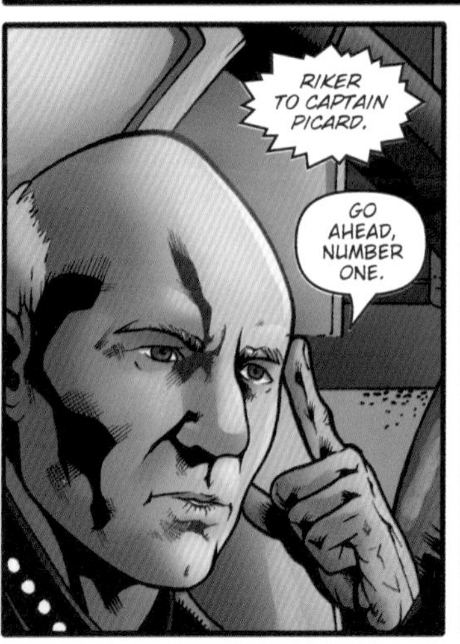

SIR, I RECOMMEND THAT LT. LA FORGE REMAIN ABOARD TO INVESTIGATE THE **CAUSE** OF THE EXPLOSION.
HMM. I WOULDN'T THINK THE JUULET COUNCIL WOULD LIKE THAT VERY MUCH, NUMBER ONE.

*I'M SURE YOU'RE **RIGHT**, SIR.*
VERY WELL, MAKE IT SO.
PICARD OUT.
CAPTAIN...

...I HATE TO PLAY DEVIL'S ADVOCATE, BUT WHY DO YOU WANT TO EXAMINE THE SHIP? THE SURVIVOR IS **SAFE**—
—AND THE JUULETIANS CAN ANALYZE THE SHIP ***THEMSELVES.***

TRUE, COUNSELOR.
I SUSPECT YOU'D SEE RIGHT THROUGH ME IF I SAID IT WAS JUST TO CHECK UP ON THE TRUTH OF THEIR ***APPLICATION.***

I SUPPOSE IT'S... THESE RESEARCHERS ARE DOING WHAT WE DO, COUNSELOR, AND THEIR SUPERIORS SEEM QUITE CASUAL ABOUT THEIR DEATHS.
TO DIE WITH NO ONE TO SPEAK FOR YOU...
...THEY DESERVE ***BETTER*** THAN THAT.

IT'S VERY THOUGHTFUL OF YOU, CAPTA—
OH!
DEANNA?

*COUNSELOR TROI, REPORT TO **SICK BAY.***
ON—ON MY ***WAY.***
DEANNA, ARE YOU ALL RIGHT?
I—I'M OKAY...

SIR, WE ARE BEING ***HAILED.***

IS IT THE JUULETIANS AGAIN?
NO, SIR.
THE HAIL IS USING AN OUTDATED FREQUENCY. THE SIGNAL REQUIRES SIGNIFICANT ***CLEAN-UP.***

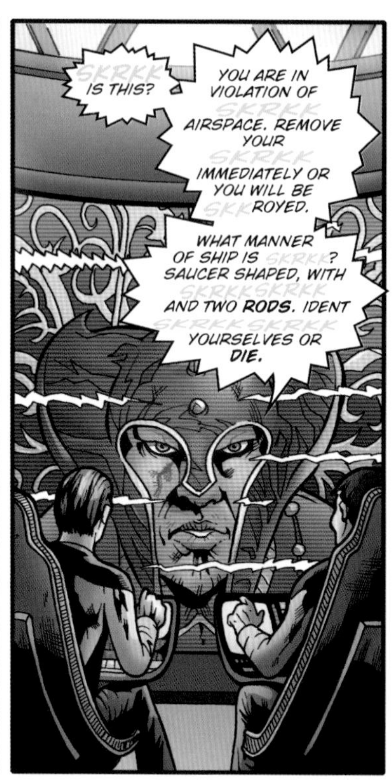

PEOPLE OF DOROSSH.
THIS IS CAPTAIN JEAN-LUC PICARD OF THE FEDERATION STARSHIP **ENTERPRISE.**
WE ARE IN THE PROCESS OF RESCUING A STRANDED SHIP IN ORBIT—WE ASK THAT YOU PLEASE PUT YOUR WEAPONS ON **HOLD.**

WE DO NOT SKRKK KNOW YOU, FEDERATION.
BUT A SHIP ABOVE US HAS BEEN SENT BY THE JUULETIAN MURDERERS, AND IF YOU ASSIST THEM—

"MURDERERS?"
THE ENTERPRISE COMES ONLY IN PEACE. WE ARE RECOVERING A WOUNDED RESEARCHER FROM A JUULETIAN SHIP, NO MORE.
OUR INTENT IS NOT TO ENCROACH ON YOUR BORDERS.
NOW, IF YOU WILL IDENTIFY YOURSELVES SO THAT WE MAY SPEAK TOGETHER PEACEFULLY...

I AM SUPREME ELDER KALKASS, FEDERATION. I AM THE SOLE REMAIN SKK ELDER, AND FOR THAT YOU MAY THANK YOUR DEAR SKRKK JUULETIANS.
BUT WE WILL NOT SPEAK ON THIS BROADCAST SHOUTING MACHINE, FEDERATION. THE TOWER IS THE ONLY PLACE FOR DISCUSSIONS OF WAR OR PEACE.

THE TOWER?
WHAT IS—
SKS ST

HE HAS ENDED THE TRANSMISSION, SIR.
MR. DATA, WHAT TOWER IS SUPREME ELDER KALKASS SPEAKING OF?

THE TOWER IS A LONG-UNUSED STRUCTURE ON THE BORDER BETWEEN JUULET AND DOROSSH, SIR.
IT WAS ONCE USED TO MEDIATE TALKS BETWEEN THE TWO NATIONS.

THE REPUBLIC OF JUULET CEASED USING IT ELEVEN YEARS AGO.
OF COURSE...

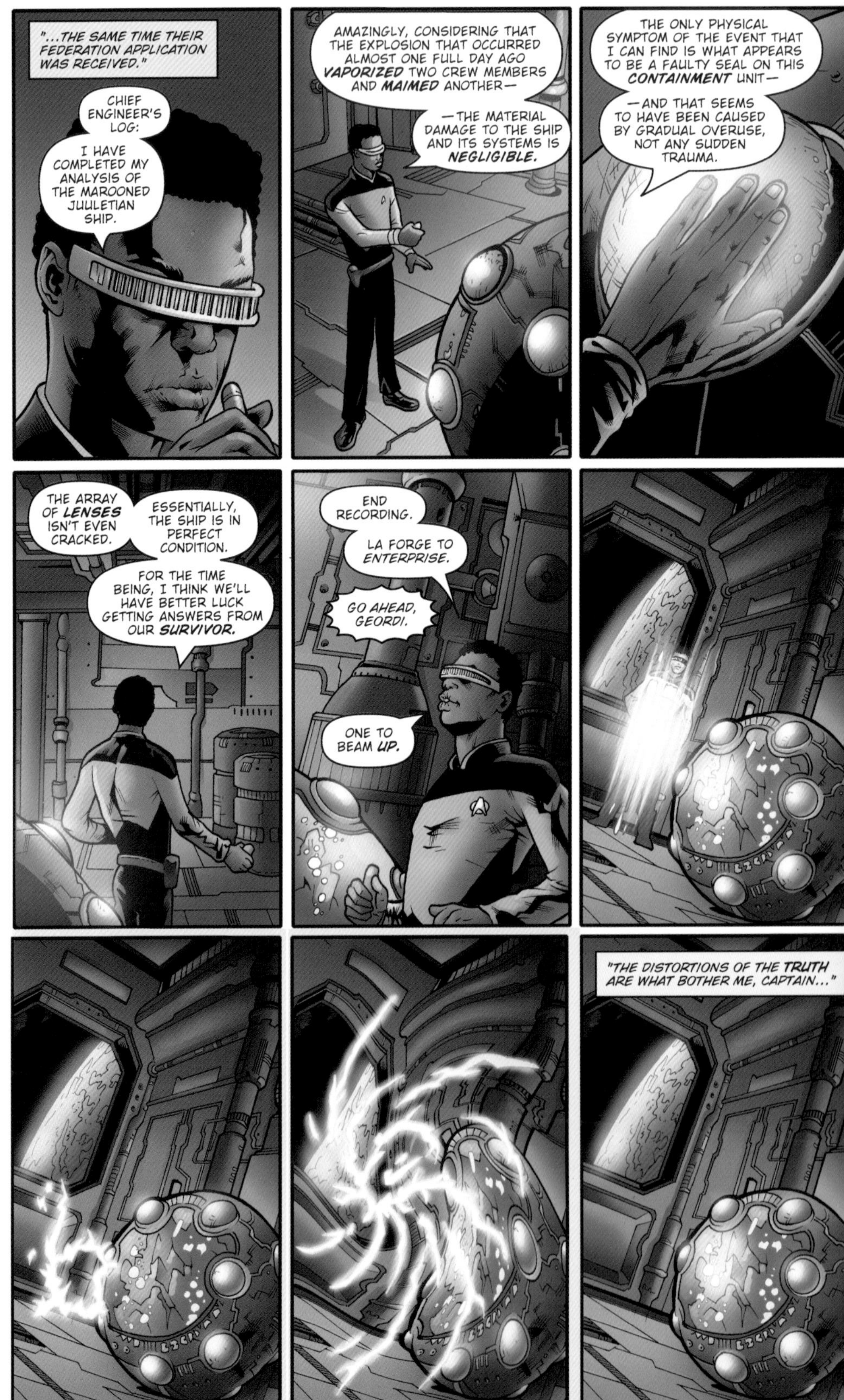
"...THE SAME TIME THEIR FEDERATION APPLICATION WAS RECEIVED."
CHIEF ENGINEER'S LOG:
I HAVE COMPLETED MY ANALYSIS OF THE MAROONED JUULETIAN SHIP.
AMAZINGLY, CONSIDERING THAT THE EXPLOSION THAT OCCURRED ALMOST ONE FULL DAY AGO VAPORIZED TWO CREW MEMBERS AND MAIMED ANOTHER—
—THE MATERIAL DAMAGE TO THE SHIP AND ITS SYSTEMS IS NEGLIGIBLE.
THE ONLY PHYSICAL SYMPTOM OF THE EVENT THAT I CAN FIND IS WHAT APPEARS TO BE A FAULTY SEAL ON THIS CONTAINMENT UNIT—
—AND THAT SEEMS TO HAVE BEEN CAUSED BY GRADUAL OVERUSE, NOT ANY SUDDEN TRAUMA.
THE ARRAY OF LENSES ISN'T EVEN CRACKED.
ESSENTIALLY, THE SHIP IS IN PERFECT CONDITION.
FOR THE TIME BEING, I THINK WE'LL HAVE BETTER LUCK GETTING ANSWERS FROM OUR SURVIVOR.
END RECORDING.
LA FORGE TO ENTERPRISE.
GO AHEAD, GEORDI.
ONE TO BEAM UP.
"THE DISTORTIONS OF THE TRUTH ARE WHAT BOTHER ME, CAPTAIN..."

YOUR POINT IS NOTED, NUMBER ONE, AND I SHARE IT, BUT...
...WE MUST GIVE THEM THE CHANCE TO TELL THEIR SIDE OF THE STORY.
SOUNDS LIKE THEY'VE BEEN TELLING THEIR SIDE FOR ELEVEN YEARS.
AGAIN, NOTED.
THAT'S PRECISELY WHY WE'LL MEET IN THE TOWER ON THE BORDER OF THE TWO COUNTRIES.
THE PEOPLE OF DOROSSH SEEM COMPLETELY UNAWARE OF THEIR PLANET'S CONSIDERATION FOR THE FEDERATION.
AT LEAST THIS MEETING WILL CORRECT THAT.
THE ACCUSATIONS ARE ANOTHER MATTER. PERHAPS THE OPENNESS THAT FEDERATION MEMBERSHIP REQUIRES WILL ENCOURAGE THEM TO SHED SOME LIGHT ON WHAT KALKASS HAS SAID.
HELLO, SIR. COMMANDER. THE SPEAKER OF JUULET HAS SENT COORDINATES FOR THEIR PALACE.
WE WON'T BE NEEDING THEM, O'BRIEN.
NO?
PUT US INTO THE TOWER THAT SITS ON THE WALL BETWEEN THE TWO COUNTRIES.
YES, SIR, LOCATING...
NUMBER ONE, WHAT IS THE STATUS OF THE SURVIVOR?
CONSIDERING THE EXTENT OF HIS INJURIES, SIR, HE'S DOING WELL. DR. CRUSHER HASN'T FOUND ANY INFECTION AND HIS SIGNS ARE STABLE.
THE PROBLEM IS HIS MIND.
HIS MIND?
HE'S CONVINCED HE SEES... GHOSTS... AND IT TERRIFIES HIM.
DR. CRUSHER HAS TO KEEP HIM SEDATED, SO HE CAN'T BE QUESTIONED YET...

"...IT'S SILENCE OR LUNACY AT THIS POINT."

REALLY, CAPTAIN PICARD...

...FOR DISCUSSIONS OF *JUULET* AND THE *FEDERATION,* WE HAVE *MUCH* MORE COMFORTABLE ACCOMMODATIONS WITHIN THE *CITY.*

I'M SURE YOU DO, SPEAKER KEJAAL.

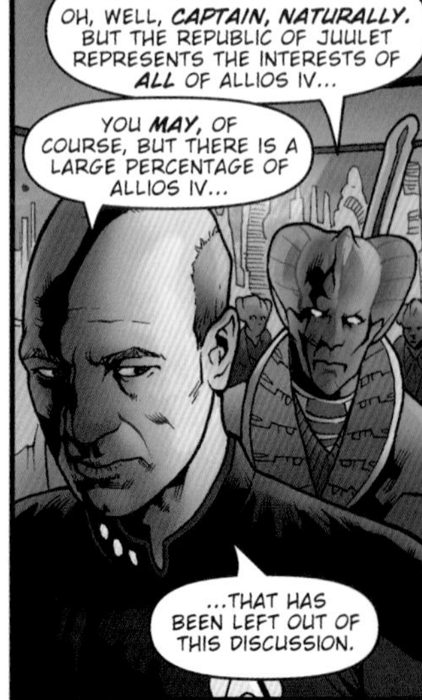

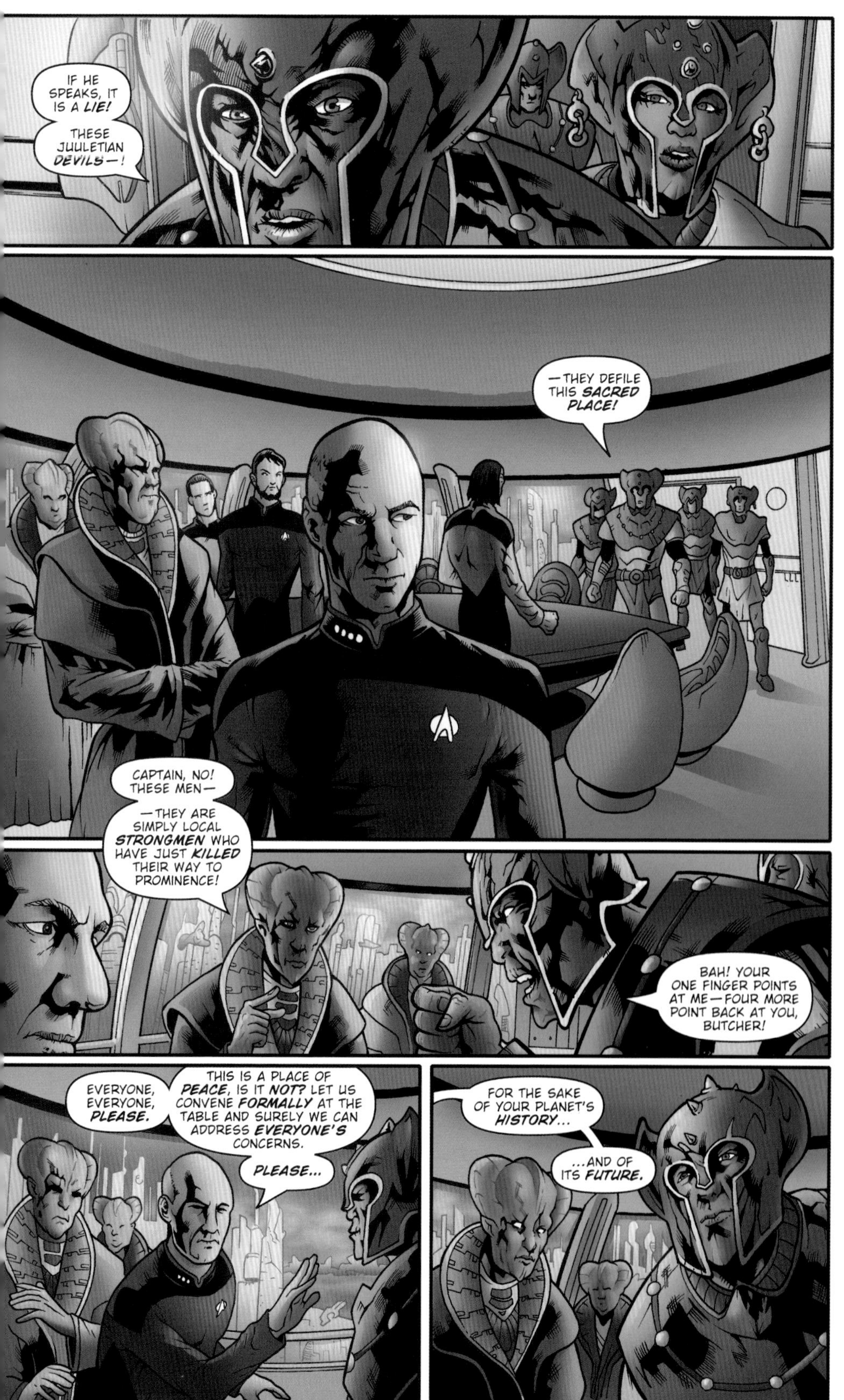

IF HE SPEAKS, IT IS A LIE!
THESE JUULETIAN DEVILS—!
—THEY DEFILE THIS SACRED PLACE!
CAPTAIN, NO! THESE MEN—
—THEY ARE SIMPLY LOCAL STRONGMEN WHO HAVE JUST KILLED THEIR WAY TO PROMINENCE!
BAH! YOUR ONE FINGER POINTS AT ME—FOUR MORE POINT BACK AT YOU, BUTCHER!
EVERYONE, EVERYONE, PLEASE.
THIS IS A PLACE OF PEACE, IS IT NOT? LET US CONVENE FORMALLY AT THE TABLE AND SURELY WE CAN ADDRESS EVERYONE'S CONCERNS.
PLEASE...
FOR THE SAKE OF YOUR PLANET'S HISTORY...
...AND OF ITS FUTURE.

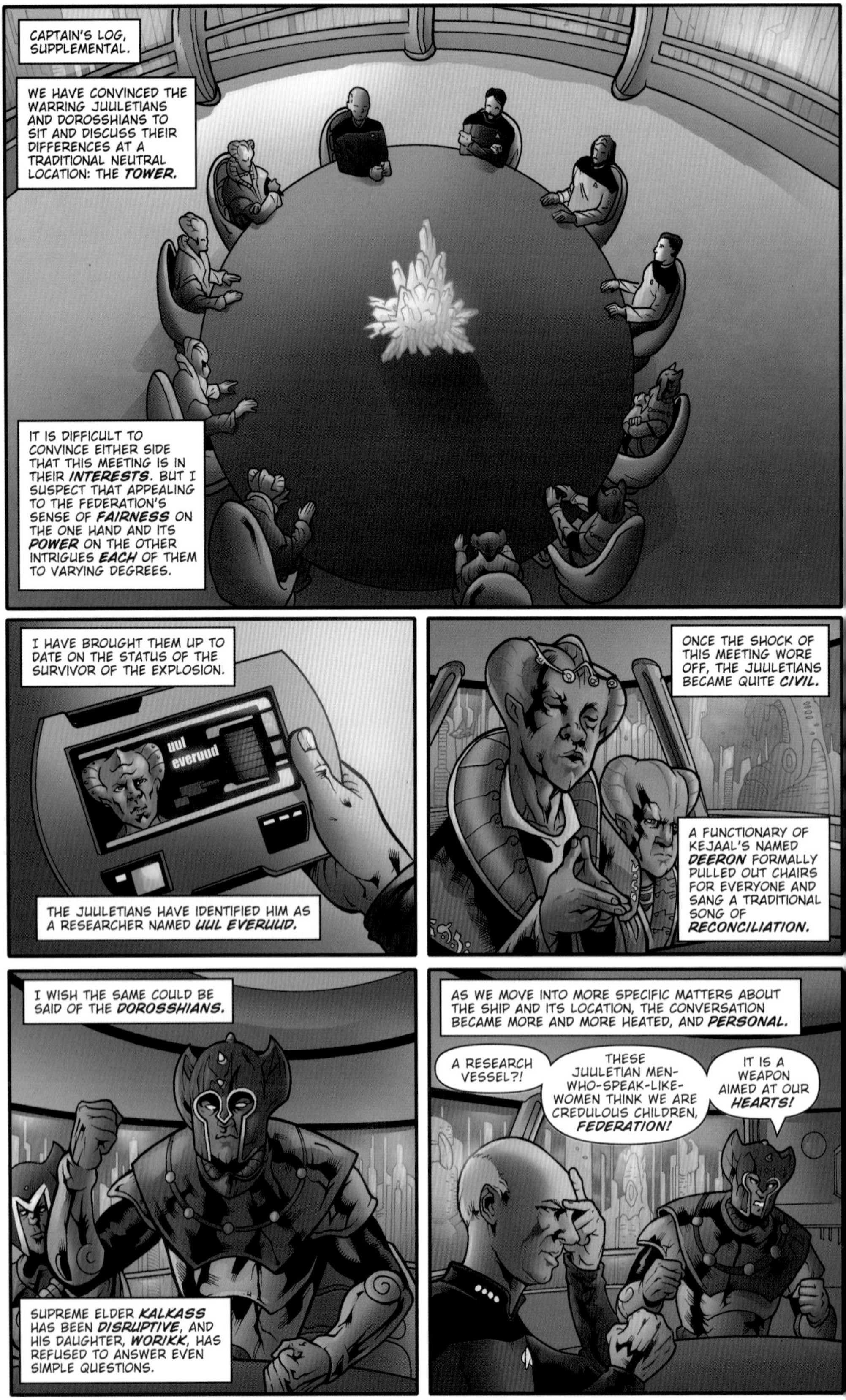

CAPTAIN'S LOG, SUPPLEMENTAL.

WE HAVE CONVINCED THE WARRING JUULETIANS AND DOROSSHIANS TO SIT AND DISCUSS THEIR DIFFERENCES AT A TRADITIONAL NEUTRAL LOCATION: THE ***TOWER.***

IT IS DIFFICULT TO CONVINCE EITHER SIDE THAT THIS MEETING IS IN THEIR ***INTERESTS***. BUT I SUSPECT THAT APPEALING TO THE FEDERATION'S SENSE OF ***FAIRNESS*** ON THE ONE HAND AND ITS ***POWER*** ON THE OTHER INTRIGUES ***EACH*** OF THEM TO VARYING DEGREES.

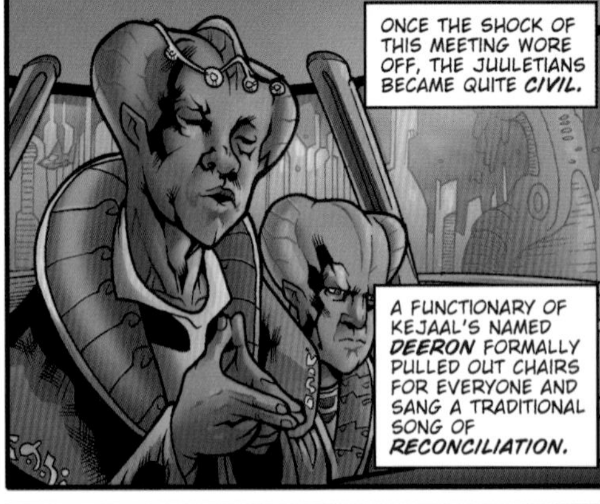

RIDICULOUS.
CAPTAIN PICARD, THESE ACCUSATIONS ARE BASELESS, LIKE THEIR CLAIMS OF SOVEREIGNTY.
OUR SHIP HAS NO WEAPONS, AS YOUR AWAY TEAM CAN ATTEST.

SUPREME ELDER, COMMANDER RIKER WAS ABOARD THE SHIP, HE REPORTED NO WEAPONS.
YES, THAT'S TRUE.
BUT I—
IT DOES NOT MATTER! THE SHIP IS JUULETIAN!

WORIKK?
IF IT WERE ONLY A LITTLE BIT BIGGER WE WOULD HAVE BLASTED IT FROM THE SKY—
—NO MATTER WHAT ITS PURPOSE!

IDIOT!
OXYGEN-DEPRIVED INFANT!
FOOL!
SMACK
OW!
FATHER!
WILL YOU TELL ALL OUR LIMITATIONS?

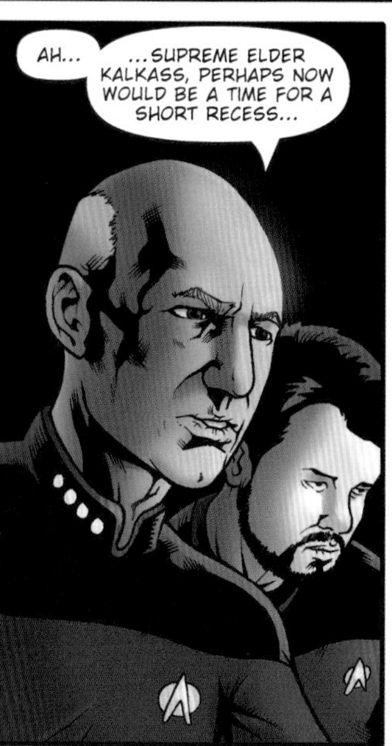
AH...
...SUPREME ELDER KALKASS, PERHAPS NOW WOULD BE A TIME FOR A SHORT RECESS...

NO.
ALL SIX OF MY FELLOW ELDERS HAVE VANISHED IN THE PAST TWO YEARS, FEDERATION.
THESE ASSASSINS AND THEIR SHIP ARE TO BLAME.

DO YOU HAVE ANY PROOF OF THIS, ELDER KALKASS?
-SIGH-
CAPTAIN, OF COURSE HE DOESN'T...

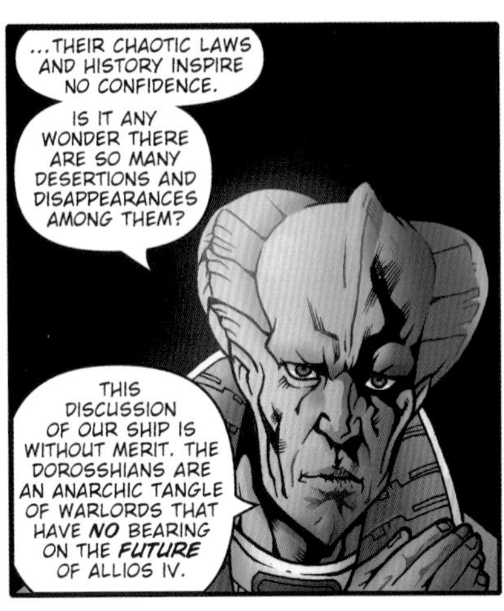
...THEIR CHAOTIC LAWS AND HISTORY INSPIRE NO CONFIDENCE.
IS IT ANY WONDER THERE ARE SO MANY DESERTIONS AND DISAPPEARANCES AMONG THEM?
THIS DISCUSSION OF OUR SHIP IS WITHOUT MERIT. THE DOROSSHIANS ARE AN ANARCHIC TANGLE OF WARLORDS THAT HAVE NO BEARING ON THE FUTURE OF ALLIOS IV.

I MOVE WE CONTINUE THE DISCUSSION OF OUR APPLICATION TO THE FEDERATION BACK INTO OUR CAPITOL PALACE, AND—
ONE MOMENT, SPEAKER KEJAAL.

THERE WERE NO WEAPONS ABOARD YOUR SHIP, TRUE...
...BUT THE VIEWPORTS HAD AN ELABORATE ARRAY OF LENSES...
...AIMED DIRECTLY AT THE DOROSSHIANS.

CAN YOU EXPLAIN THAT?
-SIGH-
COMMANDER—

HA! AS WE SAID—A WEAPON!
A SURVEILLANCE SHIP, KALKASS.
IT IS SIMPLY A SURVEILLANCE SHIP.

CAN YOU BLAME US, CAPTAIN PICARD? COMMANDER RIKER? THESE ARE OUR NEIGHBORS...
...AND ALL THAT SEPARATES US IS SOME THIN WALL...
...AND THE DOZENS OF BROKEN PROMISES THEY HAVE LEFT US WITH IN THIS ROOM.

PROMISES OF DISARMAMENT.
PROMISES OF SCHOOLS.
PROMISES OF EQUITABLE DISTRIBUTION OF SOPPAN LIQUID.
ALL IN TREATIES SIGNED OVER DECADES...
...AND ALL IGNORED.

SO CERTAINLY WE WATCH THEM.
AND IT MAY WELL SEEM A HOSTILE ACT, BUT TO WATCH AND LISTEN FOR WAR IS NOT TO WAGE IT.
HMPH.
"PROMISES."

ELDER KALKASS, IS WHAT SPEAKER KEJAAL SAYS *TRUE?*
BAH.
THEIR WEAKNESS SHOWS IN THEIR... *REQUIREMENT* OF SUCH NICETIES.

HMM.
PERHAPS WE MIGHT RETIRE FOR TODAY AND PICK UP AGAIN TOMORROW.
CAPTAIN...

...WHEN WILL WE BE ABLE TO RECEIVE RESEARCHER EVERUUD?
HIS ACCOUNT OF THE DISASTER WILL PROVIDE VALUABLE DATA TO OUR SHUTTLE CREW.

I'M AFRAID IT WON'T BE POSSIBLE TO RETURN HIM UNTIL OUR MEDICAL OFFICER HAS DONE A FEW MORE SCANS.
I'M SORRY FOR THE DELAY, BUT WE'D LIKE TO BE THOROUGH.

AND *US*, FEDERATION?
WILL YOU DO WHAT *WE* DEMAND, AND MOVE THIS GUNSHIP OUT OF OUR *SKY*?
NO. WE WILL NOT.

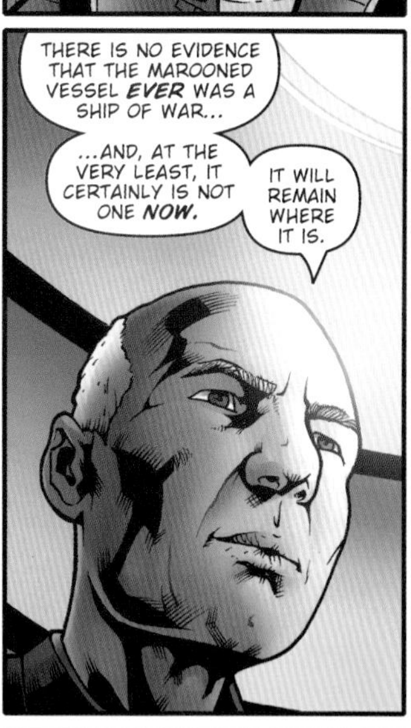
THERE IS NO EVIDENCE THAT THE MAROONED VESSEL *EVER* WAS A SHIP OF WAR...
...AND, AT THE VERY LEAST, IT CERTAINLY IS NOT ONE *NOW.*
IT WILL REMAIN WHERE IT IS.

NOW, IN PREPARATION FOR TOMORROW'S MEETING, WE WISH TO TASK SOME OF OUR CREW TO ACT AS *LIAISONS* WITH YOUR COUNTRIES.
BUT—
FURTHER STUDY OF YOUR CULTURES WILL HELP SPEED THE APPLICATION PROCESS.

"STUDY."
"DELAY."
THESE "LIAISONS."
THIS IS NOT *DECISION*, FEDERATION—

—IT IS *NOTHING.*
YOU HAVE TAKEN NO ACTION, *CAPTAIN*—

"—AND WHO BUT A ***DEAD MAN*** TAKES NO ***ACTION***?"

I CAN'T BELIEVE YOU'RE TELLING ME THIS ISN'T AS BAD AS IT LOOKS.

WELL, IT'S CERTAINLY ***BAD.***

BUT THIS GLOW AROUND HIS WOUNDS—IT'S NOT AN ENERGY SIGNATURE WE'VE EVER RUN INTO BEFORE.

WHATEVER CAUSED IT SEEMS TO HAVE CAUTERIZED HIS WOUNDS AND HAS COMPLETELY PROTECTED HIM FROM ANY OPPORTUNISTIC INFECTIONS.

CAUTERIZED?

DOCTOR CRUSHER.
THE HIGH-DENSITY SCANS OF THE WOUNDS ARE IN.
GOOD, THANK YOU, XIAN.
CAN YOU SEND THE RESULTS TO THIS STATION?

I CAN'T BELIEVE THIS.
WHAT DO YOU SEE?
THESE SCANS ON THE CELLULAR LEVEL...

...IN THIS IMAGE OF THE WOUND'S SURFACE, THESE CAROLUS CELLS, THE EQUIVALENT TO OUR RED BLOOD CELLS, ARE ACTUALLY SLICED IN HALF BY THE EXPLOSION'S ENERGY.

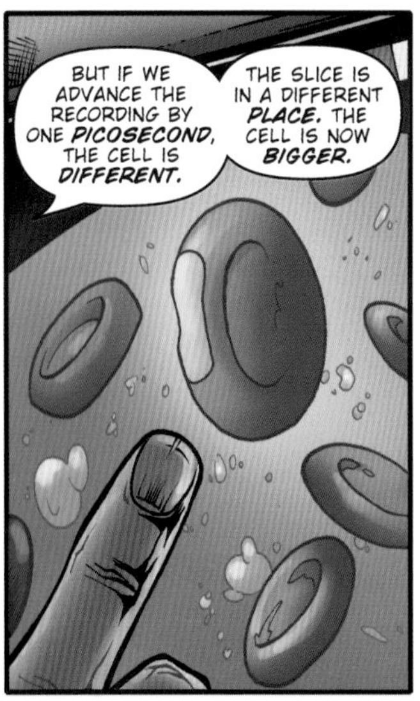
BUT IF WE ADVANCE THE RECORDING BY ONE PICOSECOND, THE CELL IS DIFFERENT.
THE SLICE IS IN A DIFFERENT PLACE. THE CELL IS NOW BIGGER.

WHAT DOES THAT MEAN?
I DON'T KNOW... IT'S LIKE THE ADDITIONAL MASS IS COMING FROM SOMEWHERE ELS—
BEE-BEEP

BEVERLY, HE'S COMING OUT OF SEDATION.
RESEARCHER EVERUUD?

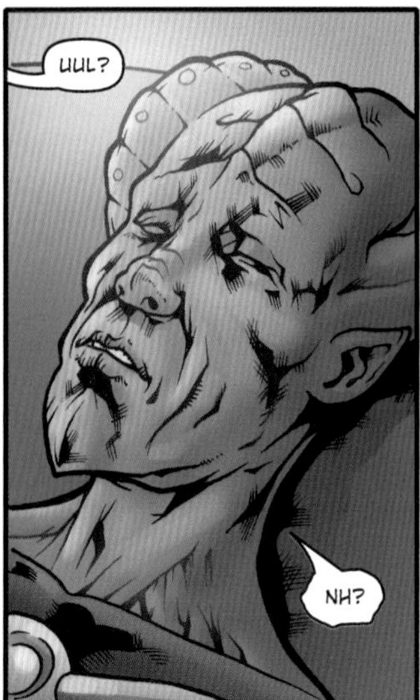
UUL?
NH?

UUL, CAN YOU HEAR ME?
NH... K-KEER?

KEER? I-IS THAT Y—
OH, NO— OH WH-WHERE AM I??
SHH... SHH... YOU'RE SAFE.

YOU'RE ON THE FEDERATION STARSHIP ENTERP—
NO!

WHY? WHY ARE THEY HERE?
THEY'RE STILL HERE!
TH-THE GHOSTS!
IT'S ALL RIGHT!
UUL, IT'S ALL RIGHT!

SHH... SHH...
NO... NO, I CAN'T...
PLEASE...
TH-THEY JUST WON'T GO AWAY...

DOCTOR—
I KNOW, HE'S BEEN LIKE THIS SINCE WE BROUGHT HIM BACK.
N-NO...

I'D HOPED THAT YOU COULD CALM HIM DOWN.
IT SEEMS TO HAVE WORKED. AT LEAST A LITTLE.
PERHAPS, BUT I DON'T KNOW IF I'LL GET MUCH OUT OF HIM.

HE'S TERRIFIED, BUT MORE THAN THAT, HE'S COMPLETELY CONFUSED.
HIS SENSES ARE OVERWHELMED WITH... SOMETHING.

SOMETHING WE CAN'T SEE, OR EVEN SENSE.
YES, I NEED TO LOOK INTO THIS SOME MORE... MAYBE GEORDI WILL HAVE SOME INSIGHT.
TELL XIAN IF YOU FEEL HE NEEDS TO BE SEDATED AGAIN.

CRUSHER TO LA FORGE.
GO AHEAD, DOCTOR.
WELL, GEORDI...

"...I'VE GOT QUITE A MYSTERY FOR YOU."
OKAY...
...SO YOU THINK THAT THIS ENERGY HAS CREATED A FIELD OF SOME KIND THAT...

...WHAT, SHIFTS THINGS INTO OTHER DIMENSIONS?
I DON'T KNOW— I MEAN, WE DON'T EVEN KNOW WHAT THIS ENERGY IS, RIGHT?
IT DOESN'T EVEN SHOW UP ON OUR SENSORS.
OR... IT DOES, BUT THE SENSORS DON'T KNOW HOW TO INTERPRET IT.

HMM.
COMPUTER.
LIST ALL KNOWN ENERGIES THAT HAVE A PHASE-SHIFTING EFFECT.
THERE ARE 725 KNOWN ENERGIES WITH THAT EFFECT.

ALL RIGHT, HOW MANY OF THOSE WOULD NOT SHOW UP ON A STANDARD SCAN—OR A TRICORDER?
377.
AND PRODUCES A WHITE GLOW IN FLESH EXPOSED TO IT?
26.

HOW MANY OF THOSE HAVE BEEN OBSERVED IN THIS SECTOR?
4.
LIST AND SEND TO THIS TERMINAL.
BEVERLY, LOOK AT THIS.

LOOKS LIKE WE FOUND THE CULPRIT.
. STWALLIAN GLOW
FOUND: ZARC 113 CLOUD
2. GAALAN EMANATA
FOUND: EDGE OF F NEB
3. ZOOR ENERGY
FOUND: CORE OF ALLI
4. DOW BEAMS
FOUND: 66804

HMM. CAN YOU ADJUST THE TRICORDERS TO READ IT?
SURE, I'LL RETUNE THE SHIP'S SENSORS, TOO.
TROUBLE IS, WHERE DOES THAT GET US?

AND MORE IMPORTANTLY, HOW DO WE FIX IT?
RIGHT, I—
PICARD TO DR. CRUSHER.

GO AHEAD, CAPTAIN.
PLEASE REPORT TO SICK BAY. I'D LIKE TO SPEAK WITH OUR SURVIVOR.
ON MY WAY.

THANKS, GEORDI.
NO PROBLEM. I'LL BE BY TO RETUNE THE MEDICAL TRICORDERS.

HOW WAS THE MEETING?
SIGH
TRYING.
I'M NOT SURE WHY EACH SIDE HAS TO MAKE IT SO DIFFICULT, OR...

...OR WHY YOU HAVE TO CARE SO MUCH?
HMM. I SUPPOSE.
IT'S REALLY NONE OF OUR CONCERN WHETHER ALLIOS IV IS LET INTO THE FEDERATION OR NOT...

...BUT I JUST WANT TO SORT OUT EVERYONE'S STORIES AND FIND OUT WHAT HAPPENED TO THE SHIP, THEN MOVE ON.
WHY MUST PEOPLE MAKE IT HARD FOR THE TRUTH TO COME OUT?
ALL THIS BLUSTER, AND ALL THESE EVASIONS, JUST MAKE ME FEEL DEAD INSIDE.

WELL, SIR, GEORDI AND I MAY HAVE FIGURED OUT ONE ASPECT OF THE SHIP DISASTER.
DOES IT TELL US WHETHER OR NOT THE SHIP HAD WEAPONS?
AH, ACTUALLY, THERE'S SOME EVIDENCE THAT THEY INTENTIONALLY BROUGHT UP THE ELEMENT THAT CAUSED THE EXPLOSION, BUT...
YES, WELL, LET'S ASK THE SURVIVOR WHAT HE KNOWS—I'D LIKE TO GO INTO TOMORROW'S MEETING WITH SOME SOLID INFORMATION, IF I CAN.

COUNSELOR TROI IS SPEAKING WITH RESEARCHER EVERUUD RIGHT NOW.
HE'S BEEN DIFFICULT TO COMMUNICATE WITH, AS WILL MUST HAVE TOLD YOU.
YES... THESE... HALLUCINATIONS. OF DEAD PEOPLE.
YES, BUT NOW, CAPTAIN, IF GEORDI AND I ARE CORRECT...

...WE MAY BE DEALING WITH A DIMENSIONAL SHIFT THAT'S SPECIFIC TO THE SURVIVOR. BASICALLY—

—THEY MAY NOT BE HALLUCINATIONS.
THE GHOSTS MAY BE REAL.

HMM. ALL RIGHT.
HERE WE ARE.

I—THE UM... THEY'RE TALKING TO ME. I-I JUST... CAN'T UNDERSTAND WHAT THEY WANT—
BUT WHO ARE THEY?

DO YOU KNOW ANY OF THEM? FRIENDS?
I-IT'S TOO HARD TO SEE... I DON'T KNOW...

COUNSELOR.
CAPTAIN. LET ME INTRODUCE YOU TO OUR SURVIVOR, UUL EVERUUD.
PLEASED TO—

NO!
NNO!
YOU! WHAT ARE YOU DOING HERE?!

HE—
HE'S ONE
OF **THEM!**

H—HE'S
ONE OF THE
GHOSTS!

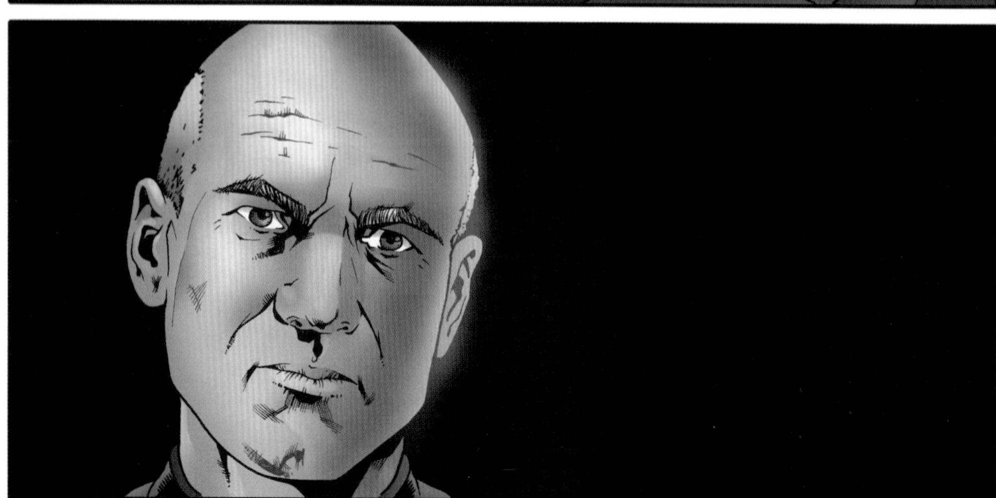

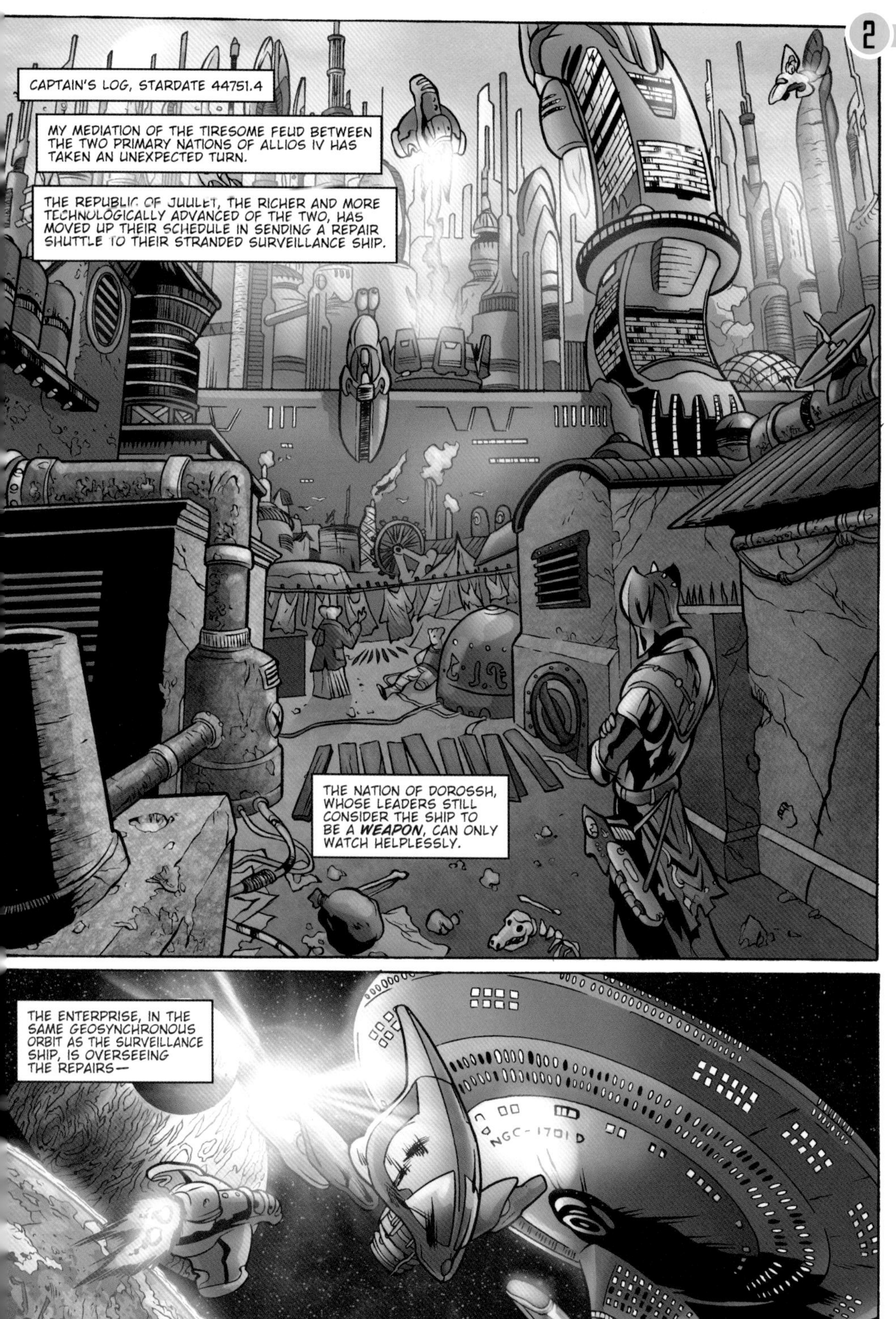
CAPTAIN'S LOG, STARDATE 44751.4
MY MEDIATION OF THE TIRESOME FEUD BETWEEN THE TWO PRIMARY NATIONS OF ALLIOS IV HAS TAKEN AN UNEXPECTED TURN.
THE REPUBLIC OF JUULET, THE RICHER AND MORE TECHNOLOGICALLY ADVANCED OF THE TWO, HAS MOVED UP THEIR SCHEDULE IN SENDING A REPAIR SHUTTLE TO THEIR STRANDED SURVEILLANCE SHIP.
THE NATION OF DOROSSH, WHOSE LEADERS STILL CONSIDER THE SHIP TO BE A *WEAPON*, CAN ONLY WATCH HELPLESSLY.
THE ENTERPRISE, IN THE SAME GEOSYNCHRONOUS ORBIT AS THE SURVEILLANCE SHIP, IS OVERSEEING THE REPAIRS—
NCC-1701 D
—AN IMPOSITION AND SHOW OF DISTRUST THAT THE JUULETIANS WOULD NO DOUBT FIND *INTOLERABLE* IF THEY DID NOT SO FERVENTLY WISH TO JOIN THE FEDERATION.

I HAVE DISPATCHED COMMANDER DATA AND LIEUTENANT WORF TO INVESTIGATE THE HISTORIES AND CLAIMS OF JUULET AND DOROSSH, RESPECTIVELY.
I SURMISE THAT THEIR TEMPERAMENTS WILL SUIT THEM TO THE CHOSEN COUNTRIES.
WITH THAT—AND THE TREATMENT OF THE SURVEILLANCE SHIP'S SOLE SURVIVOR PROGRESSING APACE—WE HAVE A RARE QUIET MOMENT ABOARD THE ENTERPRISE.
BEEBOOP
COME.

HELLO, CAPTAIN.
COUNSELOR!

AH... WHAT BRINGS YOU HERE?
IS THE PATIENT CONTINUING TO BE LESS-THAN-FORTHCOMING ABOUT THESE... HALLUCINATIONS HE SEES?
WELL, HE'S ASLEEP—SEDATED. HE STILL FEELS SO CONFUSED. HE CAN'T CONCENTRATE LONG ENOUGH TO TELL US ANYTHING.

BUT IT WAS YOUR EMOTIONS THAT BROUGHT ME HERE, SIR.
MY EMOTIONS?

IT SEEMS THAT YOU'VE EXPERIENCED SOME DARK THOUGHTS SINCE YOUR ENCOUNTER WITH OUR PATIENT, CAPTAIN.
WHAT? OH, NO, NONSENSE.
JUST A MOMENT OF REFLECTION.

SIR—BEING SINGLED OUT BY RESEARCHER EVERUUD AS ONE OF THE... PEOPLE THAT ARE HAUNTING HIM...
...THAT COULD MAKE ONE FAIRLY INTROSPECTIVE.
THOUGHTS OF MORTALITY... OF FINALITY...

COUNSELOR, I APPRECIATE YOUR CONCERN, I REALLY DO, BUT...
...IT'S JUST THAT IT'S BEEN A WEARYING THIRTY-SOME HOURS HERE.
I'M PERFECTLY FINE.

YOU CAN LEAVE ME HERE WITH MY DARK THOUGHTS.

OF COURSE THIS IS FASCINATING, SIR...
...BUT THE HISTORY I'M HERE TO REVIEW IS MEANT TO BE... THE STORIES OF ALL OF YOUR PEOPLE.
BAH.
WHY WOULD YOUR FEDERATION **CARE** ABOUT THE TREACHEROUS FAILED USURPERS AND ADDICTED FOOLS, KLINGON?
THE DEEDS OF THE MIGHTY AND WISE ELDERS ARE THE SOIL OUR DOROSSH HAVE SPRUNG FROM.

FOR A FULL HISTORY...
...YOU WILL WANT TO SEE VOLMOLOKK, THE SINGER. HE IS ON THE FAR SIDE OF—
-GROAN-
FATHER...

WHAT IS IT, WORIKK, YOU LAZY CHILD?
VOLMOLOKK IS TOO OLD! HE IS A FOOL WHO ONLY THINKS OF THE OLD DAYS!
BAH.
IF ONLY YOU WOULD THINK OF THE OLD DAYS...

...INSTEAD OF WISHING FOR THINGS YOU CANNOT HAVE. THEN YOU MIGHT BE AN ELDER ONE DAY.
AN UNLIKELY OUTCOME AT BEST.

WH—?
YOU SEE, FEDERATION, WHAT I MUST CONTEND WITH? I, THE LAST ELDER? AN HEIR THAT IS A FOOL! THESE INFERNAL JUULETIANS AND THEIR LIES!
IT'S...
...IT'S ENOUGH TO MAKE ME WISH THAT GUN IN THE SKY WOULD JUST TAKE ME TOO.

THE DOROSSH I KNOW IS LONG GONE. DEAD WITH THE OTHER ELDERS.
IF IT WERE A CHOICE BETWEEN RAISING A CUP WITH OLD FRIENDS IN OUR WARRIOR HEAVEN AND LISTENING TO IDIOTS AND ASSASSINS...

...IT WOULD BE NO CHOICE AT ALL.
GO TALK TO VOLMOLOKK, FEDERATION. HE WILL TELL YOU HOW WE CAME TO THIS SORRY STATE.
I'M TIRED.

THE OLD FOSSIL—
HE KNOWS NOTHING OF WHAT MUST BE DONE TO KEEP DOROSSH MOVING. NOTHING.
WORIKK, WHAT—
HE KNEW ALL THE ELDERS, AND SO USED TO ACCOMPLISH WHAT HAD TO BE DONE THAT WAY.

...BUT NOW THAT THE ELDERS ARE DEAD, AND THIS IS A NEW TIME, HE IS JUST A RELIC.
SEE, FEDERATION? HE STILL WEARS THE SAME ARMOR FROM THAT MEETING WITH YOUR JUULETIANS YESTERDAY.

THE DUST AND DETRITUS FROM THEIR CUSHIONED CHAIRS IS STILL ON HIS BACKSIDE.
LOOK AT HIM.
HE IS RIDICULOUS, A CLOWN WHOSE WORLD HAS—
WORIKK, PLEASE.

YOUR FATHER MAY BE HARD ON YOU, BUT YOU MUST NOT SPEAK OF HIM LIKE THIS.
YOU ARE A WARRIOR PEOPLE, AND RESPECT FOR ONE'S FATHER IS THE WARRIOR'S WAY.

HAH.
PERHAPS FOR WHAT PASSES FOR WARRIORS IN YOUR FEDERATION, IT IS THE WARRIOR'S WAY.
YOU MAY BE SENTIMENTAL IN YOUR HOUSES-IN-THE-SKY.

THEY ALLOW YOU TO FLOAT ABOVE US IN JUDGMENT...
...WHILE EVERYTHING YOU WANT IS PLACED IN YOUR MOUTHS BY YOUR OVERLORDS.

NOT LIKE US. NOT LIKE DOROSSH.
WHERE WE FOUGHT FOR EVERYTHING WE OWN...
...AND THEN FOUGHT AGAIN TO KEEP IT.

MM
WORIKK, LET ME TELL YOU THIS.
I KNOW SOMETHING OF LOSS...
...AND THE LOSS OF A FATHER YOU HAVE MALIGNED AND DISRESPECTED IS IMPOSSIBLE TO BEAR.

IT IS A MARK OF SHAME ON ANY WARRIOR, NO MATTER HIS OR HER ORIGIN.
YOU HAVE INSULTED ME, WORIKK...
...AND NORMALLY I WOULD SEEK TO SETTLE SUCH AN INSULT HERE, ON THESE DESERTED STREETS.

BUT MY SUPERIORS HAVE REQUESTED I PERFORM AN AUDIT OF YOUR NATION'S HISTORY.
SO I WILL DO THAT.
BUT KNOW THIS—FROM ONE HEIR TO ANOTHER—NOTHING IS FOREVER. MUCH AS WE THINK IT CAN NEVER HAPPEN, WORIKK...

...FATHERS EVENTUALLY DIE.

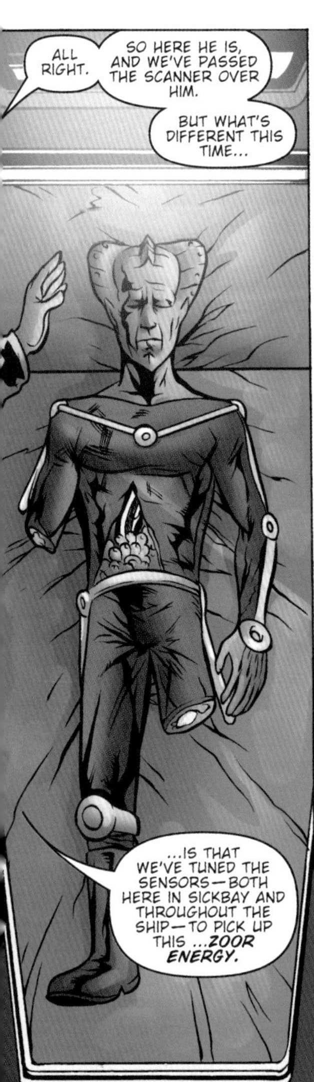
ALL RIGHT.
SO HERE HE IS, AND WE'VE PASSED THE SCANNER OVER HIM.
BUT WHAT'S DIFFERENT THIS TIME...
...IS THAT WE'VE TUNED THE SENSORS—BOTH HERE IN SICKBAY AND THROUGHOUT THE SHIP—TO PICK UP THIS ...**ZOOR ENERGY.**

OF COURSE, YOU CAN SEE THE WHITE GLOW AROUND HIS WOUNDS WITH NO ENHANCEMENT AT ALL.
BUT IF WE ADJUST THE FILTER LIKE SO...

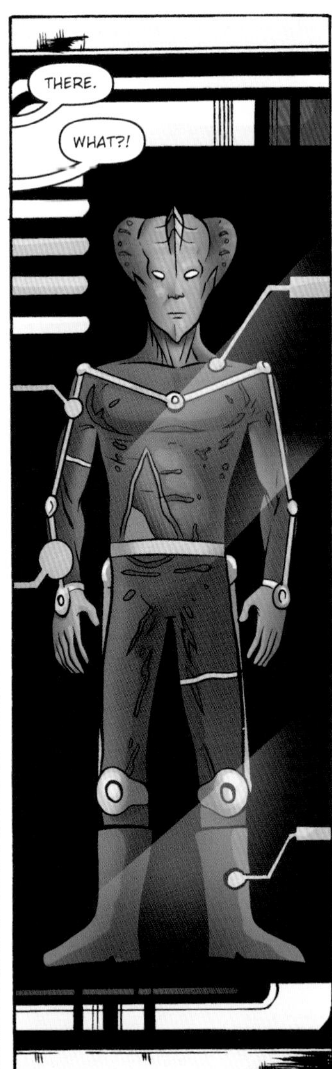
THERE.
WHAT?!

GEORDI—HE'S **COMPLETE.** IT'S LIKE HE HASN'T BEEN MAIMED AT **ALL.**
BUT HIS **LIMBS**—
—WHERE ARE THEY?

THAT I DON'T KNOW.
WE DON'T KNOW MUCH ABOUT THIS ENERGY OTHER THAN THE ORE THAT PRODUCES IT IS MINED FROM THE CORE OF THE PLANET.
SO THEY COULD BE... IN ANOTHER SPACE, WITH THIS ENERGY SIGNATURE OUR ONLY LINK TO THEM.
OR THE SIGNATURE COULD BE A MERE **APPROXIMATION** OF THE LIMBS IT DESTROYED, AND...

...AND HE REALLY DID KILL THEM ALL.

WHAT DO YOU **MEAN**, DEANNA?
AS HE SAID WHEN YOU **FOUND** HIM. "I KILLED THEM ALL, AND THEY WON'T LEAVE ME **ALONE**."

THIS BEAM THAT INJURED HIM—IT MUST HAVE KILLED THE OTHER TWO SCIENTISTS ABOARD THE SHIP.
AND OTHERS, TOO—ALL THE ACCIDENTS WITH THIS ORE OVER THE YEARS...
...PERHAPS EVEN IN THE **FUTURE**.

THE ENERGY IS SOME HOW LINKING HIM TO THEM...
...AND HE CAN PERCEIVE WHAT IS TOO SUBTLE EVEN FOR THE **TRICORDERS**.
IT'S HIS **GUILT**. HIS **GUILT** LETS HIM SEE WHAT WE **CAN'T**.

HM. I DON'T KNOW IF I **BUY** THAT, COUNSELOR.
I MEAN, GUILT'S **POWERFUL**, BUT AS FOR SEEING **THINGS**?
I'LL TAKE MY **VISOR** ANY DAY.
WELL...
BRIDGE TO LA FORGE.

LA FORGE HERE, COMMANDER. GO AHEAD.
GEORDI, OUR SENSORS PICKED UP A BIG SPIKE OF THAT ENERGY YOU WERE TALKING ABOUT.
WHAT? FROM WHERE?

IT'S FROM THE JUULETIAN SURVEILLANCE SHIP.
COMMANDER, MY SCHEDULE SAYS NO ONE'S DUE ABOARD UNTIL 1400 HOURS.
-SIGH- YES, MINE TOO.

I CAN'T BELIEVE THEY'D JUMP THE GUN LIKE THIS WHEN THEY'RE SO HUNGRY FOR FEDERATION APPROVAL, COMMANDER.
DEANNA? ARE YOU ALL RIGHT?
YES, I...

I'M FINE. I JUST—I FEEL A LITTLE HELPLESS. I WENT TO SEE THE CAPTAIN EARLIER...
...AND HE STILL WON'T COME DOWN AND SPEAK WITH OUR SURVIVOR?

IT'S MORE THAN THAT. HE HAS SUCH DARK FEELINGS ABOUT BEING SEEN AS A GHOST—FEELINGS THAT HE WON'T ACKNOWLEDGE.
WHATEVER IT MEANS TO OUR MYSTERY, HE NEEDS TO FACE HIS FEARS, FOR HIS OWN SAKE.

WELL, DEANNA, I AGREE, BUT IT'S THE CAPTAIN'S OWN BUSINESS, ISN'T IT?
OF COURSE, OF COURSE. I'M JUST... I'M SORRY.
BEING UNABLE TO COMMUNICATE WITH OUR SURVIVOR—IT MAKES ME TRY FOR SUCCESS IN OTHER AREAS, I SUPPOSE.

ACKNOWLEDGED, COMMANDER. LA FORGE OUT.
IF ONLY THERE WERE SOME WAY TO—TO TURN OFF HIS GUILT FOR A MOMENT. TO CLEAR AWAY THE CLUTTER FROM HIS MIND...

WAIT.
WHAT WAS THAT, COUNSELOR? WHAT DID YOU SAY?
JUST... TURN OFF HIS GUILT FOR A MOMENT. GEORDI, I KNOW IT SOUNDS SILLY, I WAS JUST—

NO, NO.
THAT'S JUST RIGHT. I DON'T KNOW WHAT I WAS THINKING. I WAS SO FOCUSED ON LETTING US SEE MORE...
...THAT I IGNORED THE FACT THAT WHAT WE NEEDED WAS FOR HIM TO SEE LESS.

"—AND HIS FELLOW COUNTRYMEN WON'T."

NCC 1701 D

AH!

COMMANDER RIKER, HOW GOOD OF YOU TO JOIN US!

ASTOUNDING, THAT TRANSPORTER TECHNOLOGY OF YOURS, COMMANDER.
IF ONLY JUULET HAD ACCESS TO SUCH A THING, IT WOULD—
DEERON!

WHAT THE HELL ARE YOU THINKING!?
C-COMMANDER?

AS IF IT WEREN'T ENOUGH THAT YOU MOVE UP YOUR SCHEDULE WITHOUT NOTIFYING US—
—OR THAT YOU BOARDED THE SHIP THREE HOURS EARLY—
—BUT TO HAVE ANOTHER EXPOSURE OF THE SAME ENERGY THAT CAUSED THE FIRST ACCIDENT...!!

YOU PEOPLE REALLY ARE BEYOND BELIEF. YOU WANT TO BE IN THE FEDERATION SO BADLY, AND TO HAVE ALL OF THE THINGS THAT MEMBERSHIP CAN PROVIDE...

...BUT YOU HAVE NO NOTION OF HOW TO CONDUCT YOURSELVES. CONTINUED UNSAFE PRACTICES, CONTEMPT FOR INQUIRIES INTO YOUR METHODS, AND LIES UPON LIES.

I'VE LOST MY PATIENCE WITH YOU, DEERON, AND YOUR COUNCIL. IT'S JUST—
COMMANDER, PLEASE.
ONE MOMENT.

WE ARE IN THE MIDST OF AN EXCEEDINGLY RARE ARMISTICE WITH THE DOROSSHIANS, WHOSE GENERAL PATTERN OF BEHAVIOR YOU YOURSELF HAVE WITNESSED.
RUDE, PRIMITIVE, MERCENARY, SELFISH.

ELDER KALKASS IS THE WORST OF THE COLLECTION OF WARLORDS; HE IS A STRONGHOLD IN THEIR OLD WAY OF THINKING—A WAY THAT EXPLOITS THE WEAK AND EMPOWERS THE STRONG.
YOU MUST KNOW OF THIS PHILOSOPHY, COMMANDER—

—IT WAS THE MILLSTONE AROUND YOUR SOCIETY'S NECK AS YOU ACHIEVED WARP CAPABILITY.
WERE YOU NOT STILL FIGHTING THOSE ELEMENTS ON YOUR WORLD WHEN YOU JOINED THE FEDERATION?

THAT HASN'T ANSWERED ANY OF MY—
BY NO MEANS ARE WE A PERFECT CULTURE, COMMANDER. THE STRUGGLE TO KEEP OUT THE CREEPING TENDRILS OF CHAOS LEADS ONE TO SOLUTIONS THAT OTHERS MAY FIND... UNPALATABLE.

DO WE WISH TO ORBIT THE PLANET AND SPY ON THE DOROSSHIANS?
NO.
WOULD WE PREFER TO TRUST THEM TO KEEP THEIR PROMISES?
CERTAINLY.
BUT ALLIOS IV IS POISED TO TAKE A GREAT LEAP, AND THEY ARE OUR MILLSTONE, COMMANDER...

...KALKASS AND HIS CRONIES IN THE ELDER COUNCIL.
"THEIR?"
THERE'S ONLY ONE OF THEM LEFT, DEERON.

YES, WELL, OUR WORK HAS BEEN SUCCESSFUL, HASN'T IT?
HOLD IT. YOU'RE ADMITTING TO—?

I'M ADMITTING THAT THE ADVANCE OF OUR CIVILIZATION MEANS THAT THE GLORY DAYS OF THOSE WHO WOULD LIVE IN LUXURY AT THEIR PEOPLE'S EXPENSE IS DRAWING TO A CLOSE.
THEIR REWARDS WERE WANING.
MY GUESS IS THAT THEY HAVE TAKEN WHAT THEY COULD AND LEFT.

PRETTY THIN, THIS THEORY OF YOURS, DEERON.
NO THINNER THAN THAT WE HAVE SOMEHOW OBLITERATED THEM WITHOUT A TRACE, COMMANDER.

TOUCHE.

COMMANDER, COME. THIS MUTUAL ANTAGONISM IS TIRESOME.
MEET THE CREW, AND PLEASE, INSPECT OUR REPAIRS.

YES, WELL, IT IS QUITE A CREW YOU HAVE.
YES. OF COURSE, ONE HATES TO SHOW PREFERENTIAL TREATMENT...

...BUT FEMALES OF OUR SPECIES HAVE SUCH AN APTITUDE FOR MECHANICS.
AS FOR ME, I MERELY SUPERVISE. MY TECHNICAL KNOWLEDGE IS MINIMAL.

LEADERSHIP HAS ITS OWN CHALLENGES WITHOUT MIRING ONESELF IN TECHNICALITIES, DON'T YOU AGREE?
I AGREE ENTIRELY. I'M NOT TERRIBLY TECHNICAL MYSELF.
AH!

HERE'S WHAT YOU'RE HERE TO SEE.
THE ZOOR LENSES.
ALL RIGHT...

...OUR READINGS ON THE ENTERPRISE DETECTED WHAT SEEMS TO BE A HUGE OUTPUT OF THE SAME ENERGY THAT CAUSED THE FIRST EXPLOSION, DEERON.
CARE TO COMMENT ON THAT?
AH, YES.

WHEN WE CAME ABOARD, OUR TEMPORARY HOUSING FOR THE ZOOR ORE PIECES WERE APPROACHING THE END OF THEIR WINDOW OF USE, AND WE THOUGHT IT BEST TO PUT THEM INTO THE PERMANENT CASING HERE ON THE SHIP.

HMM.
THE DAMAGE TO THE CASING WAS SIMPLY A WORN-OUT SEAL AND **BOLT.**
AS YOU HAVE SEEN, OF COURSE, THE COST IN LIVES WAS **HIGHER.**

RIGHT, SO THE SPIKE IN **ENERGY...?**
UH, YES... THE BRIEF TRANSITION BETWEEN THE TWO SHIELDED COMPARTMENTS RELEASED SOME ENERGY.
OUR TECHNICIANS WHO WERE WITHIN THE RADIUS OF THE TRANSFER WERE WEARING SHIELDED SUITS, COMMANDER.
WE WON'T MAKE THE SAME MISTAKE TWICE.

-SIGH-
ALL RIGHT, I HAVE TO SAY: YOUR EXPLANATIONS ARE VERY **THOROUGH.**
AND THE SUSPICIONS OF THE DOROSSHIANS—AND I'LL ADMIT, MINE AS WELL—SEEM TO BE BASED ONLY ON A LACK OF UNDERSTANDING.
BUT AFTER ALL THIS, WHY DO YOU HAVE THE ORE ABOARD?
WHY IS IT **HERE?**

OH, WELL, COMMANDER RIKER, ISN'T IT **OBVIOUS?**
POWER.

UH...
THIS SHIP DOESN'T OPERATE ITSELF, OF COURSE. AND THE MECHANISMS ABOARD NEED A PRIME MOVER TO DO ANYTHING AT ALL.
YES, COMMANDER.
POWER.

THE DISCOVERY OF THIS ORE DEEP IN THE CENTER OF OUR PLANET HAS **REVOLUTIONIZED** OUR CULTURE.
JUST TWENTY QUADS AGO WE WERE SCARCELY AHEAD OF THE **DOROSSHIANS.**
NOW WE ARE POISED TO ENTER THE **FEDERATION.**

THIS ORE HAS BEEN THE KEY TO SO MANY ADVANCEMENTS.
WITHOUT IT, WE WOULD BE NOTHING MORE THAN ONE MORE WARRING PLANET ON THE OUTER RIM.
IT'S AMAZING, COMMANDER, WHAT SUCH A SIMPLE THING LIKE **POWER** CAN DO FOR A PEOPLE—

"—IT LETS THEM SEE SOLUTIONS SO CLEARLY."
OKAY, GEORDI—A LITTLE MORE IS OKAY...

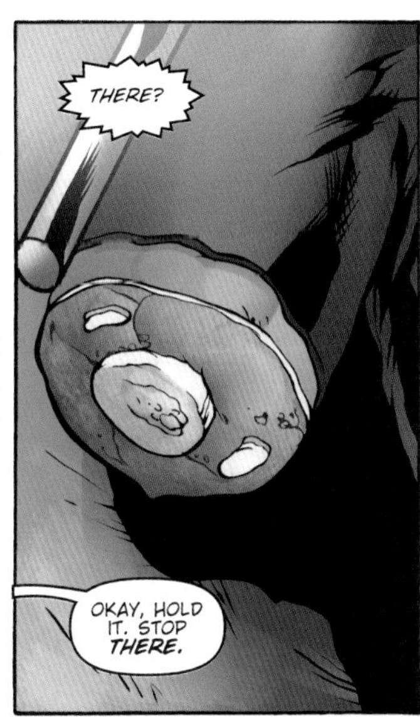
THERE?
OKAY, HOLD IT. STOP THERE.

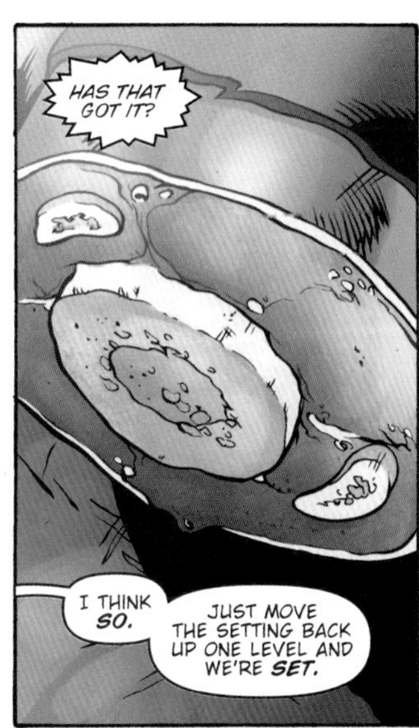
HAS THAT GOT IT?
I THINK SO.
JUST MOVE THE SETTING BACK UP ONE LEVEL AND WE'RE SET.

GREAT. I'LL BE DOWN THERE IN A FEW MINUTES.
EXCELLENT. THANKS, GEORDI. CRUSHER OUT.
SO, BEVERLY...
...DO YOU THINK IT WILL WORK?

IT SEEMS REASONABLE. THE DISPLAY SHOWS THAT THE ENERGY SCARCELY EXTENDS BEYOND HIS WOUNDS.
I THINK WHEN HE COMES OUT OF SEDATION, YOU SHOULD BE ABLE TO SPEAK WITH A FAR MORE LUCID PATIENT.

WELL, THAT WOULD BE WONDERFUL.
IT WILL MAKE EVERYTHING SO MUCH EASIER—AT LEAST FOR ME AND HIM.
FOR THE CAPTAIN, THOUGH—I JUST WISH HE'D COME DOWN HERE TO TALK.

HE'S SO CONCERNED ABOUT BEING A ROCK FOR THE CREW TO HOLD ON TO IN ALL THIS CONFUSION—
—THAT HE'S CUT HIMSELF OFF FROM THE PEOPLE HE WANTS TO HELP.
IF HE JUST WOULD HELP HIMSELF FIRST, HE...

...HE WOULD BE A FAR BETTER *CAPTAIN.*

ER... YES.
NOW, RESEARCHER EVERUUD, CAN YOU SEE THE GHOSTS THAT WERE SURROUNDING YOU BEFORE?

N-NO, I CAN'T. TH-THEY'RE GONE. I—
I CAN'T BELIEVE IT. THEY'RE—

OH, NO, WAIT.
THERE'S ONE.

OH, NO, NO, RESEARCHER EVERUUD—
THIS IS OUR CAPTAIN, AND HE'S VERY MUCH ALIVE.
HOW DO YOU DO. I AM JEAN-LUC PICARD, THE CAPTAIN OF THIS STARSHIP.
I'M GLAD WE CAN FINALLY TALK.

SO LET US TALK ABOUT YOUR GHOSTS.
NHH... I'M SO TIRED...
...THEY JUST TALKED AND TALKED TO ME, TELLING ME SECRETS... NUMBERS...

"NUMBERS?"
BUT WHO WERE THEY, UUL? AND WHY WAS OUR CAPTAIN ONE OF THEM?

THAT LEADER—ELDER WITH THE ANGRY HEIR—
WHAT—? KALKASS IS ONE OF YOUR GHOSTS?
Y-YES. KALKASS.
MM.

ONE MOMENT.
PICARD TO WORF. IS ELDER KALKASS WITH YOU?
NO, CAPTAIN. HE BECAME UPSET AND LEFT US. THEN WORIKK INSULTED ME SO I HAVE BEEN FINISHING MY RESEARCH IN AN EMPTY BUILDING.
AN INSULT? AH... I HOPE YOU WERE ABLE TO TAKE APPROPRIATE STEPS...?

YES, SIR.

ABSOLUTELY.

SO, FEDERATION.
AN ASSASSIN FOR JUULET.
I SHOULD HAVE SEEN IT.

WHAT—?
YOU ARE MISTAKEN, WORIKK.
I HAVE KILLED NO ONE.

AH, BUT DON'T YOUR MASTERS SAY THERE IS NO WEAPON IN THE SKY?
THERE IS NO SIGN OF MY FATHER—
—SAVE FOR HIS BOOT—

—AND DO YOU NOT HAVE, FEDERATION—
HEY!

—A WEAPON THAT VAPORIZES ITS TARGET, LEAVING NO TRACE?

WORIKK, I HAVE DONE NOTHING TO YOUR FATHER.

FEDERATION ASSASSIN—BY OUR ELDER LAWS...
...YOU ARE OUR PRISONER. YOU WILL COME WITH US.
WORF TO ENTERPRISE. ONE TO BEAM—

HUH.
WHAT'S THE MATTER, FEDERATION? DO YOU RUN AWAY FROM A FIGHT TO YOUR RETURN TO YOUR "WARRIOR CULTURE?"

NO, IT WAS JUST HALF A MESSAGE, CAPTAIN.
HE STOPPED IN THE MIDDLE OF HIS SENTENCE.
ALL RIGHT, MR. O'BRIEN. GET HIM OUT OF THERE.

SIR, HIS COMMBADGE, IT'S COME OFF.
JUST HONE IN AND BEAM HIM UP, O'BRIEN.
SIR—THERE'RE DOZENS OF THEM, ALL OVER.
I CAN'T TELL WHICH ONE IS **WORF!**

EVERYONE'S **MOVING**—WE'VE GOT **INJURIES**—
ONE'S VITALS AT HALF-STRENGTH—

GET HIM **OUT** OF THERE, O'BRIEN!
SIR, I'M **TRYING**—I CAN'T LOCK ON TO **ANYONE!**
I CAN'T TELL WHO'S WHO!
ALL STATIONS—

—RED ALERT.
ERRTERRTERRTERRTERRTERRTERRTERRTERRT
ENSIGN, CAN YOU CONFIRM WHAT CHIEF O'BRIEN IS SEEING?
YES, SIR—A HUGE MOB—HUNDREDS NOW.
WHAT'S *HAPPENING?*
O'BRIEN SAYS WORF'S LOST HIS COMMBADGE—WHERE *IS* HE—!
NUMBER ONE—I NEED YOU TO TAKE A SECURITY DETAIL AND—
SIR, WE'RE BEING *HAILED.*
ON SCREEN!

SKKKTAIN PICARD, I CAN ONLY BLAME MYSELF FOR MY NAIVETE—
—YOU SPEAK AS THE GIRLISH JUULETIANS DO—
—AND YOU SEND US A FALSE WARRIOR TO KILL FOR THEM.

WELL, SPEAKER KEJAAL...
...YOU WERE NOT LYING ABOUT THE SIZE OF YOUR COUNTRY'S ARCHIVES.
INDEED, COMMANDER DATA...

3

...WE'RE QUITE PROUD THAT OUR LIBRARY IS THE MOST COMPLETE—
NO.
I MEAN THAT **HONESTY** IS A KEY FACTOR IN CONSIDERATION FOR FEDERATION MEMBERSHIP.

OH, UH...
-AHEM-
YES, **OF COURSE.**

MY REPORT ON YOUR COUNTRY IS NEARLY COMPLETE. THANK YOU, SPEAKER KEJAAL, FOR ALL YOUR ASSISTANCE.
I HOPE MY COLLEAGUE, LIEUTENANT **WORF**, FINDS YOUR NEIGHBORS THE **DOROSSHIANS** AS COOPERATIVE.
YES, WELL...
...I'M NOT CERTAIN HE **WILL**. OUR FEUD HAS—

ENTERPRISE TO **DATA.**
EXCUSE ME, SPEAKER KEJAAL. YES, DATA HERE.
COMMANDER, PREPARE TO BEAM UP. THERE HAS BEEN AN EMERGENCY THAT NEEDS YOUR ATTENTION.

RIGHT AWAY, CHIEF O'BRIEN.
AND, DATA, IS SPEAKER KEJAAL WITH YOU?
YES.
THE CAPTAIN'S ASKED THAT I BEAM **HIM** UP AS WELL—

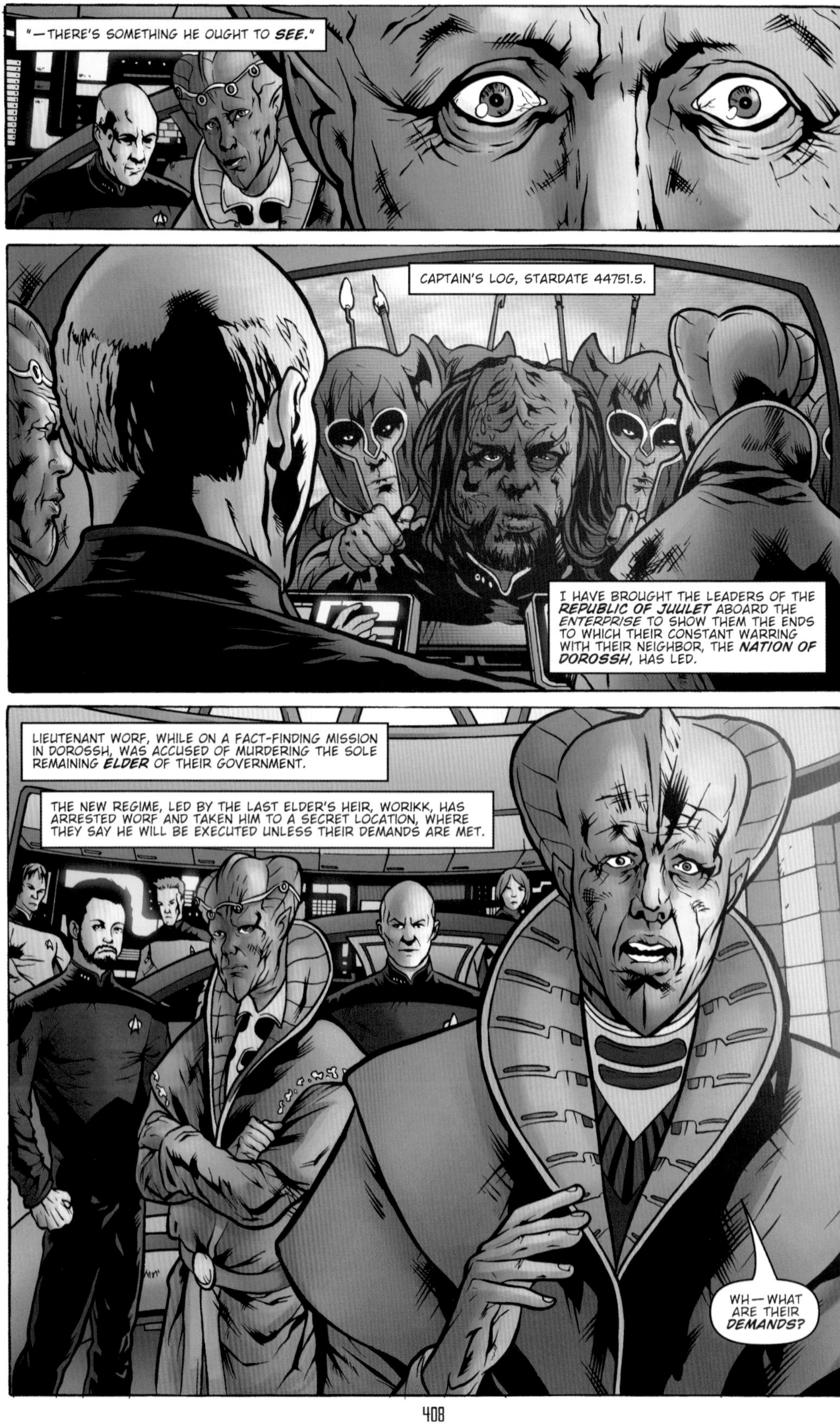

LIEUTENANT WORF, WHILE ON A FACT-FINDING MISSION IN DOROSSH, WAS ACCUSED OF MURDERING THE SOLE REMAINING ***ELDER*** OF THEIR GOVERNMENT.

THE NEW REGIME, LED BY THE LAST ELDER'S HEIR, WORIKK, HAS ARRESTED WORF AND TAKEN HIM TO A SECRET LOCATION, WHERE THEY SAY HE WILL BE EXECUTED UNLESS THEIR DEMANDS ARE MET.

WH—WHAT ARE THEIR ***DEMANDS?***

THEY'VE DEMANDED THAT WE MOVE YOUR SURVEILLANCE SHIP OUT OF THE GEOSYNCHRONOUS ORBIT ABOVE THEIR NATION, AND—
WELL, CERTAINLY. LET'S GET STARTED RIGHT AWAY, CAPTAIN.

ABSOLUTELY NOT. THE FEDERATION DOES NOT ACCEDE TO THE DEMANDS OF TERRORISTS, NOT EVEN IF—
OH, BUT CAPTAIN, PLEASE...

...YOUR OFFICER'S LIFE IS IN DANGER— WE MUST MOVE IT.
I UNDERSTAND YOUR UNWILLINGNESS TO SET A PRECEDENT, BUT...

...YOUR OFFICER'S PRESENCE THERE IS AN ANOMALY TO BEGIN WITH. ONCE HE'S RETURNED, I CAN ASSURE YOU, NO JUULETIAN WILL PUT HIMSELF IN THAT POSITION.
JUST THIS ONCE, CAPTAIN, WE MAY GIVE IN TO THEIR DEMANDS.

YOU MAKE A PASSIONATE ARGUMENT, SPEAKER KEJAAL.
THEN IT IS SETTLED. WHAT ARE THEIR OTHER DEMANDS?

JUST ONE.
THAT WE TURN YOU BOTH OVER TO THEM.

UH, WAIT, WAIT, WAIT...
RELAX, SPEAKER KEJAAL.
AS THE CAPTAIN SAID, THE FEDERATION WILL NOT GIVE IN TO RANSOMS OR TO DEMANDS MADE BY THOSE WHO THREATEN US.

YOU'RE SAFE WITH US.
BUT WE DO NEED TO GET OUR OFFICER BACK.
THAT'S WHERE YOU COME IN.
YOU KNOW THE DOROSSHIAN CULTURE.

THERE ARE NEARLY A MILLION INDIVIDUALS IN DOROSSH'S CAPITAL, WITHIN A KILOMETER OF WHERE WORF WAS ARRESTED.
WHERE CAN HE HAVE BEEN TAKEN? I MEAN—

"—HE CAN'T HAVE JUST VANISHED INTO THIN AIR."

HERE WE PROVIDE YOU A CHAIR YET YOU KNEEL ON THE FLOOR IN DEFERENCE.
OH, WOULDN'T YOUR "WARRIOR ANCESTORS" BE ASHAMED?

IT IS NOT YOU TO WHOM I KNEEL, WORIKK.
NO?
YOU HAD BETTER, FEDERATION. MY DEAD FATHER CALLS FOR JUSTICE...
...AND MY MERCY MAY BE ALL THAT SAVES YOUR NECK FROM THE AXE.

YOUR SOCIETY IS ANYTHING BUT JUST, WORIKK.
IF THE ONLY WAY FOR ME TO LIVE IS TO PLEAD FOR YOU TO SPARE ME...
...THEN I WILL DIE.

SO IT IS NOT YOU I KNEEL TO...
...BUT MY WARRIOR ANCESTORS AND MY WARRIOR GOD.
TO PLEAD WITH THEM TO SEE THE HONOR IN MY DEATH—

—DESPITE THE FACT THAT I AM SOON TO DIE BY YOUR TREACHERY.
WHAT?

YOU ARE NOT THE SIMPLE BARBARIAN YOU PRETEND TO BE.
YOU KNOW VERY WELL I DID NOT KILL YOUR FATHER.
BUT IT WAS SIMPLE TO PLAY ON YOUR PEOPLE'S IGNORANCE IN ORDER TO GET YOURSELF A BARGAINING CHIP.

HM.
I DISAGREE, MURDERER.
BUT IF THE FEDERATION SEES FIT TO SEND OVER THOSE WHO ORDERED MY FATHER'S DEATH—

—THEN I SHALL SEE FIT TO RETURN THEIR ERRAND BOY.
PERHAPS YOU SHOULD PRAY YOUR CAPTAIN EVEN WANTS YOU BACK...

"...WHEN HE SEES WHAT YOU'VE BEEN REDUCED TO."
NNH...

QUITE A LONG SLEEP YOU HAD.
I BET *THAT* CLEARED AWAY SOME COBWEBS.
HOW ARE YOU FEELING?
OHH...

I-I'M FEELING FINE, I GUESS. B-BUT WHAT *HAPPENED* TO ME?
OH—OH, BY THE *CORE*—WHERE'S MY *HAND*—WHERE'S MY *LEG?!*

RESEARCHER EVERUUD, I'M SORRY, YOU APPEAR TO HAVE BEEN INJURED IN AN *EXPLOSION.*
A VERY *STRANGE* EXPLOSION...
...BECAUSE WHILE IT SEEMS TO HAVE VAPORIZED YOUR CREWMATES, THE SURVEILLANCE SHIP ITSELF IS UNTOUCHED.

OHH, I FEEL SICK—I DON'T—
A-AND—WHAT SURVEILLANCE SHIP? M-MY CREW AND I WERE ON A MILITARY MISSION TO—
AH! SO HERE IS OUR LONG-LOST LOYAL COMRADE!

FINALLY WE CAN SEE OUR BRAVE SURVIVOR!
YOU HAVE A MEDAL COMING TO YOU, UUL. FORTITUDE IN THE FACE OF EXTREME PERIL!

BEVERLY— HIS FEAR RESPONSE...!
I SEE IT TOO, DEANNA—THE READINGS ON THE INSTRUMENTS JUST JUMPED OFF THE CHARTS!
H-HELLO, SPEAKER KEJAAL. D-DEERON.

HELLO, DR. CRUSHER, COUNSELOR TROI.
GOOD TO SEE YOU IN SUCH CAPABLE HANDS, UUL.
WE'VE ONLY HEARD BITS ABOUT HOW YOU WERE DOING...

...SOMETHING ABOUT GHOSTS HAUNTING YOU?
UNSETTLING. PARTICULARLY FOR SOMEONE SO SCIENTIFIC.
ER, Y-YES, VERY UNSETTLING.

NOW, DR. CRUSHER, MAY WE EXPECT RESEARCHER EVERUUD BACK DOWN PLANET-SIDE ANYTIME SOON? HIS FAMILY DEARLY WISHES TO SEE HIM.

WELL, WE DON'T RECOMMEND HE BE MOVED FOR SOME TIME.
HIS WOUNDS ARE EXTENSIVE, AND WE'VE ONLY JUST RECENTLY GOTTEN A SUPPRESSION FIELD IN PLACE TO FILTER OUT THE ZOOR ENERGY, AND THE GHOSTS, SO HE CAN SPEAK WITH US.
WE CERTAINLY DON'T WANT TO KEEP HIM FROM HIS FAMILY, BUT—

WELL, YES, EXTENDED FAMILY. AUNTS, UNCLES. NO SPOUSE, NO CHILDREN.
HE HASN'T TOLD YOU HE'S A BACHELOR? SURPRISING.
TWO PRETTY GIRLS LIKE YOU, I WOULD HAVE THOUGHT HE'D BRING IT UP.

UH, WELL, NO.
ANYWAY, WE SHOULD CARRY ON. WE WILL HAVE THE CAPTAIN CONTACT YOU WHEN WE KNOW MORE ABOUT WHEN HE CAN GO HOME.
SO, IF YOU'LL EXCUSE US...

OF COURSE. JUST A FINAL, TRADITIONAL SEND OFF. DEERON?
YES, SIR.
TAKE MY HAND, UUL.

CITIZEN, O CITIZEN, GREAT HAS BEEN YOUR SERVICE TO THE REPUBLIC. SHOULD YOU FALL, OR SHOULD YOU BE RESTORED FULLY TO US, YOU WILL HAVE THIS HONOR.
YOU HAVE SUFFERED. YOU FIND IT DIFFICULT TO SPEAK. YOU FIND IT DIFFICULT TO SEE.

YOU FIND IT DIFFICULT TO REMEMBER. YOU FIND IT DIFFICULT TO UNDERSTAND. THESE ARE ALL WOUNDS YOU HAVE SUFFERED IN OUR NAME.

BUT ON THE DAY WHEN ALL ARE ONE, THESE WOUNDS ARE TAKEN AWAY, AND THERE WILL BE NO SUFFERING.
TWO PATHS LEAD THERE.
MAY WE ALL TAKE THE CORRECT ONE.
FAREWELL, CITIZEN, O CITIZEN.

THANK YOU, DR. CRUSHER. COUNSELOR TROI.
GOOD TO SEE OUR RESEARCHER IN SUCH GOOD CARE.

STRANGE.
SO...
...UUL, YOU WERE SAYING, SOMETHING ABOUT A MILITARY MISSION...

...UH, UUL?
HELLO?

UUL? CAN YOU HEAR ME?

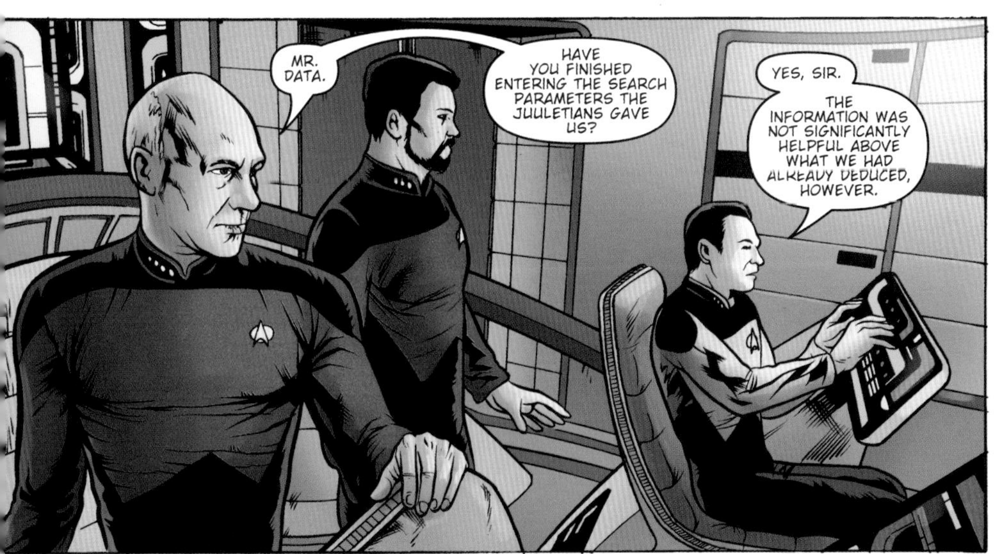
MR. DATA.
HAVE YOU FINISHED ENTERING THE SEARCH PARAMETERS THE JUULETIANS GAVE US?
YES, SIR.
THE INFORMATION WAS NOT SIGNIFICANTLY HELPFUL ABOVE WHAT WE HAD ALREADY DEDUCED, HOWEVER.

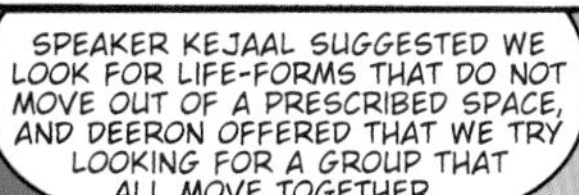
SPEAKER KEJAAL SUGGESTED WE LOOK FOR LIFE-FORMS THAT DO NOT MOVE OUT OF A PRESCRIBED SPACE, AND DEERON OFFERED THAT WE TRY LOOKING FOR A GROUP THAT ALL MOVE TOGETHER...

...BOTH OF WHICH WE HAD ALREADY ENTERED.

THEY WERE HELPFUL, SIR, AND THEIR IDEAS WERE SOUND, BUT THEY DIDN'T SHOW ANY SPECIAL KNOWLEDGE OF THE DOROSSHIANS OR THEIR CULTURE.
STRANGE FOR A COUNTRY WITH A MUCH-DISCUSSED SURVEILLANCE SHIP ABOVE DOROSSH.

WHAT'S THE STATUS OF THE SEARCH NOW, DATA?
PROGRESSING, COMMANDER. CURRENTLY THE NUMBER OF HITS THAT MATCH ALL OF OUR CRITERIA IS 361,948 AND DROPPING.
THEY'RE DROPPING FAR TOO SLOWLY FOR MY TASTE.

WHAT ABOUT KLINGON BIOSIGNS?
SURELY HE'S THE ONLY ONE DOWN THERE.
HE IS, SIR...

...BUT SCANNING TO THE DEPTH THAT WOULD DIFFERENTIATE HIM TAKES 91.44 SECONDS PER INDIVIDUAL.
WE'RE RUNNING IT CONSTANTLY BUT WITH THE HIGH VOLUME OF INDIVIDUALS, IT WILL TAKE—
—MORE TIME THAN WE'VE GOT. OKAY.

CAPTAIN, THE SEARCHES ARE ALL RUNNING AT TOP SPEED. I WILL NOTIFY YOU OF OUR PROGRESS AS WE NARROW DOWN OUR OPTIONS.
THANK YOU, DATA. CARRY ON.

WELL, DATA...
...I HAVE TO SAY, THE AMOUNT OF INFORMATION YOU'VE PUT INTO YOUR REPORT ON JUULET IS AMAZING.
THANK YOU, SIR.

HISTORIES, CULTURAL NORMS, PROGRESSION OF LANGUAGE, HAND PHYSIOLOGY, NUMBER SYSTEMS...
IT WILL TAKE A WHILE TO GET THROUGH, BUT IT WILL BE OF GREAT USE TO US ON THE BRIDGE.
THANK YOU.
I AM, HOWEVER, CONCERNED ABOUT ONE SECTION THAT IS INCOMPLETE.

REALLY? WHICH ONE?
WELL, SIR, THE DISCOVERY AND HARNESSING OF THE ORE FROM THEIR PLANET'S CENTER—THE ONE THAT PRODUCES ZOOR ENERGY—SEEMS TO BE THE DRIVING FORCE BEHIND THE JUULETIAN SOCIETY'S ADVANCEMENT...
...AND YET I WAS UNABLE TO FIND EVEN THE SMALLEST PIECE OF SCIENTIFIC DATA ON THE ORE ITSELF.

THROUGH MY STUDY OF THE COUNTRY'S HISTORY, I HAVE IDENTIFIED A NUMBER OF INDIVIDUALS WHO MADE DISCOVERIES OR ADVANCES IN THE FIELD.
CROSS-REFERENCING THAT INFORMATION WITH RAW DATA OF RESIDENTIAL AND WORK ADDRESSES, I HAVE FOUND THIS.

COORDINATES. OKAY, SO WHAT DO YOU THINK IS HERE?
THIS IS THE LOCATION THAT SAW THE MOST SIGNIFICANT ADVANCES IN HARNESSING THE PROPERTIES OF THE ORE.
IT'S AN ENTIRE FLOOR OF ONE OF THEIR HIGHEST BUILDINGS. I WAS DENIED ACCESS, THOUGH THEY DID NOT SUSPECT I KNEW ITS IMPORTANCE.

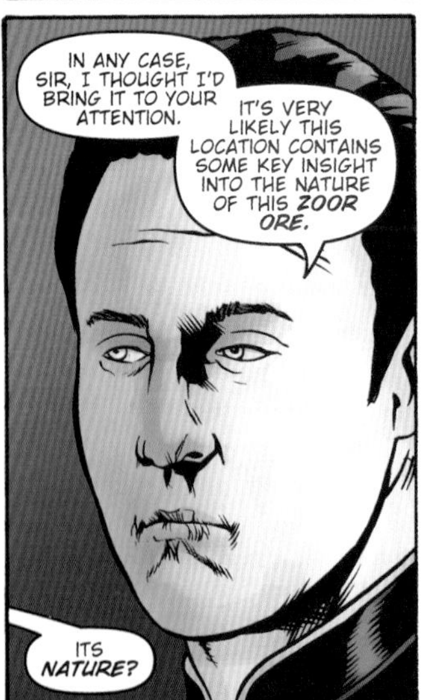
IN ANY CASE, SIR, I THOUGHT I'D BRING IT TO YOUR ATTENTION.
IT'S VERY LIKELY THIS LOCATION CONTAINS SOME KEY INSIGHT INTO THE NATURE OF THIS ZOOR ORE.
ITS NATURE?

DEERON TOLD ME IT'S A POWER SOURCE FOR THE SHIP.
I DON'T SEE WHY—
I'M SORRY, SIR, BUT I'M AFRAID YOU HAVE BEEN MISINFORMED.
WHAT?

ACCORDING TO LT. COMMANDER LA FORGE, THE JUULETIAN SHIP IS POWERED BY A MATTER/ANTIMATTER REACTION ASSEMBLY SIMILAR TO OURS.
IN FACT, SIR...

...ENERGY IS RELEASED INTO THE ORE CHAMBER ON THE JUULETIAN SHIP.
THE LIKELIHOOD IS THAT THE SHIP IS A WEAPON...
...JUST AS DOROSSH HAS SAID.

DAMN IT.
I THOUGHT WE WERE ALL LEVELING WITH EACH OTHER, BUT—
—MORE LIES. I DON'T KNOW.
AND WHAT DOES IT MATTER, WITH WORF CAPTURED?

WHAT DOES IT MATTER TO HIM WHAT THE SURVEILLANCE SHIP DOES?
WE SHOULD SEND SOMEONE DOWN TO FIND HIM, NOT WORRY ABOUT THIS CIVIL WAR.
PERHAPS, COMMANDER...

...BUT IF WE PROVE THAT THE SHIP DID KILL ELDER KALKASS—
—BY EXAMING THE RESEARCH SITE AT THESE COORDINATES—
—THE DOROSSHIANS WOULD HAVE TO SET LT. WORF FREE.

I DON'T KNOW, DATA. I DOUBT THE DOROSSHIANS EVER FEEL THAT THEY HAVE TO DO ANYTHING.
FROM WHAT I'VE SEEN, THEY'RE LITTLE MORE THAN—
MR. DATA, COMMANDER— DOROSSH IS HAILING US.

ON SCREEN.

SKKKAPTAIN PICARD, ARE YOU A DEAD MAN? ARE YOU A GHOST?
YOU FLOAT, SILENT, IN THE SKY, DOING NOTHING.
YOU HAVE NOT MOVED THE GUN-SHIP, CAPTAIN. YOU HAVE NOT GIVEN US THE JUULETIAN LEADERS.

AND WE SHALL NOT, WORIKK.
AS I TOLD YOU, THE FEDERATION AND THE ENTERPRISE DO NOT RESPOND TO THREATS.
VERY WELL.
YOU TOY WITH YOUR ASSASSIN'S LIFE, CAPTAIN.

WITH EVERY MOMENT YOU SIT THERE, STALLING, TERRIFIED TO MAKE A DECISION, YOUR "WARRIOR" TAKES THE LAST FEW STEPS INTO HIS GRAVE.
AND WHAT ASSURANCE DO I HAVE THAT HE IS NOT DEAD ALREADY?

HAH. WARRIORS OF DOROSSH! LET OUR ENEMIES SEE THEIR FAILED KILLER!
LET THEM SEE WHAT HE IS NOW!

HA HA HA HA HA
HERE HE IS, CAPTAIN.
REDUCED TO...
...A SHADOW.
IS WHAT YOU SEE BEFORE YOU STILL WHAT YOU CALL A WARRIOR?

WORIKK, I SEE A WARRIOR WHO HAS FOUGHT AGAINST IMPOSSIBLE ODDS.
I SEE A WARRIOR WHO HAS HAD HIS STRENGTH STRIPPED FROM HIM.
I SEE A WARRIOR OF GREAT VIRTUE WHO FEARS IF HE IS EXECUTED THAT HE WILL NOT BE FOUND WORTHY IN HIS FINAL JUDGMENT.

BUT HE SHOULD KNOW:

IF IT TAKES EVERYTHING THIS CREW AND THIS SHIP HAS TO GIVE, AND ALL THE TIME ANY OF US HAS LEFT—
—HE WILL ENTER HIS WARRIOR HEAVEN.

BAH!
PRETTY WORDS FROM THE WEAK AND TREACHEROUS.
THEY SIGNIFY ABSOLUTELY NOTH—
...WISHES TO DWELL IN A WARRIOR HEAVEN...
...WARRIOR...
...STOVOKOR...
...HIS DEDICATION...
COULD HE BE...
WHAT ARE YOU FOOLS TALKING ABOUT?

WORIKK—YOUR WARS AGAINST JUULET HAVE BEEN LONG AND HARD-FOUGHT. THERE IS MUCH CAUSE FOR COMPLAINT ON *BOTH* SIDES.
BUT LIEUTENANT WORF IS *BLAMELESS.*

WE DO NOT KNOW WHO, IF ANYONE, KILLED YOUR FATHER. AND THE PUNISHMENT OF THE INNOCENT, WORIKK—
—IT WILL NOT *STAND.*

YOUR DEMANDS WILL *NOT* BE MET. YOUR BULLYING WILL *NOT* BE REWARDED. YOU WILL NOT—
BAH.
TAKT

THESE FOOLS...
...AND THEIR LIES...
THEY...
...THEY WILL SEE...

THEY WILL SEE WHEN THEIR OFFICER LIES DEAD...
...THEY SHOULD NOT UNDERESTIMATE US.
YOU HEAR, MURDERER? YOUR CAPTAIN HAS SIGNED YOUR DEATH WARRANT!

THANK YOU, MY CAPTAIN.

TYPICAL.
ENSIGN, SCAN BACK 10 SECONDS.

TYPICAL OF THIS COUNTRY. THEY DON'T CARE WHO MURDERED KALKASS...
...THEY DON'T CARE ABOUT JUSTICE OR A PEACEFUL SOCIETY.
THEY JUST WANT POWER AND REVENGE AND—
PERHAPS WORIKK DOES, NUMBER ONE...

...BUT THE FACES OF THE OTHER WARRIORS SAY DIFFERENTLY.

WORIKK HAS FOOLED THEM. USING THEIR SENSE OF HONOR, SHE'S MADE THEM BELIEVE WORF IS THE KILLER.
WE KNOW AT LEAST THAT ISN'T TRUE.

I BELIEVE THAT IF WE CAN PRODUCE SOME EVIDENCE THAT WORF IS INNOCENT, THE OUTCRY FROM THESE WARRIORS WILL OVERWHELM EVEN WORIKK.
HM.
RIKER TO LA FORGE.

MEET ME IN TRANSPORTER ROOM 3, GEORDI.

WE'VE GOT SOMETHING TO PROVE.

OKAY, UUL, YOU'VE ALREADY STATED THAT TWO OF THE GHOSTS YOU'VE SEEN WERE CAPTAIN PICARD AND ELDER KALKASS OF DOROSSH.
NOW, WHO ELSE? WHO ELSE HAUNTS YOU?

-SIGH-
COME ON, UUL. THIS SILENCE ISN'T HELPING. WHY WON'T YOU TALK TO US?
WE'RE TRYING TO HELP YOU.

UUL, IF YOU FEEL LIKE SAYING SOMETHING WOULD PUT YOUR LIFE IN DANGER, THE FEDERATION CAN PROTECT YOU.
WE NEED TO GET SOME ANSWERS... IN ORDER TO HELP BOTH YOU AND THE GHOSTS.
BEVERLY—

—HAVE YOU SEEN HOW EXTENSIVE DATA'S REPORT ON JUULET IS?
SO MANY TOPICS—SO COMPLETE.
UH...
...NO, SORRY DEANNA, I HAVEN'T.

THIS IS IMPORTANT. CAPTAIN PICARD COULD BE AT RISK HERE, BUT UUL WON'T GIVE ANY MORE INFORMATION.
WE'VE TAKEN AWAY THE GHOSTS' VOICES THAT WERE DISTRACTING HIM...

...BUT NOW IT'S FEAR THAT'S KEEPING HIM QUIET.
UUL, IF YOU WOULD JUST TELL US WHO THESE GHOSTS ARE, WE COULD—
OH, YOU SHOULD SEE THIS, TOO, UUL. WHAT AN AMAZING COUNTRY YOU HAVE. ALL THE ARCHITECTURE. ALL THE SCIENCE.

ALL THE PEOPLE.

KEER EVERUUD.
EVERUUD KEER
KNOWN RELATIVES: **UUL EVERUUD,** HUSBAND.

VOCATION: GEOLOGIC RESEARCHER. ACCOMPLISHMENTS: REFINED ORE OUTPUT INTO DIRECTIONAL ENERGY STREAMS; RECIPIENT OF MUUR JUUSTAT PRIZE FOR PHYSICS.
CAUSE OF DEATH: UNKNOWN.

SO, UUL—WE THOUGHT YOU WERE A **BACHELOR.**
HH

WH-WHY ARE YOU D-DOING THIS?
WHY ARE YOU TORTURING ME WITH HER **FACE**?
WHY C-CAN'T YOU JUST LET ME **FORGET?**

SHE'S ONE OF YOUR GHOSTS, ISN'T SHE, UUL?
A LITTLE ACCIDENT WITH THE ORE YEARS AGO...
...AND NOW SHE'S **HERE,** TALKING TO YOU. **HAUNTING** YOU. BUT THIS ISN'T **GUILT,** UUL...

...IT'S **REAL.** SHE'S REAL. SHE'S TRAPPED.
AND IF YOU **TALK** TO US, YOU CAN **HELP** HER.
MAYBE EVEN BRING HER **BACK.**
PLEASE, UUL—TELL US HER **STORY.**

"W-WE MET AT THE ORE RESEARCH CENTER UP IN THE GOVERNMENT BUILDING.
"PEOPLE BEFORE US HAD DISCOVERED THE ORE HAD PECULIAR PROPERTIES—WE WERE MEANT TO HARNESS THEM.

"OUR DISCOVERIES CAME FAST, AND WERE WELL RECEIVED. EVERY DAY WE FOUND NEW USES FOR THE ORE."
OKAY, GEORDI—
—LET'S BYPASS THE LOCK AND GET IN THERE.
"EVEN OUR FIRST **DISASTER** WAS LUCKY. NO ONE WAS INJURED WHEN I SPLIT A CHUNK OF ORE AND RELEASED A MASSIVE AMOUNT OF ZOOR ENERGY.

"IT SEEMED THAT WE—AND OUR LAB—WERE BLESSED. WE MADE DISCOVERY AFTER DISCOVERY—"
ALMOST GOT IT, COMMANDER.

"—AND THE LAB ITSELF WAS A REPOSITORY OF OUR NATION'S MOST VALUABLE SCIENTIFIC SECRETS."
WHAT...?

I DON'T GET IT.
THESE ARE DATA'S EXACT COORDINATES. THERE'S NOTHING *HERE.*
"BUT THEN KEER DIED."

THEN I KILLED HER.
WE HAD FOUND ONE MORE PROPERTY OF THE ORE.

DAMN IT.
ENTERPRISE. TWO TO BEAM UP.
"THE ENERGY I HAD RELEASED IN THE ACCIDENT DIDN'T DISSIPATE AS I THOUGHT. IT DISAPPEARED, BUT...

"WHEN KEER WAS WORKING LATE ONE NIGHT, AS I HAD BEEN...
EEEEEEEEEEEE
"...AT THE SAME TIME OF NIGHT THAT I HAD MADE MY ERROR...
"...SOMETHING SWEPT THROUGH..."

"...AND SHE WAS GONE."

WE CALLED IT "ORE PROPERTY 671: CORE-RELATIVE PERSISTENCE."
THEY WANTED TO NAME IT AFTER KEER, BUT I WOULDN'T LET THEM...

WAIT—
—SO THE ENERGY ORBITS THE PLANET? IT JUST KEEPS COMING AROUND AT THE SAME HEIGHT AS WHERE IT WAS RELEASED?
NO, NO.

WE ORBIT THE PLANET. THE PLANET TURNS, AND WE TURN WITH IT. THE ENERGY JUST STAYS. SAME HEIGHT, SAME BEARING FROM THE CORE.
MAKING THAT EXACT RING AROUND THE PLANET UNLIVABLE.

IT'S LIKE THE CORE IS PUNISHING US FOR TAKING PART OF IT AWAY.
ITS ENERGY JUST STAYS, LURKING.
IT KILLED MY WIFE...
...IT KILLED MY CREW...

"...NOW IT'LL KILL ME."
BEE BOOP
COME.

CAPTAIN.
THERE IS NOTHING AT THE SITE THAT DATA GAVE US. WE WERE UNABLE TO UNCOVER ANY EVIDENCE TO HELP WORF.
RECOMMEND WE SEND AN AWAY TEAM TO THE SURFACE AND USE TRICORDERS TO LOCATE HIM.

I CAN HAVE A TEAM TOGETHER IN TEN MINUTES.
MM. IT'S RISKY, NUMBER ONE. I HAD HOPED FOR AN ELEGANT SOLUTION—JUST PLUCK HIM OUT OF THERE.

AND WE'RE STILL PUSHING FOR A DIPLOMATIC SOLUTION...
I DO STILL FEEL THE DOROSSHIANS CAN BE REASONED WITH IF—

ERRT ERRT
RED ALERT, WHAT—?

ENSIGN— WHAT'S GOING ON?
MISSILES, SIR. DOROSSH HAS LAUNCHED A FULL BATTERY OF MISSILES.
RIGHT IN FRONT OF US, COMMANDER. BEARING 005, MARK 330.
UNBELIEVABLE.
SHIELDS UP.
WHERE ARE THEY, ENSIGN?

THEY ARE AN ANCIENT DESIGN, CAPTAIN.
OUR SHIELDS CAN DEFLECT DOZENS OF THEM WITH LITTLE TO NO LOSS.
BUT THERE ARE HUNDREDS—AND THEY'RE NOT AIMED AT US.

WHAT? THEN WHAT ARE THEY—
THEY'RE AIMED AT THE JUULETIAN SHIP UNDER US, SIR—

SOUNDS LIKE WORIKK RAN OUT OF **PATIENCE.**
TACTICAL— EXTEND SHIELDS OVER THE JUULETIAN SHIP.
HELM—
—COVER THEM WITH OUR SAUCER. BEARING 000, MARK 270.

MANEUVER COMPLETED.

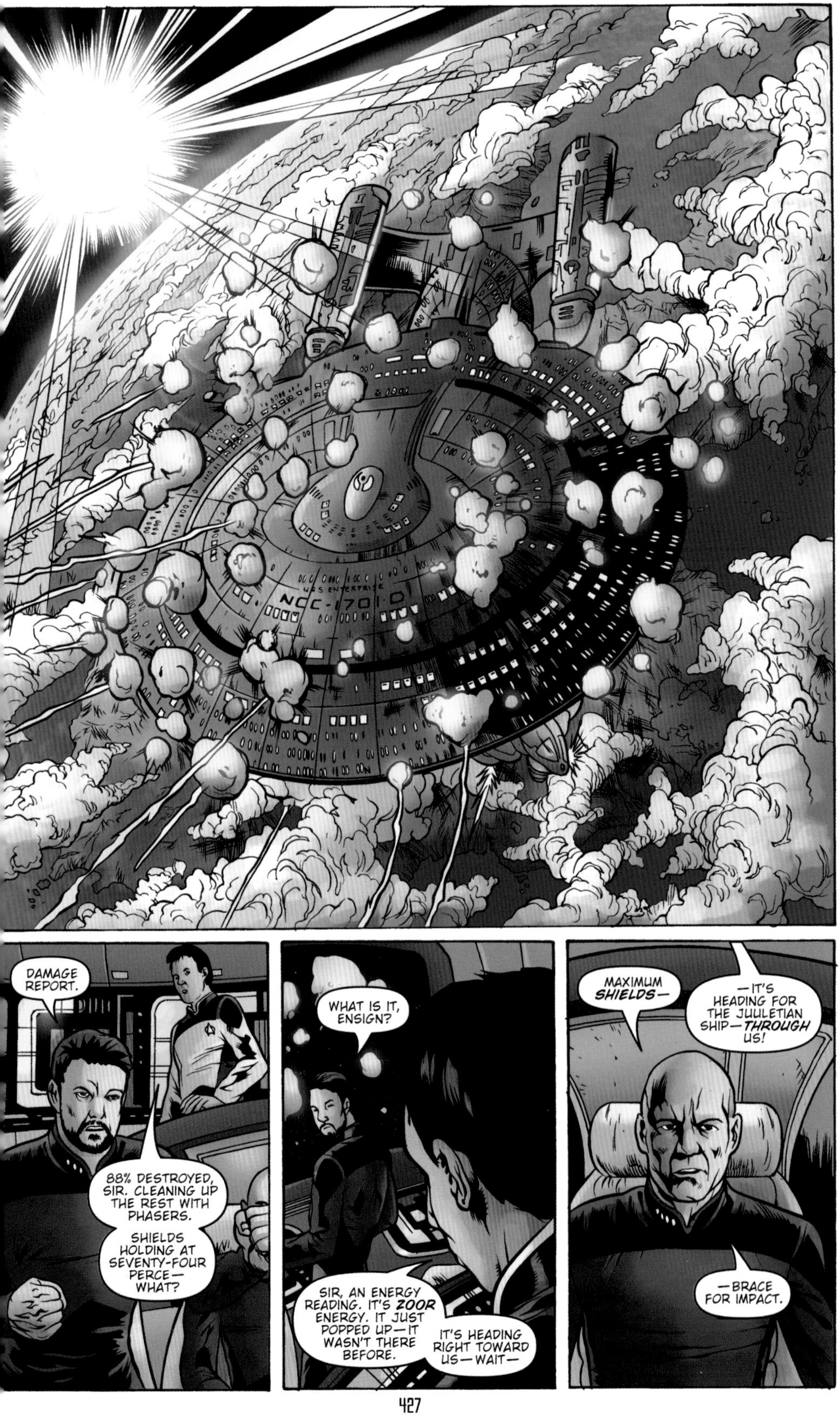

DAMAGE REPORT.
88% DESTROYED, SIR. CLEANING UP THE REST WITH PHASERS.
SHIELDS HOLDING AT SEVENTY-FOUR PERCE— WHAT?

WHAT IS IT, ENSIGN?
SIR, AN ENERGY READING. IT'S ZOOR ENERGY. IT JUST POPPED UP—IT WASN'T THERE BEFORE.
IT'S HEADING RIGHT TOWARD US—WAIT—

—IT'S HEADING FOR THE JUULETIAN SHIP—THROUGH US!
MAXIMUM SHIELDS—
—BRACE FOR IMPACT.

EEEEEEEEEEEEEE

EEEEEEOOOOOO

OOOOOOO
DAMAGE REPORT!
CAPTAIN, RECOMMEND WE—

CAPTAIN?

FIRST OFFICER'S LOG, STARDATE 44571.6.

CAPTAIN PICARD IS MISSING FOLLOWING A DEFENSIVE MANEUVER THAT PLACED THE BRIDGE OF THE *ENTERPRISE* IN THE PATH OF A ***ZOOR ENERGY CLOUD***, AN UNANTICIPATED AFTER-EFFECT OF AN EARLIER DISASTER.

WITH THE ***MISSILE ATTACK*** WHICH PROMPTED THE DEFENSIVE MANEUVER ***OVER***, AND OUR CHIEF OF ENGINEERING'S HYPOTHESIS THAT THE CAPTAIN IS LIKELY ***UNHARMED***, I HAVE PUT THE SHIP ON ***YELLOW ALERT*** UNTIL WE DETERMINE THE BEST STRATEGY FOR FINDING HIM.

WHAT ABOUT THE CLOUD? IS IT STILL INTACT?
IS IT STILL ON ITS PATH AROUND THE PLANET?

FROM OUR PERSPECTIVE, YES, SIR. HOWEVER, THE CLOUD IS ACTUALLY STATIONARY RELATIVE TO THE PLANET'S CORE.
RATHER, WE HAVE CONTINUED ON OUR ORBITAL PATH AND LEFT IT BEHIND.
ALL RIGHT, HOW LONG UNTIL WE ENCOUNTER IT AGAIN?

ONE FULL DAY, SIR. THIRTY-SIX OF THEIR HOURS, THIRTY POINT TWO SIX OF OURS.
RECOMMEND WE MOVE THE ENTERPRISE AND THE JUULETIANS' SHIP TO A HIGHER ORBIT IN ADVANCE OF THAT TIME.

AGREED. HELM, REORIENT US AND INCREASE IMPULSE BY TEN PERCENT.
TACTICAL.
YES, SIR.
HAIL THE JUULETIAN SHIP. I WANT TO TALK WITH THEM.

LA FORGE HERE, COMMANDER. GO AHEAD.
GEORDI, I THOUGHT WE'D TUNED OUR SENSORS.
WHY COULDN'T WE DETECT THAT ENERGY CLOUD UNTIL IT WAS TOO LATE?

COMMANDER, I'M SORRY. WE HAD BEEN DAMPENING THE ZOOR ENERGY ABOARD THE SHIP SO THAT DR. CRUSHER'S PATIENT COULD TALK WITH US.
HE'S OVERWHELMED WITH VISIONS OF GHOSTS OTHERWISE.

RIGHT. GHOSTS THAT INCLUDE THE CAPTAIN.
DO NOT REENGAGE THAT DAMPENER. WE NEED INFORMATION ON WHERE THESE GHOSTS ARE.
COMMANDER, I HAVE THE JUULETIAN SHIP ON SUBSPACE.

GOOD. ON SCREEN.
COMMANDER! A CLOSE CALL WITH THAT ENERGY CLOUD. I DEARLY HOPE THAT ALL OF YOUR CREW ARE—
SKIP THE PLEASANTRIES, DEERON.

FIRST, ARE ALL YOUR PEOPLE UNHARMED?
THEY ARE, THANK YOU. WE ANTICIPATED THE ENERGY CLOUD AND MOVED TO THE PERIPHERY OF THE SHIP.
AND WE ARE NOW IN THE PROCESS OF MOVING WITH YOU TO A HIGHER ORBIT.
IF THERE'S ANYTHING WE CAN DO FOR YOU, COMMANDER, PLEASE—

DEERON...
...YOU HAVE DONE ENOUGH. I NOW CONSIDER YOUR LIES AND EVASIONS A PERSONAL INSULT.
B-BUT PERHAPS IF I COULD SPEAK WITH CAPTAIN PICARD...

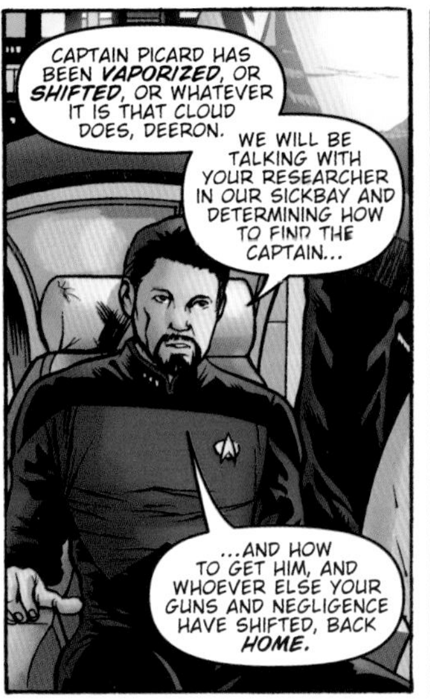
CAPTAIN PICARD HAS BEEN VAPORIZED, OR SHIFTED, OR WHATEVER IT IS THAT CLOUD DOES, DEERON.
WE WILL BE TALKING WITH YOUR RESEARCHER IN OUR SICKBAY AND DETERMINING HOW TO FIND THE CAPTAIN...
...AND HOW TO GET HIM, AND WHOEVER ELSE YOUR GUNS AND NEGLIGENCE HAVE SHIFTED, BACK HOME.

YOUR HELP IS NO LONGER NEEDED, YOUR COUNTRY IS NO LONGER A PART OF THIS MISSION.
ONLY THE FACT THAT YOUR RIVAL COUNTRY SHOT MISSILES AT US SAVES YOU FROM A FULLER EXPRESSION OF OUR ANGER.
ENTERPRISE OUT.

TACTICAL —HAIL DOROSSH.
YES, SIR.
BRIDGE TO DR. CRUSHER.
CRUSHER HERE.

WITHOUT GEORDI'S DAMPENER ENGAGED, YOUR PATIENT MUST BE SEEING GHOSTS AGAIN.
YES, SIR, HE'S VERY UPSET.
NO-NO—
ALL THE GHOSTS SEEM TO BE SPEAKING TO HIM AT ONCE.

PLEASE, SIR, RECOMMEND WE REENGAGE THE DAMPENER SO HE CAN CALM DOWN.
NEGATIVE, DOCTOR, WE NEED HIM TO HEAR WHAT THEY ARE SAYING.
IF THE CAPTAIN'S ONE OF THEM, HE WILL TRY AND COMMUNICATE WITH US.
IS COUNSELOR TROI THERE WITH YOU?

I'M HERE, WILL.
DEANNA, I NEED YOU TO REALLY LISTEN TO THE PATIENT—CUT THROUGH ALL THE NOISE AND FIND OUT WHAT HE'S HEARING.
I KNOW IT WON'T BE EASY. THERE'S A LOT TO SIFT THROUGH, BUT WE HAVE TO FIND THE CAPTAIN.

COMMANDER, I HAVE WORIKK FROM DOROSSH ON SUBSPACE.
ONE MOMENT.
DEANNA—THE CAPTAIN NEEDS US, BUT NOT AS BADLY AS WE NEED HIM.

DOROSSH WILL NOT LISTEN TO REASON. WE HAVE TO FIND KALKASS AND THE OTHER VICTIMS OF THIS ENERGY.
WE CAN ONLY DO THIS BY FINDING THE CAPTAIN...

"...WHO I ASSUME HAS BEEN SENT TO THE SAME PLACE AS THE OTHERS."
WHAT—?

WHERE THE HELL?

PICARD TO ENTERPRISE.
COME IN, ENTERPRISE.

PICARD TO—

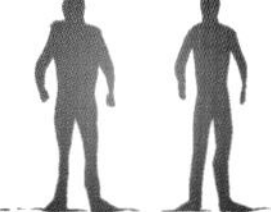

"SO, THIS IS HOW YOU OPEN NEGOTIATIONS?"

WITH A MISSILE ATTACK, WORIKK?

FIRST YOU ARREST OUR OFFICER AND SENTENCE HIM TO DEATH WITHOUT EVIDENCE OR CAUSE.
AND NOW YOU FIRE ON US, UNPROVOKED BY ANY ACTION OF OURS.
YOU MAY BE A POWERFUL COUNTRY ON YOUR PLANET, WORIKK...
...BUT HAVE YOU ANY IDEA WHOM THIS SHIP REPRESENTS?

I DO, FEDERATION.
YOU REPRESENT A COLLECTION OF LIARS, FOOLS, AND HANDWRINGERS WHO SIT MANY LIFETIMES AWAY FROM US, AND AFFECT OUR FORTUNES NOT ONE BIT.
AND YOU SHOULD KNOW AS WELL AS ANYONE THAT WE WERE PROVOKED BY YOUR INACTION.
THE BUTCHERS FROM JUULET ARE NOT DELIVERED TO US, AND THEIR WEAPON STILL HANGS ABOVE US IN THE SKY.

BE IT YOU OR YOUR CAPTAIN, OR YOUR CAPTAIN'S CAPTAIN, I KNOW WHAT YOU REPRESENT, FEDERATION.
WORDS.
TALK, AND LIES.

ALL TALK AND NO ACTION.
WORIKK, THAT'S ENOUGH.

NOW IS THE TIME WHEN YOU NEED TO LISTEN TO ME. IGNORE THE LIEUTENANTS THAT FLANK YOU.
YOU AND I MUST SPEAK AS LEADERS.

CAPTAIN PICARD IS MISSING, A VICTIM OF THE ENERGY THAT WE BELIEVE ALSO CAUSED YOUR FATHER'S DISAPPEARANCE.
TWO GREAT MEN ARE **GONE,** WORIKK...

...AND SO IT IS YOU AND I WHO ARE NOW IN CHARGE.
WE MUST SPEAK QUICKLY AND UNDERSTAND WELL, FOR WE HAVE LIVES IN OUR HANDS.

THERE IS A SOLUTION HERE, WORIKK.
WE ARE CLOSE TO IT.

THE FEDERATION WILL NOT BOW TO THREATS.
NOT **EVER.**
BUT GOODWILL GESTURES ON YOUR PART WILL BE TAKEN INTO CONSIDERATION WHEN WE DETERMINE HOW THIS PLANET SHALL FARE IN THE FEDERATION'S EYES.

GOODWILL GESTURES LIKE FREEING LT. WORF.
HA!
BEFORE YOU DO YOUR UNNAMED GOOD TURN FOR US? OH, FEDERATION...

...HOW NAIVE YOU MUST THINK WE ARE, HERE IN DOROSSH!
DO YOU WISH ME TO BE **ASSASSINATED** AS WELL, AFTER I DEMONSTRATE SUCH WEAKNESS?
I DO NOT, WORIKK.
I HAVE NO DESIRE TO SEE YOU LOSE FACE...

...BUT I MUST HAVE MY OFFICER BACK. AND I MUST NOT SACRIFICE ANY MORE LIVES TO DO IT.
THERE WILL BE NO **TRADE.** THERE IS ONLY A SHOW OF GOODWILL.
IT IS HOW CIVILIZED BEINGS **BEHAVE.**

HMH. FOR A **MOMENT,** I THOUGHT YOU WERE DIFFERENT, RIKER.
A MAN OF *ACTION,* WITH A DESIRE TO **WIN.**
WE HAVE NO NEED OF YOUR ***"CIVILIZATION,"*** RIKER...

"...NONE OF MY PEOPLE EVER HAVE."
PICARD!
WHAT IS THE MEANING OF THIS?!

SUPREME ELDER KALKASS! WHAT—
THIS FEDERATION SORCERY! HAVE YOU BROUGHT ME TO YOUR SHIP TO—TO LIVE IN A FALSE REALITY?
RECREATING THE DEAD TO FOOL ME INTO REVEALING THE SECRETS OF DOROSSH?!
KALKASS...

GET AWAY FROM ME, CREATURE!
YOUR VERY PRESENCE INSULTS THE MEMORY OF ELDER MMEMON!
B-BUT—
I-IT'S ME, KALKASS!

IT'S ME, MMEMON! KALKASS, WHERE ARE WE?
WHERE HAS MY THRONE ROOM GONE?
NO—GET AWAY—
—THIS CANNOT BE!
YOU MUST BE A SPIRIT!

KALKASS, WH-WHAT IS THIS PLACE?
A-AND YOU—WHY DO YOU LOOK SO OLD, KALKASS?
OH NO—NO—B-BY OUR ANCESTORS, KALKASS...
...A-AM I DEAD?

YES! YES, YOU DIED SIX QUADS AGO, MMEMON!
KILLED BY THE TREACHEROUS JUULETIANS!
WE MOURNED AT YOUR FUNERAL!
YOU ARE GONE, MMEMON! YOU ARE...

NO. WE ARE ALL HERE.
WE ARE ALL DEAD.
PICARD...
...TELL ME THIS ISN'T SO. TELL ME YOU HAVE BROUGHT US ALL TO YOUR SHIP AND—

NO.
NO, KALKASS, I CANNOT TELL YOU IT WAS THAT.
AS FOR BEING DEAD...

...I DON'T KNOW.
I HAVE SEEN MUCH IN MY TRAVELS. BUT NOTHING BEYOND THE DEATH OF THE BODY.
AND PERHAPS...

...PERHAPS THIS IS WHAT DEATH IS.
NOTHINGNESS. FOREVER.

ALL ALONE.

NO. NO, WE ARE NOT DEAD, KALKASS.

I'M SORRY. A MOMENTARY LAPSE.
WE ARE NOT DEAD? AND WE ARE NOT ON YOUR SHIP?
WHERE ARE WE, PICARD? TELL ME IF YOU KNOW!

I BELIEVE WE HAVE SHIFTED, KALKASS, INTO ANOTHER SPACE.
TO TELL YOU MORE IS OUTSIDE MY AREA OF EXPERTISE. FOR THE DETAILS...

"...YOU'LL HAVE TO ASK **THEM.**"
S-SO IT'S **TRUE.**
THE SPACE **EXISTS.**
WE'VE ALL READ THE THEORIES, BUT I NEVER—
MURDERERS!

WHAT—?
OH, NO...
SO, BUTCHERS, THE DEAD HAVE FOUND YOU, EH?

N-NO, AH... I AM RESEARCHER **BEEL KOSEED.**
I-I'M AS CONFUSED AS YOU—WHAT IS THIS PLACE—WHAT—
NO.

STOP YOUR **LYING,** JUULETIAN.
YOUR **ZOOR ENERGY** FROM YOUR **GUN** HAS BROUGHT US ALL HERE.
WE **KNOW.**

YOU HAVE SILENCED US, BUT NOW YOU ARE SILENT TOO, VILLAIN.
N-NOW—
AND WHO WILL COMPLAIN IN THIS PLACE IF YOU WERE TO BE **GONE? HMM?**
NO—
WHO WOULD CARE IF YOU WERE **DEAD,** MURDERER?

OH, IS THAT HOW IT IS, THEN?
THE SAVAGES HAVE TO CRUSH THE FORCE FOR PEACE THAT THEY DON'T *UNDERSTAND?*
PEACE?!

YOU HAVE *CRIPPLED* OUR GOVERNMENT!
NEARLY TURNED OUR NATION INTO A LEADERLESS *WASTELAND!*
WHAT OF IT?

IT'S JUST A PITY WE DIDN'T *FINISH* THE JOB, YOU *MONSTERS!*
STOP IT!
YOU DARE CALL *US* MONSTERS, YOU *MASS MURDERERS?*
STOP IT!

ALL OF YOU—
—BE SILENT!

THERE IS NOTHING MORE MEANINGLESS THAN *NATIONALISM* FROM THOSE WITH NO *NATION.*
WE ARE ALL *PRISONERS* HERE, MY FRIENDS. AND RIGHT NOW...
...THAT IS *ALL* WE ARE.

YES—
PRISONERS OF THESE JUULETIAN VILLAINS.
ISN'T THAT RIGHT?
NO!
WE ARE HERE TOO—THIS ISN'T OUR PRISON.
WE DON'T KNOW WHAT THIS PLACE IS!

THAT'S CORRECT. NO ONE IS IN CONTROL OF THIS SPACE. NONE OF US ARE GUARDS.
WE SHARE THE SAME IMMEDIATE GOALS.
SO STOP FIGHTING AND LET'S FIGURE OUT OUR SITUATION.

WE HAVE ALL ARRIVED HERE SIMULTANEOUSLY, DESPITE THE FACT THAT WE DEPARTED—
OR WERE ATTACKED—
YES, OR WERE ATTACKED, AT VERY DIFFERENT TIMES.

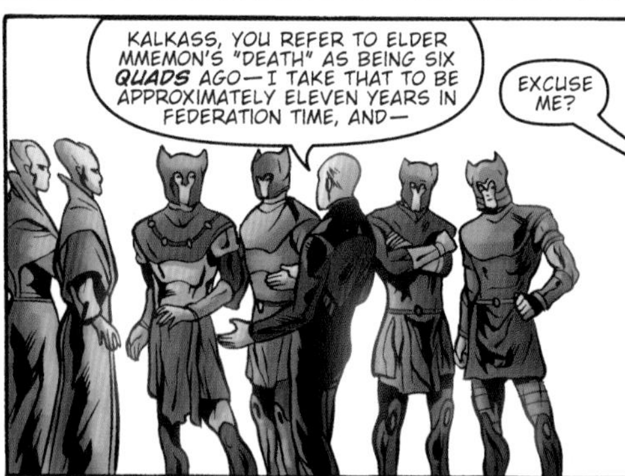
KALKASS, YOU REFER TO ELDER MMEMON'S "DEATH" AS BEING SIX QUADS AGO—I TAKE THAT TO BE APPROXIMATELY ELEVEN YEARS IN FEDERATION TIME, AND—
EXCUSE ME?

I-I DON'T KNOW WHERE I AM.
WHAT IS... P-PLEASE, CAN YOU HELP ME?

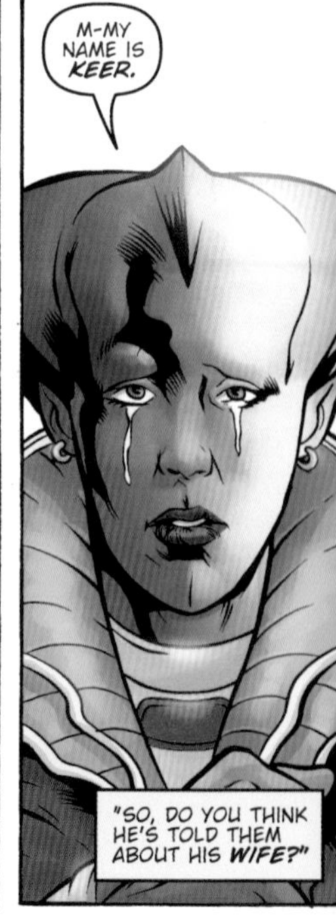
M-MY NAME IS KEER.
"SO, DO YOU THINK HE'S TOLD THEM ABOUT HIS WIFE?"

IF HE HASN'T YET, HE ALMOST CERTAINLY WILL SOON. THEY HAVE BEEN ATTENDING TO HIM NONSTOP SINCE THE ACCIDENT.
HE'S SURE TO CONFIDE IN ONE OF THEM EVENTUALLY, DESPITE OUR WARNING.
-SIGH-
WHAT IS IT, DEERON?

TERRIBLE TIMING. ANOTHER FEW DAYS AND WE WOULD HAVE CLEANED UP THIS MESS OURSELVES.
BUT THE FEDERATION HAD TO SHOW UP, AND KEJAAL IS SO INTENT ON JOINING THEM.
WITH ALL OF THE WARLORDS OUT OF THE WAY, WE DON'T NEED THE FEDERATION'S TECHNOLOGY...

"...BUT WITH THE FEDERATION WATCHING OVER US, WE HAVE TO LIVE BY THEIR RULES.
"WE'RE TOO YOUNG A COUNTRY TO DO EVERYTHING EXACTLY RIGHT. A FEW QUADS DOWN THE LINE AND OUR ETHICAL SLIPS WILL BE FORGOTTEN...
"...BUT IF UUL TELLS THEM EVERYTHING HE KNOWS, THERE'S NO SKIPPING AHEAD."

TECHNICIAN DINAAN, HAVE YOU GOT THE TRACKING CHIP'S BEARING?
YES, DEERON, AND THE FEEDBACK INDICATES IT'S STILL IN HIS HAND.
OKAY, THEN...

"...GOODBYE, UUL."
I'VE BEEN GONE...
...H-HOW LONG?

TWELVE **QUADS**, KEER. OVER TWENTY YEARS BY THE **FEDERATION'S** CALENDAR. I'M SORRY—THIS MUST COME AS A **SHOCK.**
—BUT MAYBE—MAYBE Y-YOU'VE ALL COME **BACK** TO **MY** TIME. **O-OR** WE'RE ALL COMPLETELY **DETACHED** FROM TIME.
W-WE CAN'T **KNOW**, CAN WE?
O-OUR RESEARCH IS SO INCOMPLETE O-ON THE ORE.

OH.
OH, **NO.**
UUL—M-MY **HUSBAND**. MY HUSBAND—I-IS HE...
...I-IS HE STILL **ALIVE?**

YES.
HE IS.
OHH... THANK THE **C-CORE...**
BUT, KEER...

...UUL IS THE REASON WE BELIEVE WE'RE ANCHORED IN YOUR FUTURE, MY **PRESENT.**
UUL HAS BEEN INJURED, KEER, BY THE SAME ENERGY THAT BROUGHT US HERE.

HE LIES IN MY SHIP'S SICK BAY—
—WHERE HE IS HAUNTED BY VISIONS OF **GHOSTS.**
GHOSTS?

YES, THE GHOSTS ARE **US,** KEER.
ALL OF US.

I BELIEVE HE IS **STUCK,** KEER, BETWEEN THIS WORLD AND OURS.
AND HE IS ANCHORING THEM TOGETHER.

WE NEED TO FIND HIM—OR THE PART OF HIM THAT IS IN THIS SPACE.
COMMUNICATION WITH HIM IS OUR WAY **OUT,** BACK TO THE **REAL** WORLD.
IF WE—
PICARD!

WHY DO YOU SPEND SO MUCH TIME MOLLYCODDLING THIS **ASSASSIN** FROM OUR GREAT ENEMY? WE HAVE TO RETURN TO OUR BELOVED DOROSSH—WITH **ME** GONE, WHO **KNOWS** WHAT HAS BEFALLEN IT!
KALKASS.
THIS WOMAN HAS JUST BEEN TOLD HER HUSBAND HAS LIVED HALF HIS LIFE THINKING SHE IS **DEAD.**
SHOW SOME **RESPECT.**

AND SHE IS A SCIENTIST, KALKASS.
SHE'S NO MORE AN ASSASSIN THAN I AM.
HMH.

AS FOR WHAT HAS BEFALLEN DOROSSH, YOU ARE **CORRECT.**
WORIKK HAS SEIZED POWER AND ARRESTED OUR LT. WORF—FOR YOUR **MURDER.**

SO YES, WE DO NEED TO GET BACK. IF WORF DIES, I ASSURE YOU, AND I DO NOT SAY THIS LIGHTLY...

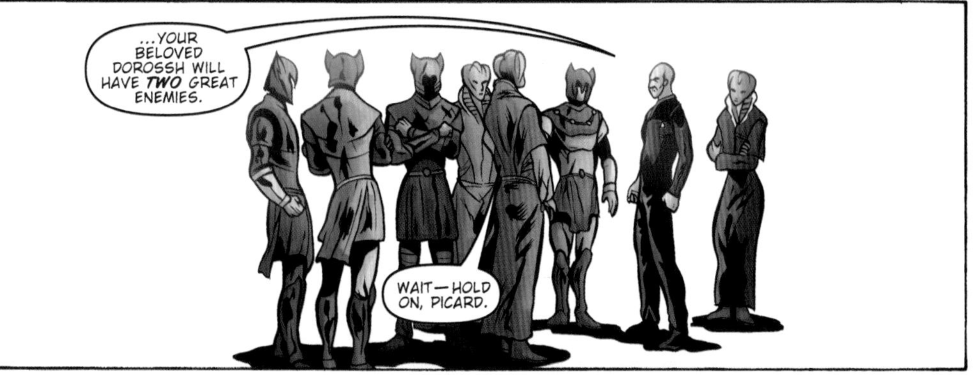
...YOUR BELOVED DOROSSH WILL HAVE **TWO** GREAT ENEMIES.
WAIT—HOLD ON, PICARD.

UUL SURVIVED THE EXPLOSION?
WELL, YES, BEEL, HE DID...
...ONLY IN THE SENSE THAT YOU DID NOT.
HE WAS MERELY INJURED IN THE BLAST—IT REMOVED AN ARM AND A LEG.
AN ARM AND A LEG THAT ARE NOW SOMEWHERE IN THIS SPACE.
ALL RIGHT. WE CAN FIND THEM MORE QUICKLY IF WE SPLIT INTO GROUPS.
STAY WITHIN SIGHT OF THE OTHER GROUPS AT ALL TIMES.
SIGNAL IF YOU FIND ANYTHING.
THANK YOU FOR WALKING WITH ME, CAPTAIN PICARD.
IT SEEMS THE ELDERS OF DOROSSH HAVE GOTTEN NO LESS TERRIFYING IN ALL THIS TIME.
OF COURSE, KEER.

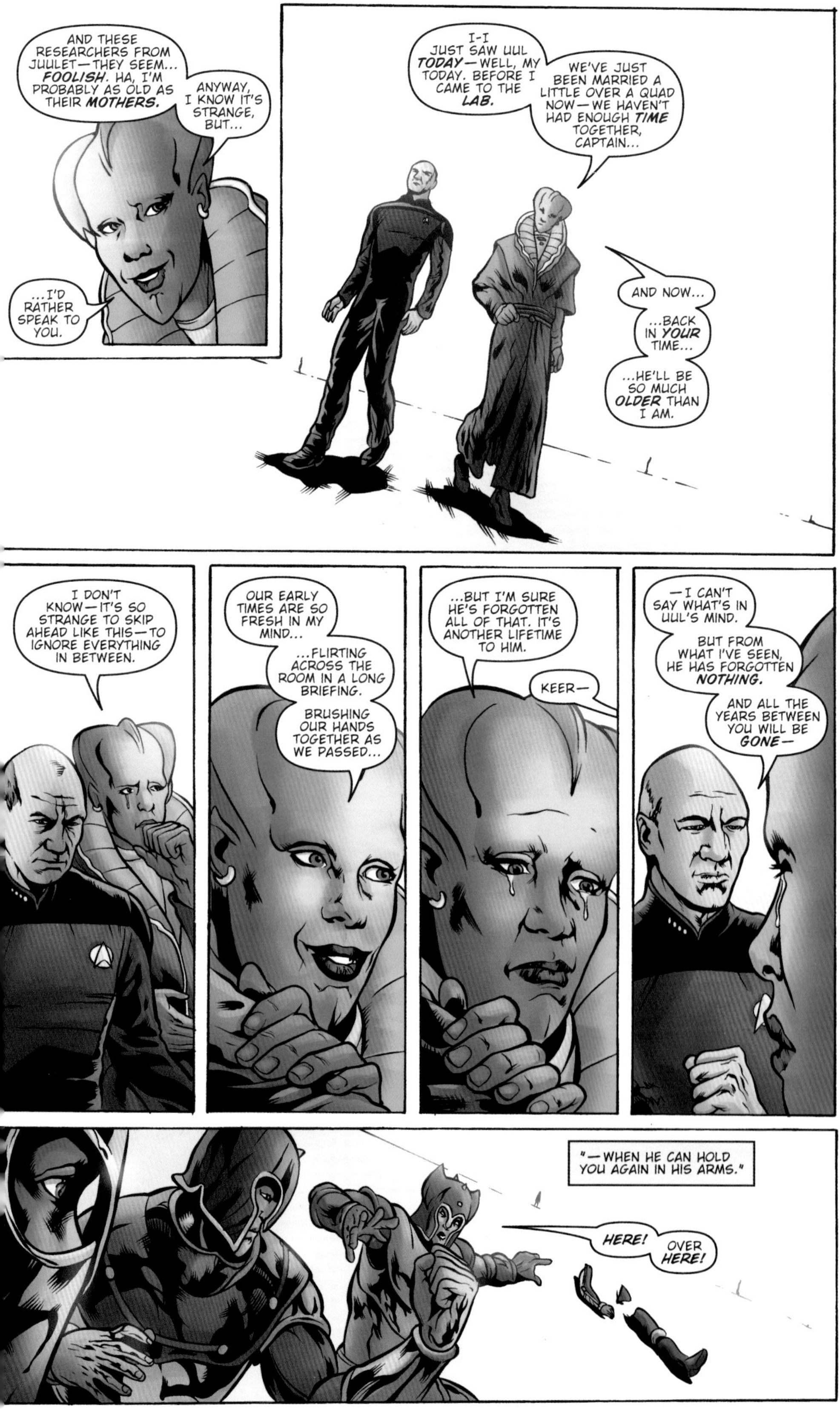

AND THESE RESEARCHERS FROM JUULET—THEY SEEM... ***FOOLISH***. HA, I'M PROBABLY AS OLD AS THEIR ***MOTHERS.***
ANYWAY, I KNOW IT'S STRANGE, BUT...
...I'D RATHER SPEAK TO YOU.

I-I JUST SAW UUL ***TODAY***—WELL, MY TODAY. BEFORE I CAME TO THE ***LAB.***
WE'VE JUST BEEN MARRIED A LITTLE OVER A QUAD NOW—WE HAVEN'T HAD ENOUGH ***TIME*** TOGETHER, CAPTAIN...
AND NOW...
...BACK IN ***YOUR*** TIME...
...HE'LL BE SO MUCH ***OLDER*** THAN I AM.

HELLO!
MURDERER! GET US OUT OF HERE!
YES! USE YOUR FOUL SORCERY TO GET US HOME!
CAPTAIN PICARD, IT'S NO USE REASONING WITH THEM...

...THESE SAVAGES DON'T UNDERSTAND THAT UUL CAN'T DO ANYTHING. THEY—
ALL RIGHT, ALL RIGHT. LET'S LET KEER SEE HER HUSBAND FOR A MOMENT.

PLEASE—LET ME THROUGH—
PLEA—

OH...
OH, UUL...

...I-IT'S WARM—IT'S ALIVE.
HE'S ALIVE—HE'S HERE WITH US.
ALL RIGHT, PICARD, NOW HOW DO WE TALK TO YOUR PEOPLE THROUGH HIM?

I SAID ONE MOMENT, BEEL.
UUL—CAN YOU FEEL THIS? WHEN I SQUEEZE YOUR HAND—
CAN YOU SQUEEZE IT B—

H-HE DID.
HE'S THERE. HE CAN FEEL ME HERE.
WE CAN TALK.

I-IT'S KEER.
SHE'S HERE.
SHE'S ALIVE.

TH-THE TALKING... ALL THE TALKING IS STILL SO CONFUSING, BUT—
B-BUT NOW SHE'S HOLDING MY HAND...
YES, I FEEL YOU CALMING DOWN, UUL...

Y-YES.
F-FOR THE F-FIRST TIME, I FEEL LIKE IT'S ALL GOING TO BE ALL R—
NNH—
UUL?!

DEANNA—HIS VITALS JUST DROPPED.
XIAN—PREPARE A HYPOSPRAY OF—
UUL?
ARE YOU ALL RIGHT?
WHAT HAPPENED?
NO—JUST A MOMENT—I FEEL HIM COMING BACK TO NORMAL.
I-I DON'T KNOW. I... UH... I JUST FELT S-S-SOMETHING HIT ME FOR A MOMENT...

...I-I DON'T KNOW WHAT IT COULD BE..

BIP
?

WHAT THE—?
ZOOR ENERGY
LA FORGE TO BRIDGE.

FOR THE LAST TIME, WORIKK, RETURN LT. WORF, OR—
HA! OR WHAT, RIKER?

YOU HAVE DEMONSTRATED ON NUMEROUS OCCASIONS WE HAVE NOTHING TO FEAR FROM THE GUTLESS FEDERATION.
REPEAT— LA FORGE TO BRIDGE.

TACTICAL— CUT AUDIO TRANSMISSION.
WHAT IS IT, GEORDI?
COMMANDER —WE'VE GOT ANOTHER ZOOR ENERGY READING.
WHAT'S THE SOURCE?

IT'S THE JUULETIANS' SHIP, SIR. IT'S A VERY WEAK BEAM—THEY PROBABLY FIGURE IT'S BELOW OUR SENSORS' THRESHOLD.
BUT IT'S AIMED AT US, SPECIFICALLY, AT SICK BAY.

THAT IS IT.
I WANT A SECURITY DETAIL TO THE BRIG.
YES, SIR.
BRIDGE TO TRANSPORTER ROOM.

O'BRIEN HERE, COMMANDER.
O'BRIEN— HOW MANY CREW MEMBERS ARE ABOARD THE JUULETIANS' SHIP?
I'M READING... THREE, SIR.

LOCK ONTO THEM AND BEAM THEM DIRECTLY TO A HOLDING CELL.
TACTICAL.
SIR.
TARGET THE SHIP.

Y-YES, SIR.
B-BUT WHAT SHALL I HAVE THE SECURITY TEAM TELL THE JUULETIANS?

LET 'EM WONDER.
FIRE.

CLAP CLAP CLAP
BRAVO, RIKER.
WHAT—?

I GUESS I WAS RIGHT ABOUT YOU ALL ALONG.
A MAN OF ACTION.

NOW, YOU'VE MET ONE OF OUR TWO CRITERIA FOR FREEING YOUR ASSASSIN WORF.
IMPOSSIBLE, YOU SAID. AND YET IT IS DONE.
TACTICAL—END TRANSMISSION.
PERHAPS IN THE END, COMMANDER—

—YOU AND I ARE NOT SO DIFFERENT—

WHAT IS HE SAYING?
USE THE KOORON MILITARY CODE, IT'S BINARY—
WHAT'S HAPPENING?
BAH. THIS WILL NEVER WORK.
NO, USE THE SIX-PART JENELUUN CODE!
JUST A MOMENT, I THINK WE'VE GOT SOMETHING—

WHAT? DID YOUR MESSAGE GO THROUGH?
WHAT IS IT, YOU FOOLISH WOMAN?
HE'S RECEIVED THE MESSAGE, I THINK, AND—

WHAT? HAS HE RESPONDED?
WHAT INFORMATION DO THEY NEED?
WHAT'S HE SAYING? IS IT IMPORTANT?

HE'S GETTING THE INFORMATION FROM THEIR TECHNICAL PEOPLE.
IT WILL TAKE A FEW MOMENTS.
AND, YES, IT'S VERY IMPORTANT.

SIGH
I'VE MISSED YOU TOO.

FIRST OFFICER'S LOG, STARDATE 44751.7.
THE SITUATION ABOVE ALLIOS IV HAS REACHED CRISIS LEVELS.
THE CURRENT WARLORD OF THE PRIMITIVE NATION OF DOROSSH, WORIKK, HAS SET A TIME FOR THE CAPTURED AND FALSELY ACCUSED LT. WORF'S EXECUTION: SUNDOWN *TONIGHT.*
ALL OF OUR DIPLOMACY HAS AMOUNTED TO NOTHING WHILE DEALING WITH A LEADER SO SHORTSIGHTED AS TO CARE NOTHING FOR CONSEQUENCES.
OUR TRACKING TECHNOLOGY HAS BEEN USELESS WHEN CONFRONTED WITH A CITY SO DENSE AND SO CHAOTIC THAT WORF COULD BE LITERALLY ANYWHERE.
ELEGANT SOLUTIONS HAVE FAILED US.
I FEEL THAT THE ANSWER LIES IN TACTICS THAT RELY LESS ON MATHEMATICS AND PROBABILITY AND MORE ON DIRECT CONTACT.
I'VE SENT A CREWMEMBER DOWN TO AGGRESSIVELY INVESTIGATE THE LIKELIEST POSSIBILITIES.
TO BRING THE *HUMAN* TOUCH.

I AM SURE CAPTAIN PICARD WOULD NOT HAVE MADE THE SAME DECISION, BUT HE IS MISSING, FOLLOWING THE *ENTERPRISE*'S ENCOUNTER WITH A CLOUD OF ENERGY, THE RESIDUE OF AN EARLIER ACCIDENT.

THE ENERGY HAS DEPOSITED HIM IN A POCKET DIMENSION, ALONG WITH A NUMBER OF OTHER VICTIMS.

OKAY, UUL, THE BEAM HAS STOPPED, YOU'RE SAFE. JUST FOCUS ON MY **VOICE.**
NOW, WHAT'S THE NEXT MESSAGE?
I-IT'S— IT'S
T-THREE SEVEN SIX NINE TWELVE FOUR ONE. TH-THEN THE NEXT S-SEQUENCE—
—FOUR TEN EIGHT FIVE ELEVEN SIX NINE.
GEORDI, ARE YOU GETTING THIS?
I'M GETTING IT DOWN, BUT IT'S NOT MAKING **SENSE.**
THESE NUMBER SEQUENCES...

UUL?
CAN YOU HEAR US?
I—
I CAN'T HEAR YOU VERY WELL.
UUL?

LOOK, I DON'T EVEN KNOW WHAT THESE NUMBERS ARE SUPPOSED TO **MEAN.**
THIS GADGET... THE IDEA OF THIS **SPACE** MAY BE SIMPLE TO **YOU**...

...BUT IT'S ALL STUFF THAT'S NEVER BEEN **DREAMED** OF IN MY TIME.
WE'VE ONLY JUST **DISCOVERED** ZOOR ENERGY.
YOU'VE HAD IT ALMOST YOUR WHOLE **LIFE.**
JUST **UPDATE** THEM, WILL YOU?

HMH.
YOU KNOW...
UUL AND I HAVE... WELL, I GUESS WE **HAD** SUCH DREAMS ABOUT WHAT TO DO WITH THIS ENERGY.

OTHER ORES IN THE CRUST OF THE PLANET WERE VALUABLE FOR TRADE, BUT **THIS...**
...THIS COULD CHANGE **EVERYTHING.** TRANSPORTATION, COMMUNICATION, WASTE-MANAGEMENT.
EVERYTHING.

WE JUST HAD TO EXAMINE ITS EFFECTS ON—
YEAH, SURE.
TYPICAL **FEMALE.**
OBSESSING OVER TECHNICAL DETAILS WHEN THE ANSWERS ARE RIGHT IN FRONT OF YOU.

WHAT?
LOOK AT THEM, KEER.

YOU THINK YOUR NOTIONS OF HOW TO USE THE ENERGY WILL DO US ANY GOOD WITH **THEM** MASSING AT OUR GATES?

DEERON HAS A VISION OF THE FUTURE, TOO. A FAR MORE REALISTIC ONE.
AND IT SOLVES THE PROBLEM WE HAVE **NOW.** THE **DOROSSHIANS.**

WAIT. THEN ALL OF US COMING TO THIS PLACE—YOU TWO, AND CAPTAIN PICARD AND I...
...WE'RE ALL HERE DUE TO ACCIDENTS, BUT—
—BUT THE DOROSSHIANS?
HOW DID ***THEY*** GET HERE?

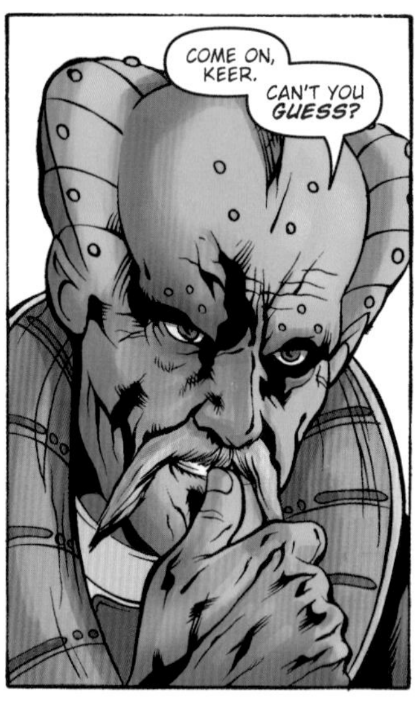
COME ON, KEER.
CAN'T YOU ***GUESS?***

Y-YOU ***MURDERED*** THEM?
MURDERED? WHAT, DON'T YOU SEE THEM THERE?

BUT THEIR FAMILIES, THEIR LIVES—EVERYONE THINKS THEY ARE DEAD, THEY ARE FORGOTTEN.
YOU DON'T CALL ***THAT*** MURDERED?

THIS ORE—THIS ENERGY—IT COULD HAVE PUT US ON PAR WITH THE CORE SYSTEMS... BUT ALL YOU COULD THINK TO DO WITH IT IS KILL OUR ***NEIGHBORS.***
HOW ***COULD*** YOU?
HOW COULD ***I,*** KEER?
DON'T BE SO MODEST...

IT'S ONLY THANKS TO YOU THAT WE COULD DO ANY OF THIS AT ALL.
YOUR EXTREME TECHNICAL EXPERTISE...

"...YOU MADE THIS POSSIBLE."
KKRK KNEW YOU WOULD HAIL US AGAIN, COMMANDER RIKER.
SO FRUSTRATING, ISN'T IT, THAT YOU STILL DON'T KNOW WHERE WE ARE?
KK SUNDOWN DRAWS **CLOSER**, RIKER.
YOUR OFFICER SITS SILENTLY, NO DOUBT CONTEMPLATING HIS DEATH. A PITY YOU HAVEN'T THE EXPEDIENCY TO PREVENT IT.

SKK YOU HAVE THE JUULETIAN FUNCTIONARY DEERON IN YOUR BRIG, COMMANDER. I KNOW THIS.
YOUR SURRENDERING DEERON...

...WOULD LIFT THE SWORD AWAY FROM YOUR LT. WORF'S NECK.
AT LEAST BUY YOU MORE **TIME.**

YOU AND DEERON DO NOT SHARE A GREAT FRIENDSHIP, RIKER. YOU DETONATED HIS GUNSHIP AT OUR REQUEST.
WOULD IT TROUBLE YOU TO TURN HIM OVER TO US?

I DO **NOTHING** AT YOUR REQUEST, WORIKK.
I SIMPLY HAVE THE FEDERATION'S REASONS, AND MY OWN.
DEERON WILL NOT BE SURRENDERED, NOT EVEN AT THE COST OF OUR CREWMAN'S LIFE.

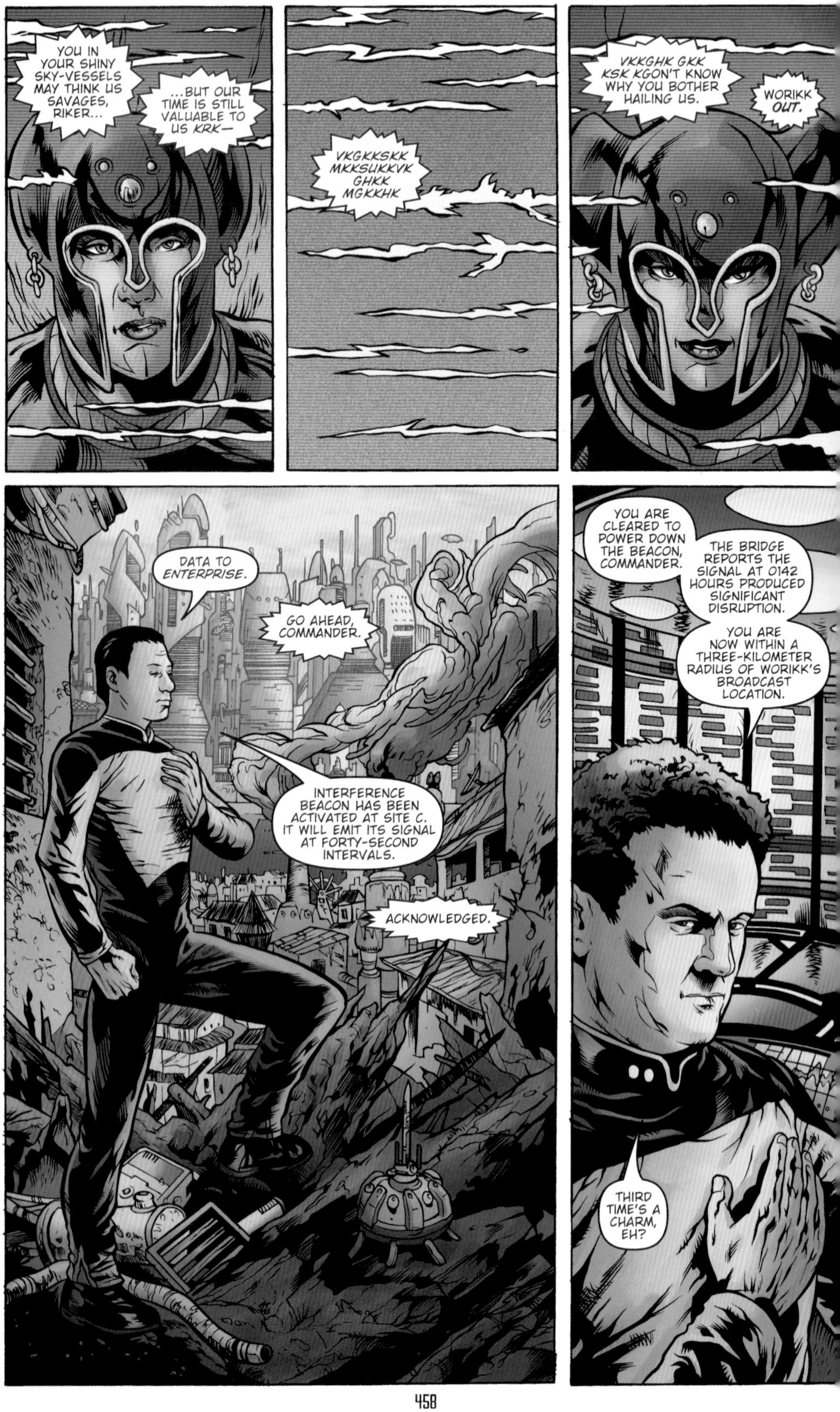

DATA TO *ENTERPRISE.*

GO AHEAD, COMMANDER.

INTERFERENCE BEACON HAS BEEN ACTIVATED AT SITE C. IT WILL EMIT ITS SIGNAL AT FORTY-SECOND INTERVALS.

ACKNOWLEDGED.

CHIEF O'BRIEN, NUMERICAL MILESTONES HAVE NO EFFECT ON THE STATISTICAL PROBABILITY OF—
—ERR,RIGHT, COMMANDER. ANYWAY, WE'RE SHOWING THAT THE SUN WILL SET ON ALLIOS IV AT 0226 HOURS.

YOU HAVE FORTY-FOUR MINUTES UNTIL WORF IS SCHEDULED TO BE EXECUTED.
WE WILL BE WORKING AS QUICKLY AS POSSIBLE TO SIFT THROUGH THE LIFE-FORMS IN THE RADIUS WITH OUR SENSORS, BUT DATA...

...WE'RE COUNTING ON YOU.

WHAT HAVE I DONE?

CAPTAIN PICARD—ALL WE WANTED WAS TO DISCOVER THIS ENERGY AND HARNESS IT—
SOMETHING TO SET ALLIOS IV—AND JUULET—APART. SOMETHING TO MAKE US MORE THAN JUST A PLANET OF ***MINERS***.
SOMETHING TO MAKE US MOVE FORWARD—***CIVILIZE*** US.
BUT YOU FEEL ALL YOU'VE ACCOMPLISHED IS TO GIVE EVERYONE MORE WAYS TO HURT EACH OTHER.

"IT IS NOT UNLIKE THIS PLACE, IN A WAY.

"WHEN I FIRST ARRIVED HERE, I TOO BELIEVED IT WAS PUNISHMENT FOR RISKING WORF—AND COUNTLESS OTHERS—OVER MY CAREER.

"BUT LIKE MANY THINGS IN LIFE, WHAT SEEMS LIKE A PUNISHMENT IS SIMPLY A ***TEST.***

"IT DOES NOT SEEM SO AT THE TIME BUT THESE MOMENTS ARE WHEN WE ARE AT OUR ***BEST.***

"WHEN WE SEE THE WORLD IN EXTRA SHARP FOCUS...

"...AND INDECISION FALLS AWAY FOR A MOMENT ...

"...SHOWING US THE STRAIGHT PATH TO THE ANSWER."

I DON'T GET IT.
WE'VE GOT THE TRANSPORTERS POWERED UP.
THE NAV COMPUTERS ARE TRACKING THE COORDINATES I'VE ENTERED.
BUT HIS NUMBERS—THEY DON'T MAKE **SENSE**.
THE DOUBLE DIGITS...
GEORDI—WE'RE LOSING UUL—HE'S FADING **AWAY.**
YOU HAVE TO **DO** SOMETHING. WE HAVE TO BEAM THEM OUT OF THERE.

EVERYONE! IN HERE!
SUBDUE THE FEDERATION ASSASSIN!!

GEORDI—UUL'S THE ONLY THING ANCHORING THOSE PEOPLE TO THE PRESENT.
IF HE'S CONSUMED BEFORE THEY'RE OUT—
I KNOW!

I'M **THINKING!**
THE ENERGY IS GOING TO GET TO HIS VITAL ORGANS, SOON.
WHEN IT WAS JUST AT HIS EXTREMITIES WE COULD DAMPEN, BUT IF IT GETS—

I KNOW, IT'S—WAIT—
HIS **EXTREMITIES!**
OF **COURSE!**

HE WAS SHACKLED AT THE **WRISTS**—
—DAMN IT, HOW DID HE SLIP **FREE?!**

THEIR HANDS!
THEY HAVE SIX FINGERS!
BUT WHAT—

TWELVE TOTAL, BEVERLY—
THEY'RE USING A BASE-12 NUMBER SYSTEM!
COMPUTER!

ADJUST ALL CALCULATIONS TO BASE TWELVE AND BEGIN LOCKING ONTO ANYONE AT THOSE COORDINATES.
WE'RE GETTING THEM OUT OF THERE NOW!

EXECUTIONER—
—YOU HAVE FAILED ME.
I WILL DO THE JOB MYSELF.
GET OUT OF MY SIGHT.

DATA TO ENTERPRISE—
—THE SEARCH HAS NARROWED.

I'M SURE THAT'S VERY INSPIRING, CAPTAIN PICARD.

IT'S CLEARLY PART OF YOUR JOB TO SPUR PEOPLE ON TO GREAT THINGS, BUT—
GREAT GODS *BELOW!*
WHAT IS *THAT?*

AH.
THE *ENTERPRISE*.
THEY'VE FOUND THIS SPACE.
BUT THEY MUST NOT BE ABLE TO LOCK ON TO US—THEY'RE JUST TAKING GUESSES WITH THE TRANSPORTERS.

BAH! IT'S *GONE!*
NO! THERE IT IS AGAIN!

KEER, YOU NEED TO GET A MESSAGE TO THEM THROUGH UUL.
BEEL CAN TELL THEM HOW TO REFINE THEIR COORDINATES.
QUICKLY!

ALL RIGHT.
OH, NO, WHAT—
—CAPTAIN PICARD!
WHAT IS IT?

IT'S UUL...
...THERE'S MORE OF HIM.

I THINK THE ENERGY'S EATING AWAY AT HIM...
...HE'S SLOWLY BEING SHIFTED HERE COMPLETELY.
THEN WE HAVE NO TIME TO WASTE!
BEEL!

UUL...
BEEL, WE NEED YOU TO UPDATE THE COORDINATES—HELP THEM REFINE THEIR GUESSES.
BUT I DON'T—

UUL... YOU'RE BEING DRAWN HERE TOO...
ANYTHING, ANYTHING YOU CAN DO TO GET THE TRANSPORTER SIGNAL TO REMAIN STATIONARY AND ACCESSIBLE.

BY THIS ENERGY WE DISCOVERED TOGETHER.
ALL RIGHT, CAPTAIN PICARD.
I'LL TRY.

OH MY HUSBAND...
...YOU'RE BEING PUNISHED, TOO.
KEER—
TELL THEM THIS SEQUENCE—
KEER...

"... DO YOU HEAR ME?!"
UUL?

UUL, IT'S ME, DEANNA.
I-I CAN'T—I-IS SOMEONE TALKING?

WH-WHO'S THERE?
P-PUNISHED? WHAT DO YOU MEAN?

N-NOW YOU'RE T-TELLING ME NUMBERS—
OH, IT'S YOU, KEER. OF COURSE, OF COURSE.
FOUR... ELEVEN... NINE... SIX... THREE... SEVEN... TEN.

GOT THAT, O'BRIEN?
GOT IT. ADJUSTING NOW...
UUL? UUL, I BELIEVE WE'VE GOTTEN ALL OF THE INFORMATION WE NEED.
NOW I HAVE TO TELL YOU SOMETHING.

THE ENERGY... IT'S TRAVELED TOO FAR UP YOUR BODY. DR. CRUSHER TELLS ME YOUR VITAL ORGANS ARE COMPROMISED.
IF... IF WE TURN ON THE DAMPER NOW... YOU WILL DIE.

I KNOW YOU'RE CONFUSED. I KNOW YOU'RE SCARED. YOU'VE BEEN SO BRAVE IN THE FACE OF DANGER...
...SO BRAVE IN THE FACE OF YOUR COUNTRYMEN'S THREATS.
I-I CAN'T—

YOU DESERVE A REST. YOU DON'T HAVE TO BE BRAVE ANYMORE.
I'M HONORED TO HAVE MET YOU.

GOODBYE, UUL.
I...

QUICKLY, ALL OF YOU!
WE DON'T KNOW HOW LONG THIS CAN LAST!
FORM GROUPS OF TWO—
ELDER KALKASS, WITH ME—
KEER, QUICKLY!
KEER, THIS SPACE IS SHIFTING CONSTANTLY—WE HAVE TO HURRY!
THIS IS OUR ONLY CHANCE—
KEER?
KEER, PLEASE, YOU HAVE TO COME WITH US.
UUL IS THE ONLY THING STABILIZING US IN TIME.
WE ONLY HAVE A FEW MINUTES.
I WANT TO SAY THANK YOU, CAPTAIN.
YOU HAVE UNITED US IN THIS SPACE. WE WOULD BE LOST WITHOUT YOU.
YOU SAVED US.
BUT I CAN'T GO. I DON'T DESERVE TO GO.
YOU ARE A FINE LEADER. YOU WILL SURELY SAVE THOUSANDS IN YOUR JOURNEYS.
BUT PLEASE, CAPTAIN, FOR ME...
...JUST DO IT FOR THOSE WHO WANT SAVING.

O'BRIEN— IT'S 0224 HOURS—WHAT THE HELL IS THE HOLDUP?
THE VICTIMS ARE COMING THROUGH, COMMANDER, BUT IT'S SLOW GOING.
THE UNPREDICTABLE NATURE OF THIS SPACE THEY'RE COMING FROM—EACH DOPPLER COMPENSATION TAKES SEVERAL MINUTES AND USES AN INCREDIBLE AMOUNT OF—
DATA TO *ENTERPRISE*—
I HAVE DETERMINED LT. WORF'S PRECISE LOCATION. HE IS SEVEN METERS DUE SOUTH OF MY ***POSITION***.

"ALL RIGHT, GET HIM, O'BRIEN. QUICKLY."
"SIR, WE CAN'T—
"—GEORDI SAYS THE ENERGY EXPENDITURE FOR THIS OPERATION IS PUSHING THE CORE TO ITS ***LIMIT***."

DAMN IT, O'BRIEN— THE SUN IS SETTING ON ALLIOS IV—WORF IS GOING TO ***DIE*** IF WE DON'T DO SOMETHING ***NOW!***
WHO IS IN THE ***BUFFER***?

IT'S CAPTAIN ***PICARD***, SIR, AND A DOROSSHIAN BIOSIGN, BUT—
WHO IS IT?
I CAN'T TELL, SIR, IT'S IMPOSSIBLE—

DOESN'T MATTER.
WORF'S ***POSITION***. SEND THEM, O'BRIEN—

NOW.
NOW IS WHEN WE GIVE A *RECKONING,* FRIENDS...
A RECKONING TO THOSE WHO WOULD INTERFERE.
TO THOSE WHO WOULD *MURDER* TO SHAPE US INTO THE TYPE OF NATION THEY *PREFER.*
AND TO THOSE WHO WOULD JOIN IN A FIGHT THAT IS NOT *THEIRS.*

VVNNNNN

"BEING FACE-TO-FACE WITH HER SUPPOSEDLY DEAD FATHER MUST HAVE BEEN A BIT OF A *SHOCK*."
"INDEED.
"AND ONCE EVERYONE REALIZED KALKASS WAS REALLY FLESH AND BLOOD—"

A GOOD NUMBER OF THE THINGS KEEPING WORIKK IN POWER STARTED TO *CRUMBLE*.
AH, DOCTOR.
HOW IS WORF?
DEHYDRATED, EXHAUSTED, SOME BROKEN RIBS.
A FEW DAYS REST SHOULD HELP GREATLY, BUT HE'LL BE FINE.

YES.
HE'S A *FIGHTER.*
NOW, CAPTAIN...
...ARE *YOU* ALL RIGHT? YOU SEEM—

FINE, THANK YOU, NUMBER ONE.
JUST THINKING ABOUT THE ONE PERSON WE LEFT BEHIND.
SHE... WOULDN'T COME, AND NOW...
...SHE'S THERE ALL ALONE. FOREVER.
ALONE? WELL, CAPTAIN...

"...I'M NOT SO SURE ABOUT THAT."
WHUH?

WHERE—?
OH, NO— SH-SHE SAID GOODBYE—AND HERE I AM.
A-AND...
UUL?

WHAT—?
OH!

OH, KEER!
KEER!
OH, FINALLY...

CAPTAIN'S LOG, SUPPLEMENTAL:

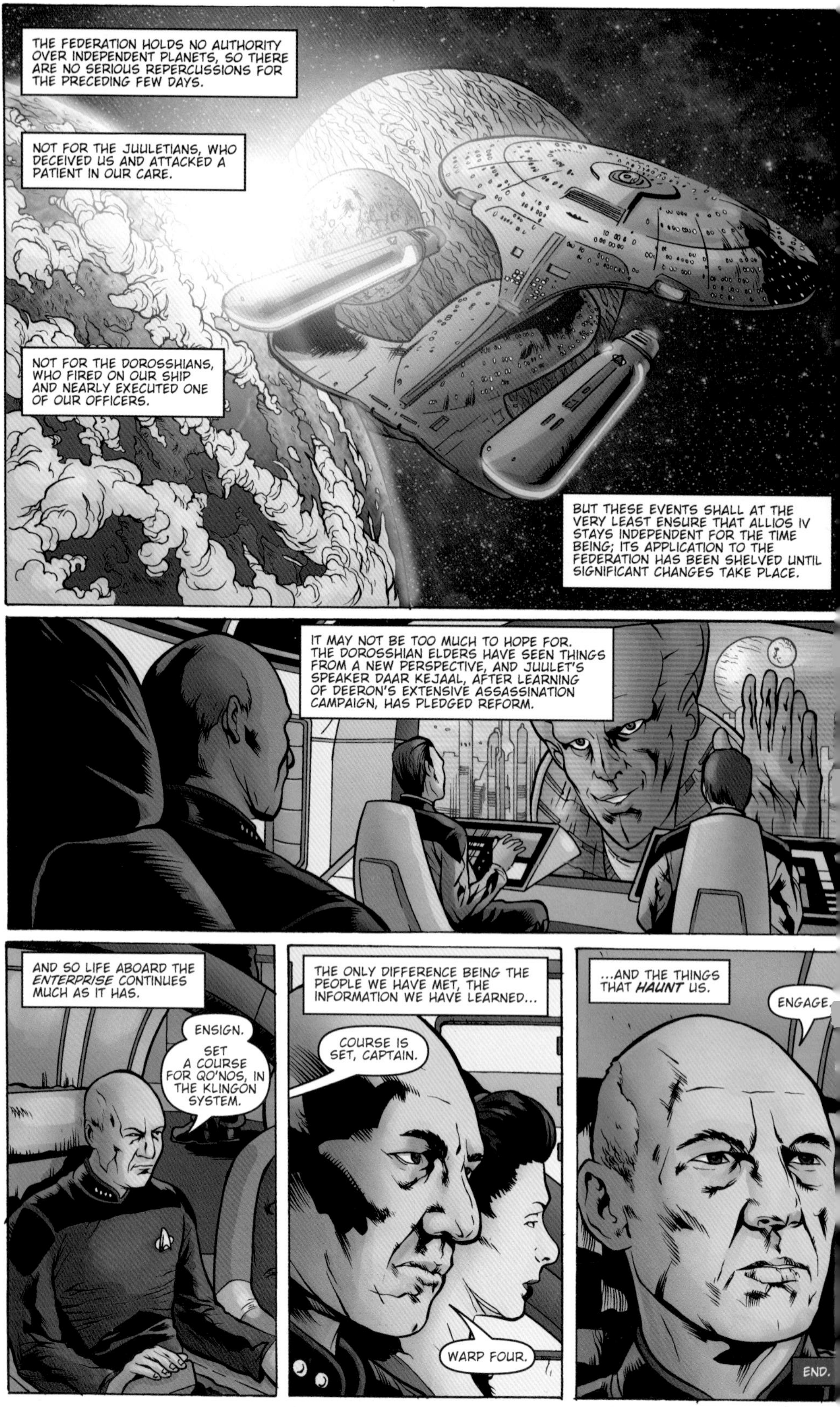

THE FEDERATION HOLDS NO AUTHORITY OVER INDEPENDENT PLANETS, SO THERE ARE NO SERIOUS REPERCUSSIONS FOR THE PRECEDING FEW DAYS.

NOT FOR THE JUULETIANS, WHO DECEIVED US AND ATTACKED A PATIENT IN OUR CARE.

NOT FOR THE DOROSSHIANS, WHO FIRED ON OUR SHIP AND NEARLY EXECUTED ONE OF OUR OFFICERS.

BUT THESE EVENTS SHALL AT THE VERY LEAST ENSURE THAT ALLIOS IV STAYS INDEPENDENT FOR THE TIME BEING; ITS APPLICATION TO THE FEDERATION HAS BEEN SHELVED UNTIL SIGNIFICANT CHANGES TAKE PLACE.